1. *Evangelical Kernels*

EVANGELICAL KERNELS

Evangelical Kernels

A Theological Spirituality of the Religious Life

DENNIS J. BILLY, C.SS.R.

ALBA · HOUSE   NEW · YORK

SOCIETY OF ST. PAUL, 2187 VICTORY BLVD., STATEN ISLAND, NY 10314

Library of Congress Cataloging-in-Publication Data

Billy, Dennis Joseph.
   Evangelical kernels : a theological spirituality of the
religious life / Dennis J. Billy.
     p.   cm.
   Includes bibliographical references.
   ISBN 0-8189-0669-3
     1. Catholic Church — Doctrines. 2. Theology, Doctrinal.
   3. Spirituality — Catholic Church. 4. Monastic and religious life.
   I. Title.
   BX1751.2.B46   1993
   230 — dc20   92-45146
                                                        CIP

Imprimi Potest:
Edward J. Gilbert, C.SS.R.

Imprimatur:
† Remigio Ragonesi, DD
Vicar General, Rome
May 14, 1992

The Nihil Obstat and Imprimatur are official declarations
that a book or pamphlet is free of doctrinal or moral
error. No implication is contained therein that those
who have granted the Nihil Obstat and Imprimatur agree
with the contents, opinions or statements expressed.

Produced and designed in the United States of America by the
Fathers and Brothers of the Society of St. Paul,
2187 Victory Boulevard, Staten Island, New York 10314,
as part of their communications apostolate.

ISBN: 0-8189-0669-3

© Copyright 1993 by the Society of St. Paul

Printing Information:

Current Printing - first digit	1	2	3	4	5	6	7	8	9	10

Year of Current Printing - first year shown

1993	1994	1995	1996	1997	1998

In memory of
Joseph A. Kenney, C.SS.R.
(1903-1982)

ABBREVIATIONS

AAS	*Acta Apostolicae Sedis*
CCCM	*Corpus Christianorum, continuatio mediaevalis*
CCL	*Corpus Christianorum, series latina*
CDD	Sacrosanctum Oecumenicum Concilium Vaticanum II. *Constitutiones decreta declarationes.* Vatican: Typis Polyglottis Vaticanis, 1966.
CIC	*Codex iuris canonici*
CSEL	*Corpus scriptorum ecclesiasticorum latinorum*
Denz.-Schön.	H. Denzinger. *Enchiridion symbolorum*, 32d ed. Revised by H. Schönmetzer. Freiburg im Breisgau: Herder, 1963.
IGP	*Insegnamenti di Giovanni Paolo II.* Vatican: Libreria Editrice Vaticana, 1979-.
PG	J.P. Migne, *Patrologia graeca*
PL	J.P. Migne, *Patrologia latina*
SC	*Sources chrétiennes*
SCDF	Sacred Congregation for the Doctrine of the Faith
SCR	Sacred Congregation of Rites
SCRSI	Sacred Congregation for Religious and Secular Institutes
SPUC	Secretariat for the Promotion of the Unity of Christians

ACKNOWLEDGMENTS

A word of sincere thanks goes to Bruce Williams, O.P. for his insightful comments, useful criticisms, and eager willingness to help with this project. Notable thanks also go to Mary O'Driscoll, O.P. and Giuseppe Phan Tan Thanh, O.P. for giving careful scrutiny to the final draft. In addition to the many friends and family members who have supported me over the years, a special word of gratitude goes to the members of the Redemptorist community at Sant'Alfonso (Rome) and to my colleagues in the Alphonsian Academy. Among the latter, I am especially grateful to Sean Cannon, C.SS.R. who, as President of the Academy, encouraged me to pursue this work in Spirituality and bring it to an effective close.

CONTENTS

ABBREVIATIONS vi
PREFACE xv
BIBLICAL ABBREVIATIONS xx
INTRODUCTION xxi
    The Meaning of Theological Spirituality xxii
    Theology and Spirituality xxv
    The Levels of Theological Spirituality xxviii
    The Distinctiveness of Kernel Spirituality xxxi
    The Method of Kernel Spirituality xxxiii
    The Witness of the Vows xxxv
    Conclusion xxxvii

1. THE THEOLOGY KERNEL 1
    The Retrieval of Theology 2
        I. Faith and the Nature of Knowing 3
        II. The Twofold Movement of Seeking 5
        III. From Understanding to Action 9
    The Theology Kernel 11
    Theology and Religious Life 13
    Conclusion 15

2. THE CHRIST KERNEL 17
    The Discipline of Christology 17
    The Christ Kernel 19

Movement One: "The Word Became Flesh"	20
Movement Two: "He Emptied Himself"	22
Movement Three: "This is My Body"	24
Movement Four: "He is Risen"	26
The Imitation of Christ	28
Conclusion	30

3. THE TRINITARIAN KERNEL 33

The Internal/External Relations of Love	33
The Relational God	35
Relation One: "The Father as Ground"	37
Relation Two: "The Son as Other"	39
Relation Three: "The Spirit as Bond"	41
The Trinitarian Dimensions of Human Solidarity	43
The Trinitarian Dimensions of Religious Life	45
Conclusion	47

4. THE CHURCH KERNEL 49

The Church's Hermeneutical Awareness	49
The Question of Models	51
A Look Beyond the Models	53
The Church Kernel	55
The Role of Religious in the Church	59
Religious and Mary	61
Conclusion	62

5. THE FALL KERNEL 65

The Classical Formulation	65
The Levels of Christian Anthropology	68
The Fall Kernel	71
Original Sin and Religious	73
Conclusion	75

6. THE GRACE KERNEL 77

Retrieving the Distinctions of Grace	77
Revising the Language of Grace	81
The Grace Kernel	84

Contents

    Grace and Religious 89
    Conclusion 91

7. THE REDEMPTION KERNEL 95

    The Problem of Development 95
    Theories of Redemption 98
    The Redemption Kernel 101
    Redemption and Religious 104
    Conclusion 107

8. THE RESURRECTION KERNEL 109

    Resurrection: Distinguishing the Idea from the Reality 109
    The Resurrection Kernel 114
    Religious and the Resurrection 118
    Conclusion 120

9. THE SACRAMENTAL KERNEL 123

    The Sacramental God 123
    The Sacramental Kernel 127
    Religious and the Sacraments 129
    Conclusion 133

10. THE BREAD KERNEL 135

    The Eucharist as a Symbolic Action 135
    In the Breaking of the Bread 138
    The Bread Kernel 143
    The Eucharist and Religious 146
    Conclusion 149

11. THE MORALITY KERNEL 151

    The Reunification of Theology 151
    Allegory, Syllogism, and Induction 153
    Theology and Liberation 156
    The Morality Kernel 158

    Religious and Moral Theology 161
    Conclusion 164

12. THE PRAYER KERNEL 167
    The Relation of Prayer to Theology 167
    The Forms of Prayer: An Anthropological Approach 170
    The Prayer Kernel 174
    Prayer and Religious 178
    Conclusion 182

13. THE ECUMENICAL KERNEL 185
    The Theological Basis of Ecumenism 185
    The Meaning of Christian Unity 188
    The Ecumenical Kernel 191
    Religious and Ecumenism 195
    Conclusion 198

14. THE MARIAN KERNEL 201
    Terminology 201
    The Marian Kernel 203
    Mary as Mothering Myth and Symbol 205
    Mary as Virgin and Theological Model 206
    Mary: Virgin and Mother 207
    Mary and Religious 210
    Conclusion 214

15. THE END KERNEL 215
    Salvation History: The Narrative Basis of Eschatology 215
    Eschatology and Hope 218
    The End Kernel 220
    Eschatology and Religious Life 223
    Conclusion 226

16. CONCLUSION 229
    Theological Kernels 229

Implications for the Religious Life 234
The Theology of the Vows 236
Conclusion 241

SELECTED BIBLIOGRAPHY 245

I. Primary Sources 245
  A. Historical Documents 245
  B. Magisterial Documents 247
    1. Papal 247
    2. Conciliar 248
    3. Ecclesiastical Law 248
    4. Vatican Congregations and Secretariats 248
    5. Reference 249
  C. Kernel Articles 249
II. Secondary Sources 250
  A. Translations 250
  B. Books 251
  C. Book Components 262
    1. Chapters 262
    2. Essays 264
  D. Journal Articles 266
  E. Encyclopedia and Dictionary Articles 271
  F. Proceedings 274
  G. Dissertations 274
  H. Unpublished Manuscripts 274

PREFACE

Much of the recent literature on the future of religious life uses expressions such as "crisis" and "refounding" (or variations thereof) for its formal point of departure. Studies have shown that, throughout the history of the Church, religious orders have undergone a recognizable (almost predictable) pattern of initial growth and expansion, followed by a period of stabilization and another of ongoing decline, which, in turn, usually leads to one of three possibilities: (1) extinction, (2) minimal survival, or (3) revitalization. This same literature insists that, since the close of the Second Vatican Council, many religious institutes — both male and female — have entered critical periods of their existence. If something drastic does not take place, many of them may not endure beyond the lifetimes of their present members.[1]

This book focuses on an element which nearly all authors in the field agree is essential for any viable project of revitalization or "refounding" of a religious institute, i.e., the spiritual transformation of its members.[2] It understands this transformation, however,

---

[1] Some of the prominent studies of this kind include: Gerald A. Arbuckle, *Out of Chaos: Refounding Religious Orders* (New York: Paulist Press, 1988); Lawrence Cada et al. *Shaping the Coming Age of Religious Life*, 2d ed. (New York: The Seabury Press, 1979), and Raymond Hostie, *The Life and Death of Religious Orders: A Psycho-sociological Approach* (Washington, D.C.: Center for Applied Research in the Apostolate, 1983).

[2] In his 1991 presidential address to the Conference of Major Superiors of Men, Marist brother Sean Sammon summarized these general sentiments thus: "The real crisis in religious life today is not our lack of vocations. No, it is our lack of spirituality and significance. A vibrant life of personal and communal prayer must be at the heart of our life; otherwise, we run the risk of being nothing more than associations that give little witness to the presence of Jesus in the

in a very particular way, i.e., as something intricately bound up with the theological tradition of the Catholic Church. The spiritual life of the individual religious, in other words, should not be understood as existing apart from the vast interlocking web of theological insights which down through the centuries represent the accumulation of the Church's reflection on the mystery of the Christ event. If the Gospel is "the supreme rule"[3] for religious in their attempts to effect the internal renewal of their institutes, then the Church's theological tradition — the result of its contemplation and proclamation of the Gospel over time — challenges religious to interiorize that rule by penetrating ever more deeply the mystery of the Christian reality as it has been preserved and safeguarded within the Church. In this respect, the ecclesial dimension of the religious life can be thought of as pertaining not only to the external organization of religious life in its various institutional aspects, but also to the interior life of its members. It is in this context that religious have been encouraged to "think with the Church and always act in union with her."[4]

This insight has important implications for classifying this work. In its "enlightened" attempt in recent centuries to imitate the empirical sciences, theology has sought an objective methodological "control" to validate and bring internal consistency to the plurality of its sacred claims. More often than not, it has resorted to a very narrow understanding of rationality (i.e., as univocal logic) to perform the lion's share of the work. This reductive tendency has resulted in a proliferation of seemingly discon-

---

world." See "The Transformation of Religious Life," *Origins* 21 (1991): 190. In the Second Vatican Council documents, the call for the "spiritual renewal" of religious is explicitly mentioned in *Perfectae caritatis*, no. 2 [*CDD*, 336] (for abbreviations in the Preface, see the general list on vi); English translation: *Vatican Council II: The Conciliar and Post Conciliar Documents*, gen. ed. Austin Flannery (Northport, N.Y.: Costello Publishing Co., 1975), 613 (This translation of conciliar documents will hereafter be referred to as Flannery, *Vatican Council II*).

[3] Vatican Council II, *Perfectae caritatis*, no. 2 [*CDD*, 335]; English translation: Flannery, *Vatican Council II*, 612.

[4] John Paul II, *Redemptionis donum*, no. 14 [*AAS* 76 (1984): 539]; English translation: "*Redemptionis Donum*: An Expression of Love for Religious," *Review for Religious* 43 (1984): 14.

nected theological disciplines mastered by a relatively small number of specialists who, in turn, have themselves lost touch with the underlying unity that informs the whole of theology.[5] It has also led to a dissociation (a "disengagement," if you will) of whatever unity did exist among the various theological disciplines from the spiritual life of the individual believer.[6]

To offset these disturbing tendencies, this book asserts a broader understanding of rational inquiry and its role in the ongoing quest of faith. It seeks to balance the critical precision of scientific method with the appropriation of Christian wisdom, to integrate the centrality of prayer in the spiritual life with the exigencies of theological scholarship. In an effort to help the reader to appreciate better the interconnected nature of the various theological disciplines, it employs a broad panoramic approach to the Church's theological tradition. This approach surfaces most clearly in the author's methodological option for treating a wide variety of disciplines in a concise manner (instead of giving more extensive coverage to a much smaller selection). In doing so, the reader has a greater opportunity of seeing what a spirituality of the religious life rooted in the *whole* of the Church's theological tradition might be like. The book, one might say, offers a "sapiential" study of the theological spirituality of the religious life: it seeks to convey to its readers (and to religious, in particular) the great importance of personally appropriating the Church's theological tradition before focusing on the critical analysis of its various details. "The whole," if you will, "is greater than the sum of its parts."

As a sapiential study, the intent of this book is not to uncover an entirely new way of looking at the religious life (the latest

---

[5] "Over-specialization has made us mistake the fake breach for a genuine one. We are like the heretics Farinata and Celvalcanti trapped in the *same* tomb in the Inferno, yet each oblivious of the other's presence." See Alan Jones, "Spirituality and Theology," *Review for Religious* 39 (1980): 165.

[6] The term "dissociation" is borrowed from Andrew Louth, who, echoing the thought of T.S. Eliot, speaks more precisely of a "dissociation of sensibility" having taken place in the relationship between theology and the spiritual life in Western culture. See *Discerning the Mystery* (Oxford: Clarendon Press, 1983), 1-2.

insights are not necessarily the best), but to deepen the reader's awareness of the intrinsic continuity that exists between the Church's theological formulations and the life dedicated to the evangelical counsels. This continuity is most clearly reflected in the insight (mentioned often in the book) that the religious life offers a *radical* witness — both countercultural and eschatological — to the spiritual and moral message of Jesus Christ. Derived from the Latin word *"radix"* (meaning "root"), the term "radical" possesses vibrant organic undertones and is not intended in any quantitative or comparative sense (as if a tree's roots were "more important" than its trunk, or limbs, or leaves, or fruit). In one sense, the theological depth of this book comes not so much from the variety of ways in which specific connections can be drawn between a particular discipline of theology and the religious life as such (although many have been drawn to good advantage— and in a number of different contexts), but by firmly "rooting" this one fundamental insight in the vast array of disciplines themselves (and, in doing so, in the whole of theology). By grounding their lives more firmly in this and similar insights, religious renew their commitment to the underlying Gospel narrative that informs their lifelong calling. In doing so, they are able to understand more clearly the important part they play as bearers of the Church's theological tradition.

As the Church nears its third millennium, the Catholic faithful have been called upon to cultivate three essential qualities of mind and heart: (1) loyalty to the Church, (2) creativity within the Church, and (3) a spirit of contemplation.[7] The author has sought in this work to foster all three of these important values, both for his own benefit and for those interested in the theology of the religious life. The chapters were originally written as a series of individual essays, many of which have already been published in the *Review for Religious* — beginning as far back as the year 1984 ("The Kernel Series," as many are wont to call it).[8] The fruit of

---

[7] Joseph Bernardin, "Dimensions of the Church in the Third Millennium," *Origins* 20 (1992): 596.

[8] These articles are listed as primary sources in the Bibliography, 249-50.

much prayer and personal reflection, they represent the author's attempt to make sense out of his own religious vocation during a time when many of the traditional safeguards of religious life in general (and of his own Congregation, in particular) had been cast aside—with virtually nothing left in their place. Gathered in this work with expanded notes designed to refer the reader to pertinent primary and secondary texts and a selected bibliography focusing on the religious life, they demonstrate one man's endeavor to arrive at a synthetic understanding of his own vocation in the larger context of the Church's theological tradition. The title of this book, "Evangelical Kernels: A Theological Spirituality of the Religious Life," points to the integrated (albeit approximating) claims of this otherwise modest attempt.

BIBLICAL ABBREVIATIONS

OLD TESTAMENT

Genesis	Gn	Nehemiah	Ne	Baruch	Ba
Exodus	Ex	Tobit	Tb	Ezekiel	Ezk
Leviticus	Lv	Judith	Jdt	Daniel	Dn
Numbers	Nb	Esther	Est	Hosea	Ho
Deuteronomy	Dt	1 Maccabees	1 M	Joel	Jl
Joshua	Jos	2 Maccabees	2 M	Amos	Am
Judges	Jg	Job	Jb	Obadiah	Ob
Ruth	Rt	Psalms	Ps	Jonah	Jon
1 Samuel	1 S	Proverbs	Pr	Micah	Mi
2 Samuel	2 S	Ecclesiastes	Ec	Nahum	Na
1 Kings	1 K	Song of Songs	Sg	Habakkuk	Hab
2 Kings	2 K	Wisdom	Ws	Zephaniah	Zp
1 Chronicles	1 Ch	Sirach	Si	Haggai	Hg
2 Chronicles	2 Ch	Isaiah	Is	Malachi	Ml
Ezra	Ezr	Jeremiah	Jr	Zechariah	Zc
		Lamentations	Lm		

NEW TESTAMENT

Matthew	Mt	Ephesians	Ep	Hebrews	Heb
Mark	Mk	Philippians	Ph	James	Jm
Luke	Lk	Colossians	Col	1 Peter	1 P
John	Jn	1 Thessalonians	1 Th	2 Peter	2 P
Acts	Ac	2 Thessalonians	2 Th	1 John	1 Jn
Romans	Rm	1 Timothy	1 Tm	2 John	2 Jn
1 Corinthians	1 Cor	2 Timothy	2 Tm	3 John	3 Jn
2 Corinthians	2 Cor	Titus	Tt	Jude	Jude
Galatians	Gal	Philemon	Phm	Revelation	Rv

INTRODUCTION

The whole of Catholic theology (both speculative and practical) has important implications for a proper understanding of vocation in the life of the Church. By way of a distinctive new approach known as "Kernel Spirituality," this book will examine what these implications are for those called to serve Christ and his Church through their profession of the religious vows.[1] As its name suggests, Kernel Spirituality seeks first to identify the most fundamental principle (i.e., "kernel") of a particular field of theological inquiry. It then reflects upon the significance of this principle for a specific way of Christian life. As might be expected, this integrated focus on theology and spirituality can be applied to any of the vocational states in the Church (i.e., priestly, religious, and lay).[2] For religious, it would mean trying to understand the nature of the relationship between the theological discipline in question and the evangelical counsels of chastity, poverty, and obedience.[3]

---

[1] In this work, the term "religious" refers to those individuals who publicly profess the evangelical counsels of chastity, poverty, and obedience and have official canonical status in the Catholic Church. For questions pertaining to religious institutes of non-canonical status, see Emily George, "Canonical Status," in *Turning Points in Religious Life*, ed. Carol Quigley (Wilmington: Michael Glazier, 1987), 174-88.

[2] For how these states of life interrelate, see William J. McDonald, gen. ed. *The New Catholic Encyclopedia* (New York: McGraw-Hill,1967), s.v. "States of Life," by S.V. Ramge. For the religious life as "a state of life" in the Church, see Sandra M. Schneiders, "Reflections on the History of the Religious Life and Contemporary Development," in *Turning Points in Religious Life*, ed. Carol Quigley (Wilmington: Michael Glazier, 1987), 37.

[3] For the evangelical counsels as constitutitive elements of the religious life, see Vatican Council II, *Lumen gentium*, no. 44 [*CDD*, 177] ; English translation: Flannery, *Vatican Council II*, 405. See also Jean Daniélou, "Il carattere specifico della vita religiosa," *Vita consacrata* 10 (1974): 525.

Such an attempt to relate sound theological reflection to lived Christian experience is a distinctive mark of what today is generally classified under the heading of theological spirituality. In some small way, the kernel approach adopted in these pages seeks to contribute to the Church's exposition and ongoing development of a balanced theological spirituality of the religious life.

THE MEANING OF THEOLOGICAL SPIRITUALITY

In these pages, the term "theological spirituality" refers to a particular approach to Christian spirituality that uses the classical theological formulations of the Church for its formal point of departure.[4] Rather than relegating human experience to the background by the imposition from above of the Church's traditional pronouncements (as at least one author seems wont to portray it),[5] this approach starts off with the conviction that the Church's theological formulations are themselves the products of sustained theological reflection upon the mystery of the Christ event. As such, they offer each generation of Christians a wealth of spiritual

---

[4] These formulations must be understood in the light of: (1) the "hierarchy of truths" in defined Catholic teaching (e.g., the theological priority given to Christ's divinity over the Church's official sacramental teaching), and (2) the varying "degrees of certitude" in the Church's ongoing exposition of its faith (e.g., teachings pertaining to the faith and theological opinions of lesser grades of certainty). For the main reference of the "hierarchy of truths" in magisterial teaching, see Vatican Council II, *Unitatis redintegratio*, no. 11 [*CDD*, 260]; English translation: Flannery, *Vatican Council II*, 462. For a study of the "hierarchy of truths" in the post-Vatican II Church, see William Henn, "The Hierarchy of Truths Twenty Years Later," *Theological Studies* 48 (1987): 439-71. For an exposition of the varying theological grades of certainty, see Ludwig Ott, *Fundamentals of Catholic Dogma*, 4th ed. trans. James Canon Bastible (Rockford, Ill.: Tan, 1960), 9-10. Ott's work represents the manualist tradition as it endured down to the period immediately preceeding the Vatican II period.

[5] Sandra M. Schneiders, for example, argues against the first and opts for the second of two basic aproaches to spirituality: "a dogmatic position supplying a 'definition from above' and an anthropological position providing a 'definition from below.'" See "Spirituality in the Academy," *Theological Studies* 50 (1989): 682.

Introduction

insight that must be appropriated anew and incorporated into the fabric of their daily Christian existence. From this perspective, theological spirituality moves present human experience not to the background of Christian life and worship, but to its proper place as the living receptacle of the Church's theological tradition. By encouraging today's Christians to assimilate the theological wisdom of the Church, this approach encourages a process of ongoing dialogue and creative adaptation that is essential for any feasible future reformulations.

In some respects, it is easier to characterize "theological spirituality" by way of negation, i.e., by comparing it to what it is not. It encompasses, for example, a much wider scope than the traditional discipline of spiritual theology. While the latter focuses on what theology manuals ever since the 17th and 18th centuries have referred to as the fields of ascetical and mystical theology,[6] the former touches upon any aspect of Catholic theological inquiry — from the most esoteric to the most utterly practical — that has some relevance to daily Christian living. This would include concrete moral norms as well as the tenets of the faith and the measured interaction between the two that makes for fruitful theological reflection. Theological spirituality, in fact, is not so much a theological discipline or subdiscipline as a way of approaching the whole of theology. It starts off with the assumption that the Church's theological formulations have something to

---

[6] While ascetical theology focuses on the motives and means by which the soul undergoes active purification first by freeing itself from sin and then by living the life of the virtues, mystical theology teaches the ways of union by means of passive purifications and the action of the Holy Spirit in the soul. Since active purification and the active pursuit of perfection take place not only in beginners but throughout the whole course of the spiritual life, many have opted for the more embracive term of spiritual theology. This theological discipline "studies the organic structure of the spiritual life and the awareness we have of it, explains the laws of its progress and development, and describes the process of growth which leads the soul from the beginning of its Christian life to the summit of perfection." See René Latourelle, *Theology: Science of Salvation*, trans. Sister Mary Dominic (Staten Island, N.Y.: Alba House, 1969), 146-47, 149. Similar insights appear in Antonio Royo Marin, *Teología de la perfección cristiana*, 5th ed., Biblioteca de autores cristianos, no. 114 (Madrid: La editorial catolica, 1968), 34-37.

contribute to a Christian's perception of reality and to his or her vocation in the world. By entering into the theological mindset that produced these statements, it seeks to penetrate their meaning, discover their contemporary relevance, and make them a vital part of a person's daily life.

Just as it is related to the whole of theology and cannot be reduced to just another of its many subdivisions, theological spirituality is also related to but more than a mere branch of human and cultural anthropology. As stated earlier, theological spirituality takes traditional Church teaching as its formal point of departure. For this reason, it cannot accept any approach to spirituality that seeks only a "definition from below" through an exclusively subject-oriented (and, hence, relativistic) understanding of historical truth and human existence.[7] To do so would be to overlook the implicit anthropological orientation of theological spirituality's most basic premise, i.e., that the Church's doctrinal formulations represent the sustained and theologically accurate reflections of preceding generations of Christians on the meaning of the Christ event. In this respect, theological spirituality provides Christians with a well-founded anthropological context through which they can interpret and make sense out of their present lives. These hermeneutical experiences can themselves be reflected upon and used to further refine the Church's unfolding theological tradition. What results from all of this is a circular relationship between the Church's past and present Christian experience that propels the Catholic theological tradition forward.[8] In this respect, theological spirituality provides its adherents with a characteristic anthropological orientation toward the future.

---

[7] Such as that proposed by Jean-Claude Breton "Retrouver les assises anthropologiques de la vie spirituelle," *Studies in Religion/Sciences religieuses* 17 (1988): 97-105.

[8] For a description of the foreward-moving character of the Church's theological tradition, see Vatican Council II, *Dei verbum*, no. 8 [*CDD*, 429-30]; English translation: Flannery, *Vatican Council II*, 754.

Introduction

THEOLOGY AND SPIRITUALITY

Up until now, little has been said in this treatment of theological spirituality about the actual relationship between theology and spirituality themselves. To get into the substantial amount of material written on this subject [9] would take the discussion far afield and divert attention away from the most relevant fact that, throughout Christian history, theology and what is today referred to as "spirituality" have related to one another in a variety of ways. That for the major part of this history such a question about the relationship between theology and spirituality would have made little sense to even the most astute of theological minds — either because they would not have understood the meaning of one or more of the terms or (as is more likely the case) because the relationship would have been obvious (indeed, quite natural) to them — points to the relatively recent origins of the problem. [10]

Generally speaking, the field of Christian spirituality arose in direct proportion to and as a way of complementing an increasingly rationalized understanding of the nature of Christian theology. If during the patristic era and for most of the medieval epoch an overly rationalized theology was looked upon with outright suspicion and the threat of Church *anathema* (as evidenced by the charges of heresy against Arius, Pelagius, Abelard, and Siger of Brabant),[11] beginning with the time of Scotus' rejection of all theological equivocations, of Ockham's theological nominalism,

---

[9] This literature is amply laid out by Eugene Megyer, "Theological Trends: Spiritual Theology Today," *The Way* 21 (1981): 55-67; Rachel Hosmer, "Current Literature in Christian Spirituality," *Anglican Theological Review* 66 (1984): 423-41; and Regina Bechtle, "Convergences in Theology and Spirituality," *The Way* 23 (1985): 305-14.

[10] The French term "spiritualité" was not applied to the interior Christian life until the seventeenth century. Prior to that time, theology was understood as both an intellectual *and* spiritual pursuit. See Jean Leclercq, "Spiritualitas," *Studi medievali* 3 (1963): 279-96; for more on the history of the term's meaning, see Walter Principe, "Toward Defining Spirituality," *Studies in Religion/ Sciences religieuses* 12 (1983): 130-35.

[11] Arius was condemned for his rational simplification of the Trinitarian doctrine ("There was a time when he was not"); Pelagius, for failing to incorporate a role for grace in the practical working out of humanity's salvation; Abelard, for what was considered an overextended application of logic to scholastic

which ushered in a breakdown of theology into separate and seemingly disconnected disciplines,[12] and certainly by the time of Descartes' "enlightened" *Cogito*, which influenced a corresponding search for clear and distinct theological ideas, it had largely displaced the Neoplatonic emphasis on symbol and allegory that had characterized so much of earlier Christian theology.[13] Over time, this increasingly rationalized approach to theology entered the religious mainstream, and was looked upon, at least in intellectual circles, as the preferred way by which to unravel and expound the fullest meaning of the Christian faith.[14]

One of the adverse effects of Reason's apparent "coming of age" was a gradual shift in the concept of rationality itself (i.e., from the analogous to the univocal).[15] With the arrival of Kant's famous *Critique*, these quiet murmurs and erstwhile cracks turned into a cataclysmic rift in the relationship between pure and practical reason.[16] In the theological sphere, this was accompanied by an increasing separation of theological reflection and devotion.

---

methodology; Siger of Brabant, for his propounding a theory of "double truth." All four were perceived in their respective days as having overstepped the legitimate bounds of reason by means of their unchecked theological reductionism.

[12] For the role of both Scotist thought and late medieval nominalism in changing the shape of later medieval theology, see Amos Funkenstein, *Theology and the Scientific Imagination: From the Middle Ages to the Seventeenth Century* (Princeton: Princeton University Press, 1986), 57-63.

[13] For the various opinions on how the division between theology and spirituality developed in the West, see Louth, *Discerning the Mystery: An Essay on the Nature of Theology* (Oxford: Clarendon Press, 1983), 4-11.

[14] According to Louth, it was the Enlightenment's universal and overly confident application of method by thinkers such as Descartes and Locke that, when applied to theological knowledge, would hammer in succeeding centuries a definitive wedge between theology and spirituality. See *Discerning the Mystery*, 7.

[15] Note, for example, Alasdair MacIntyre's discussion of Aquinas' analogical and Descartes' univocal treatments of the philosophical concept of "truth" in *Whose Justice? Which Rationality?* (Notre Dame: University of Notre Dame Press, 1988), 359.

[16] This break has been described as a "Copernican revolution in the practical order." It gives the human person autonomy in both the practical and theoretical orders. See Louis Dupré, *A Dubious Heritage: Studies in the Philosophy of Religion After Kant* (New York: Paulist Press, 1977), 2. For a critique of Kant's moral imperative, see Alasdair MacIntyre, *After Virtue: A Study in Moral Theory*, 2d ed. (London: Duckworth, 1985), 45-6.

Introduction

Theology was thought of more and more as an exclusively rational discipline; the theologian's spiritual life, while important for his or her own personal piety, moved more and more to the periphery of the theological enterprise. The classical definition of theology as "faith seeking understanding" (*fides quaerens intellectum*) was summarily inverted, exchanging subject for predicate. Faith became an experience to be verified; the content of revelation, material to be quantified. Fallen from its once exalted role as "the queen of the sciences," theology resorted to the imitation of its distantly related cousins, i.e., the empirical sciences. Promulgated through the development and systematic use of the historical-critical method, theology's newly gained authority was shaken but not unnerved by the so-called masters of suspicion (i.e., Marx, Nietzsche, and Freud). Suffering in this postmodern era[17] from a damaging and unprecedented loss of self-confidence, it has existed for a long time in a weakened, almost disillusioned state, desperately in need of a comprehensive act of retrieval.[18] By trying to reintegrate the Church's theo-

---

[17] The term "postmodernism" has recently been described as "a slippery concept" used to refer to "the widespread breakdown of certain icons of secular modernity — the belief in progress, in utilitarian reason, in science as cure-all — and along with this collapse, the sense that the mainline 'mother churches' are not capable of responding to the cultural crisis." From a report on the Omaha conference on postmodernism cited in Agnes Cunningham, "Modernity/Postmodernity: The State of the Question for Contemporary Catholic Theology," in *The Catholic Theological Society of America: Proceedings of the Forty-Sixth Annual Convention (Atlanta, June 12-15, 1991)*, ed. Paul Crowley (Santa Clara: The Catholic University of America, 1991), 156.

[18] Hence Paul Ricoeur's well-known call for "a hermeneutics of retrieval" to balance the more pervasive "hermeneutics of suspicion" of contemporary interpretation theory. See *De l'interprétation: essai sur Freud* (Paris: Éditions du Seuil, 1965), 40. For theology, this need is well-described by David Tracy: "...the very ambiguity of the religious phenomenon suggests the need for both hermeneutics of retrieval and hermeneutics of suspicion in the conversation elicited by religious classics — classics which, far more than the classics of art, are concretized and often institutionalized in concretely ambiguous religious traditions." See *The Analogical Imagination: Christian Theology and the Culture of Pluralism* (London: SCM Press, LTD, 1981), 19 n. 71. See also Walter H. Principe, "Presidential Address: Catholic Theology and the Retrieval of Its Intellectual Tradition: Problems and Possibilities," in *The Catholic Theological Society of America: Proceedings of the Forty-Sixth Annual Convention (Atlanta, June 12-15, 1991)*, ed. Paul Crowley (Santa Clara: The Catholic University of America, 1991), 84-87.

logical formulations with Christian life and worship, theological spirituality hopes to participate in this difficult act of reclamation.

THE LEVELS OF THEOLOGICAL SPIRITUALITY

Thus far, the discussion has proceeded by way of *description*, without any attempt to provide an actual *definition* of the term "spirituality" or of how its accompanying modifier "theological" might adjust it. The reason for this calculated way of proceeding is to underscore the embracive character of the field and to point out the tacit manner in which most people appropriate knowledge, i.e., by intuiting the parts before delimiting the whole. Useful as it is on most levels of practical and speculative knowledge, the way of definition can and has been taken to extremes by the unconscious tendency in today's Western technocratic culture to filter all of reality through an exclusive emphasis on the rational. This overemphasis is symptomatic of the very same narrowing of the concept of rationality that has, since the Age of the Enlightenment, relegated theological inquiry more and more to an ever diminishing group of specialized academicians. The Catholic theological tradition, by way of contrast, seeks to sustain a creative tension between the kataphatic (i.e., positive) and apophatic (i.e., negative) approaches to theology. In doing so, it recognizes the indefinable character of the ultimate source of reality and is able to maintain a healthy respect for the limitations of human reason. [19]

---

[19] The source of this creative tension goes back to the writings of Pseudo-Dionysius, a sixth-century Syrian monk, whose Neoplatonic synthesis of Christian theology reserved a place for both the kataphatic *and* apophatic approaches to the penetration of the divine mysteries. Considered to have subapostolic authority by virtue of their close (albeit untrue) association with Dionysius the Areopagite of Acts 17, these Greek writings made at least three entries into the Latin West: (1) 593-825, through a Greek codex possibly transported to Rome from Constantinople by Gregory the Great in 585 and then translated at the Lateran Council of 649; (2) during Carolingian times when two translations were made, first by Abbot Hilduin in 832 and then by John Scotus Erigena from 851-62; and (3) during the twelfth and thirteenth centuries with respective translations made by John the Saracen and Robert

Introduction

Recent years have witnessed a number of attempts to provide an adequate definition of "spirituality."[20] The differences among them — sometimes subtle; at other times, considerable — point to the comprehensive nature of the field and the great difficulty which otherwise like-minded scholars have had in reaching a consensus. Probably the greatest difference in those trying to formulate a definition of spirituality is between those who emphasize the formal doctrinal roots of spirituality and those seeking a more anthropological foundation.[21] When concerned with Christian spirituality, these approaches do not appear to be mutually exclusive. With certain adaptations, they can be used to complement each other and help to avoid an otherwise truncated form of life in the Spirit. Theology, in other words, is not fully realized until it is enfleshed; human experience, not adequately oriented to God without reference to dogma.[22]

Given the above qualifications, spirituality has aptly been defined as "the way in which a person understands and lives within his or her historical context that aspect of his or her religion, philosophy or ethic that is viewed as the loftiest, the noblest, the

---

Grosseteste. With Commentaries on such works as *The Divine Names* by scholastic theologians of such high repute as Albert the Great and Thomas Aquinas, this approach to theology earned a respected place in the Catholic tradition. Without a doubt, its greatest influence has been in the area of mystical theology, influencing such diverse authors as Bonaventure, Meister Eckhart, and the author of *The Cloud of Unknowing*. It was only with the critical literary skills of Erasmus (d. 1536) and Laurentius Valla (d. 1547) that the association of these writings with the the Apostle Paul's Greek convert at the Areopagus were proven false (hence, the term, "Pseudo-Dionysius"). See Walter H. Principe, *Introduction to Patristic and Medieval Theology*, 2d ed. (Toronto: Pontifical Institute of Mediaeval Studies, 1982), 161-70.

[20] For the spectrum of definitions, see Jon Alexander, "What Do Recent Writers Mean by Spirituality," *Spirituality Today* 32 (1980): 247-56; Antonio Queralt, "La espiritualidad como disciplina teológica," *Gregorianum* 60 (1979): 333-39; Schneiders, "Spirituality in the Academy," 684.

[21] See above xxii n. 5 .

[22] The term "dogma" comes from the Greek root, δόγμα — meaning "teaching, decree, or ordinance." Catholic dogmas give solemn expression to the truths of divine revelation and act as secure guides for authentic Christian living. For the development of the Roman Catholic theological nomenclature and the various tensions involved in contemporary usage, see Gerald O'Collins, *The Case Against Dogma* (New York: Paulist Press, 1975), 39-67, 86-100.

most calculated to lead to the fullness of the ideal or perfection being sought."[23] The word "theological" would modify this definition by focusing on the person's religious (in the present case, explicitly Christian) convictions and by seeking to extract from the Church's theological formulations their specific relevance for his or her present situation in life. When taken together, both noun and modifier convey the importance of striking a balance between the doctrinal emphasis on theological formulation and the anthropological focus on human experience. In this respect, the approach taken by theological spirituality may be said "to propose from above," while all the time working judiciously "to modify from below." Here, there is no artificial division between doctrine and devotion, theological reflection and the life of prayer.

Equally as helpful as the above definition is the way in which its author distinguishes three different yet related levels of spirituality: (1) a real or existential level, which focuses on the way a person or group brings to life in their own historical circumstances a specific religious or spiritual ideal; (2) the formulation of a teaching about this lived reality; and (3) the study by scholars of the first two levels of spirituality, with special reference to the second.[24] The value of these distinctions is the way in which they allocate appropriate fields of competence and, at the same time, highlight the intricate connection between human experience and theological reflection.

These same three levels are also applicable to what may be termed a strictly *theological* spirituality. In such an approach, the first level normally encountered by most individuals is the second, i.e., that of a formulated teaching about the lived reality. The assumption here is that the theological formulations of the Church convey not only intellectual content, but also vital experience of its lived reality in Christ. When viewed from this angle, the very purpose of theological spirituality is to counterbalance the over-intellectualized understanding of Church doctrine (now recognized as a product of the changing conception of rationality in

---

[23] Principe, "Toward Defining Spirituality," 136.
[24] Ibid., 135-36.

Introduction

Western culture) by penetrating its rational veneer and by getting in touch with the lived spiritual experience that gave rise to it. To do so, great leaps of imagination, reinvigorated preaching and educational programs, as well as long periods of study and quiet contemplation will be required to help bring about a change in the common impressions most people have of the Church's theological tradition. The classical connection between liturgy and doctrine (*lex orandi lex credendi*) will have to be brought to the fore for believers to ponder; the relationship between theology and prayer, strengthened; the ever-widening gap between the professional theologian and the simple believer, narrowed. The hope of such efforts would be to help others to experience the theological formulations of the Church as a lived spiritual reality. Only by moving from level two to level one will level two itself convey renewed meaning to future generations of Christians. And only by maintaining a continuity with levels one and two will the study by scholars of the Church's theological formulations (level three) aspire to anything more than mere antiquarian interest.

THE DISTINCTIVENESS OF KERNEL SPIRITUALITY

The kernel approach adopted in these pages is just one of many possible forms that an authentic theological spirituality could take. As such, it displays the common traits of theological spirituality mentioned in the above paragraphs, as well as a number of its own distinctive characteristics.

Kernel spirituality is most noted for its attempt to identify "fundamental principles" of particular areas of theological inquiry (e.g., Christology, ecclesiology, Trinitarian theology) and reflecting upon their significance for a specific way of Christian life. It does so with the understanding that each of these disciplines are already intimately connected at their source (as a reflection on the Church's ongoing experience of the Christ event) and vary from one another by virtue of limitations inherent in the nature of human understanding.

By "fundamental," it is not meant to be implied that theology

—in general or in any of its particulars—possesses an immutable, unchanging character (as if it existed solely in the mind of God without recourse to human experience). A thing is "fundamental" to theology to the extent that it reveals an underlying structure of rational discourse that opens itself up to historical adaptation and personal appropriation.

By "principle," the impression is not meant to be given that theology is a purely theoretical science, with a predetermined set of theorems and axioms that can be applied at all times in a detached, mathematical manner without averting to human experience. A "principle" of theology goes to the roots of a particular field of study, uncovering permanence in the midst of change, continuity in the midst of discontinuity — and vice versa. The point of departure for its own self-critique, it seeks to generate theological growth by encouraging reflection on the significance of the past for the present with an eye toward possible future reformulations.

By the expression "fundamental principle," that which is most essential to the theological disciplines in question is brought to the fore, i.e., what it most needs in order to function and exist. Since all of theology is intimately related at its source, it follows that each of these principles should be examined not only in themselves, but also in relation to each other, and in connection with the whole of theology.

These fundamental principles are called "kernels" because they represent an important source of growth ("theological seeds," if you will) for the Church's ongoing reflection on the meaning of the Christ event. By trying to uncover and make relevant the theological foundations of the Catholic faith, they hope to make the lived reality that gave rise to them be experienced anew with each generation.

Introduction

THE METHOD OF KERNEL SPIRITUALITY

As far as methodology goes, each "kernel" opens with a specific question: "Is there a fundamental principle of _____?" (The blank would be filled in by the name of the particular area of theological inquiry under consideration.) Simple, direct, easy to understand, this question underscores the importance of making the Church's theological tradition as much as possible openly accessible to all.

The type of response given to any such opening query will largely depend on the historiographical assumptions (conscious or unconscious) that guide the act of theological interpretation. A strict deconstructionist stance will seek to unravel any threads of continuity woven by the craft of the historical theologian. A firm fundamentalist position (either Biblical or dogmatic) will disallow any development that seems to depart from its untouchable canon of sacrosanct truths. A position of naive historical progressivism (either that of Enlightened humanism or of the Marxist analytical sort) will filter the Church's theological tradition through its limited understanding of human rationality. A devolutionary attitude toward the movement of world history (e.g., Gold, Silver, and Bronze Ages) will measure theology according to the standards of some previous age of unparalleled religious achievement. Each of these stances (and only a few have been mentioned) would answer questions about fundamental principles quite differently.[25]

The historiographical position adopted here is one that recognizes the analogical dimensions of human reason and takes for granted the ability of this important faculty of the human person to discern patterns of both continuity and discontinuity in the theological thought of successive historical periods. It retains

---

[25] Other historiographical assumptions are provided in Van A. Harvey, *The Morality of Historical Knowledge and Christian Belief* (Philadelphia: The Westminster Press, 1986), 68-99. Note especially his caution (84) against treating terms such as "presupposition" and "assumption" in a monolithic manner — as if "there is but one kind of presupposition and that all are equally arbitrary or well-founded."

an openness towards the presence of the transcendent in human history and maintains that, even though the past is not entirely reconstructible, the historical theologian can enter into dialogue with the beliefs and theological viewpoints of past generations. Its aim is to arrive at a sufficient degree of historical understanding that will allow the historical theologian to construct a valid principle applicable to the whole of the theological discipline in question. Such a principle will attempt to incorporate elements of continuity and discontinuity within its formulation. It will also seek to identify and formulate the essential elements of the classical theological position in a way that is relevant for the present generation of Christians.[26]

In the context of the above historiographical considerations, there follows in the kernel methodology an examination of the discipline's classical theological formulations in light of the original question posed. This invites a study of the various models used throughout Christian history to express the particular theological truth under investigation. Because of limitations due to the historical circumstances in which it was formulated, each model normally presents only a glimpse of the mystery under consideration. As a result, a sharp distinction must be drawn between the

---

[26] Helpful criteria for this process of theological correlation between the past and present are provided by Roger Haight, *The Dynamics of Theology* (New York: Paulist Press, 1990), 226-32. Note especially his emphasis (228, 230) on both appreciating the historical context of the Church's past theological formulations and understanding the present historical context in and for which the theological interpretation is being made.

[27] According to Ewert Cousins, "The use of the concept of model in theology... breaks the illusion that we are actually encompassing the infinite within our finite structures of language. It prevents concepts and symbols from becoming idols and opens theology to variety and development just as the model method has done for science, "Models and the Future of Theology," *Continuum* 7 (1969): 78-91. For the need for models in contemporary theology, see David Tracy, *Blessed Rage for Order: The New Pluralism in Theology* (Minneapolis: The Seabury Press, Inc., 1975), 22-23; Robert M. Scharlemann, "Theological Models and Their Construction," *Journal of Religion* 53 (1973): 68. The classic works on the subject are I.T. Ramsey, *Models and Mystery* (London: Oxford University Press, 1964) and Max Black, *Models and Metaphor* (Ithaca: Cornell University Press, 1962). See also T.S. Kuhn, *The Structure of Scientific Revolutions* 2d ed. (Chicago: University of Chicago Press, 1970).

Introduction

particular model employed and the theological truth it seeks to express.[27] Other, equally valid dimensions escape the model's epistemological grasp and can easily be overlooked. In this context, the goal of the historical theologian is to analyze each successive model and distill from it the particular aspect of the truth it is trying to convey. From the resulting array of insights, a new synthesis is attempted that seeks to incorporate all of these dimensions into a single comprehensive principle. Needless to say, not even this revised formulation will exhaust the truth of the mystery it is seeking to express. The hope is only to move the tradition of the Church's theological formulations forward by setting in place an interlocking logical web of orthodox judgments about a particular field of God's revelatory action.

The final step in the method of the kernel approach to theological spirituality is to focus upon the significance of its newly devised principle for a specific way of Christian living — in the present case, the religious life. The intent here is to reflect upon the newly reformulated theological truth in such a way that it connects with the lived experience of a particular vocational state in the Church. For the religious life, this is best achieved by drawing connections, making observations, and ultimately drawing conclusions about the implications these new theological insights have for the vows of chastity, poverty, and obedience. [28]

THE WITNESS OF THE VOWS

In these pages, the religious life is understood as a vocational state within the Catholic Church which participates in the universal call to Christian holiness by means of a permanent, vowed consecration to the evangelical counsels of chastity, poverty, and

---

[28] Whether it moves from the abstract to the concrete or vice versa, theology is a futile exercise if it fails to connect with the lived experience of the Church community, in this case those called to serve God's people as religious. For more on method in the field of Spirituality, see Edward Kinerk, "Toward a Method for the Study of Spirituality." *Review for Religious* 40 (1981): 3-19. See also Schneiders, "Spirituality in the Academy," 694 n. 66, 695.

obedience. Mutually inhering, these vows presume an ecclesial context, are ordained to varying forms of communal expression, and, depending on the character of the religious institute involved, allow for a variety of apostolic orientations (i.e., active, contemplative, mixed). In adapting itself to changing historical circumstances, this consecrated form of religious commitment preserves its continuity through time by a dual orientation of countercultural challenge and eschatological consolation to the world, to those variously incorporated into the Church, and to Church members themselves.[29] To the latter, religious life beckons each individual to a renewed dedication to the particular path of Christian holiness (i.e., married, priestly, single) which he or she has chosen. In this respect, the religious life serves as a leaven within the Church, constantly calling it, both individually and communally, to remain steadfast in its commitment to Christian holiness. As leaven, the religious life reminds all believers that this commitment is nourished and sustained through the universal sacrament of the Church and its Eucharistic worship. Around the table of the Lord, Catholic believers of all vocational states participate in and give expression to the Church's universal prophetic mission which religious, as members of the Church and by means of the countercultural and eschatological focus of their vows, seek to offer in a radical vocational form.[30]

---

[29] Using the insights of Walter Brueggemann's *Prophetic Imagination* (Philadelphia: Fortress Press, 1978), Juliana Casey says of this twofold dimension of the religious life that "it makes public the death and dying in the dominant culture; it energizes for a new vision of the alternative culture." See "Toward a Theology of the Vows," in *Turning Points in Religious Life*, ed. Carol Quigley (Wilmington: Michael Glazier, 1987), 121. See also Sandra M. Schneiders, *New Wineskins: Re-imagining Religious Life Today* (New York: Paulist Press, 1986), 266-84. For the prophetic dimension of the religious life, see Jean Galot, "Profetismo della vita religiosa," *Vita consacrata* 13 (1977): 487-96, 529-42; Diarmuid O'Murchu. *The Prophetic Horizon of Religious Life* (London: Excalibur Press, 1989).

[30] The Second Vatican Council documents avoid using comparative language (e.g.,"better than," "a higher stater than," etc.) when describing the relationship between the religious life and the other states in the Church. Instead, it seeks to describe the unique qualities of religious life in its own right by employing

Introduction

CONCLUSION

By identifying fundamental principles of particular areas of theological inquiry and then reflecting on their significance for those committed to the evangelical counsels, the "kernel" approach adopted in these pages opens the way for a comprehensive theological spirituality of the religious life. It does so by tapping into the well of spiritual experience beneath the soil of the Church's classical formulations, siphoning out their theological relevance for today, and taking in whatever insights (both new and old) they bring to the understanding of the religious vows. This attempt to bring theology back to its experiential roots, provide a coherent reformulation, and relate the religious life to the whole of theology constitutes one of the distinctive elements of the kernel spirituality developed in this book.

That is not to say that the kernels themselves will cover all theological bases and correspond to the experience of every religious who reads them. Considerations of space have war-

---

phrases such as "manifests in a special way," "a striking witness," and "to derive still more abundant fruit". See Vatican Council II, *Lumen gentium*, nos. 39, 42, 44 [*CDD*, 165, 172, 175]; English translation: Flannery, *Vatican Council II*, 396, 401, 403. The closest the Council comes to a strictly comparative approach is its affirmation that religious consecration is "a fuller expression" of a person's baptismal consecration. See Vatican Council II, *Perfectae caritatis*, no. 5 [*CDD*, 337-8]; Flannery, *Vatican Council II*, 614. Even this statement, however, must be understood in the context of previous declarations that "holiness is one" and that "all the faithful are called to the perfection and holiness of their own state in life." See Vatican Council II, *Lumen gentium*, nos. 41, 42 [*CDD*, 167, 173]; English translation: Flannery, *Vatican Council II*, 398, 402. The same can be said for John Paul II's nuanced (by numerous Scriptural quotations) and qualified (i.e., "in this sense the apostle teaches...") reference to the Pauline teaching that they "do better who choose virginity" (1 Cor 7:38). See John Paul II, *Redemptionis donum*, no. 11 [*AAS* 76 (1984): 260]; English translation: "*Redemptionis Donum: An Expression of Love for Religious*," 493. On the special value of the evangelical counsels, see Karl Rahner, "On the Evangelical Counsels," chap. in *Theological Investigations*, vol. 8, *Further Theology of the Spiritual Life 2*, trans. David Bourke (London: Darton, Longman and Todd, 1971), 133-67. For their radical nature, see Hans Urs von Balthasar, "Radicalisme évangélique," *Vie consacrée* 47 (1975): 238-40; B. Rollin, "Le radicalisme des conseils évangéliques," *Nouvelle revue théologique* 108 (1986): 532-54; Thomas F. O'Meara, *Holiness and Radicalism in Religious Life* (New York: Herder and Herder, 1970).

ranted a selection of only a handful of areas for careful theological scrutiny (15 out of a possible 25-30) — those deemed especially appropriate for a study of this kind. Nor is there any guarantee that the kernels themselves, taken either individually or as a whole, will affect every religious in quite the same way. To be sure, the primary purpose of these kernels is not to indoctrinate the novice to a new understanding of the vows or to shore up the veteran religious with a relevant theological updating, but to offer pertinent insights into how the religious life itself relates to the whole of theology. In this respect, the actual task of transforming these insights into lived religious experience depends largely on the strength of individual and group initiatives. Be that as it may, the hope still persists that, once duly appropriated, the kernels developed in the following chapters will bring added theological depth to the religious outlook of those already living a consecrated evangelical commitment to Christ and his Church. Only from such depth, is a thoroughly coherent and comprehensive theological spirituality of the religious life ever likely to arise.

The book itself is composed of sixteen chapters. The first fifteen are so constructed that they can stand either alone as individual essays or as interrelating parts of a larger theological synthesis. Each adheres to roughly the same organizational structure and can be read both in its specific details and as a part relating to a whole. The kernel sections, in particular, should be read side-by-side, as well as within their own proper literary settings. Those dealing with the significance of these principles for the religious life are intended to be read in a similar manner. The final chapter provides a summary of the findings, a brief reflection on the theology of the vows, and some concluding remarks about the role of religious as bearers of the Church's theological tradition.

Finally, when studying the following material, readers of *other* vocational states are encouraged to embark upon their own process of theological reflection and to draw out the significance of these principles for their own Christian calling. Although its focus in these pages rests on the religious vows of chastity, poverty, and obedience, kernel spirituality can and (with time and space permitting) should be extended to all lifelong callings

Introduction

within the mystery of Christ's Body, the Church. Needless to say, such a task goes beyond the clearly specified goal of the book's title (i.e., "A Theological Spirituality of the Religious Life"), the concrete implementation of which has now been properly introduced and can finally get under way.

EVANGELICAL KERNELS

1

THE THEOLOGY KERNEL

Is there a fundamental principle of theology? Part of the difficulty in answering this question comes from the great variety of uses now given to the term itself. Today, "theology" can have any one of a number of meanings, falling anywhere along a wide spectrum of historical, political, economic, religious, philosophical, and social concerns.[1] Influenced by the scientific outlook of a highly technologized Western culture, theology has suffered the uncertain and rather dubious fate of overspecialization, a phenomenon which has brought the discipline to its present unrelated and fragmented state.[2] It would not be an exaggeration to say that many of the controversies in the Church today are reducible to questions concerning the nature and purpose of theology itself.[3]

---

[1] Tracy outlines five basic models in contemporary theology: (1) orthodox theology, (2) liberal theology, (3) neo-orthodox theology, (4) radical theology, and (5) the revisionist model. Each makes different assumptions about the interrelation and priority of these concerns. See *Blessed Rage for Order*, 22-42.

[2] According to William Johnston, "The great temptation of theology has always been to divorce itself from mystical experience...This was a very real problem in the Middle Ages; and it is a very real problem today. Particularly so, since in the last few centuries theology has been greatly preoccupied with controversial issues, has become extremely academic, and has largely divorced itself from spirituality. Contemplative experience has been relegated to the pious writers of pious books...This is scarcely a healthy situation; for a theology which is divorced from the inner experience of the theologian is arid and carries no conviction." See *The Inner Eye of Love* (London: Collins, 1978), 56-57.

[3] To cite a few: (1) The controversy between theologians and the magisterium over theological dissent comes down to who has the right to determine the

THE RETRIEVAL OF THEOLOGY

Given this unfortunate state of affairs, perhaps now more than ever, is the time to look back into the treasury of the Christian past with a view toward recapturing that element of coherence which, for whatever reason, was first overlooked, then simply ignored, and has long since fallen from the rational structure of most modern theological discourse. The purpose of this retrospective view would not be to impose an antiquated theological principle upon the concerns of the present, but to discover an appropriate contemporary analogue.[4]

The point of departure for this act of historical retrieval and the constituent element of what in this essay will come to be known as "The Theology Kernel" is Anselm of Canterbury's well-known definition of theology as *fides quaerens intellectum* ("faith seeking understanding").[5] This statement has much to offer the study of theological foundations. Rooted in Holy Writ [6] and the tradition of the Fathers,[7] formulated by a person who represents,

---

legitimate limits of theological inquiry; (2) The tension between the Vatican and third world liberation theologies revolves around what means may be used to free the poor from oppressive societal structures; (3) Radical feminist concerns over the role of women in the Church bring into question the legitimacy of theological formulations which, for most of the Church's history, were fashioned by a male clerical world with a vested interest in promulgating a patriarchal model of Church.

[4] To be accomplished by interpreting critically the tradition-mediated event. See Tracy, *The Analogical Imagination*, 405.

[5] Anselm's precise words read: "Neque enim quaero intelligere ut credam, sed credo ut intelligam" ("For I do not seek to understand in order that I may believe; but I believe in order that I may understand"), *Proslogion*, 1 in *Anselmi opera omnia*, ed. F.S. Schmitt, vol. 1 (Stuttgart: Friedrich Frommann, 1984), 100 [Translation mine]. More recently, theology has been defined as "...the construal of reality in the light of Christian symbols." See Haight, *Dynamics of Theology*, 216.

[6] The Vulgate version of Is 7:9 reads: "...si non credideritis non permanebitis" ("If you do not believe, you will not stand firm"), *Biblia sacra vulgata*, ed. Robert Weber, vol. 2 (Stuttgart: Württembergische Bibelanstalt, 1969), 1103 [Translation mine].

[7] See especially Augustine, *De trinitate*, 8.5.8 [*CCL* 50:277-79; *PL* 42:952]; *Epistola*, 120.1.3 [*CSEL* 33:706; *PL* 33:453]; *Sermo*, 89.4 [*PL* 38:556]; *Sermo*, 212.1 [*PL* 38:1059]; *Tractatus in Iohannis evangelium*, 40.9 [*CCL* 36:355-56; *PL* 35:1690].

at one and the same time, both the greatest achievements of the monastic schools and the first fruits of scholastic method,[8] the three elements of Anselm's definition provide a valuable heuristic device for explaining the current nature and function of the discipline.

I. *Faith and the Nature of Knowing*

Today's theologians understand the phenomenon of faith in an intellectual, fiducial, or performative sense, depending on whether or not they associate it primarily with rationality and intellect (in the spirit of Thomistic thought), affectivity and will (in the spirit of Lutheran belief), or human solidarity and action (in the spirit of liberation theology).[9] Since the Second Vatican Council, many have also emphasized the social character of faith, offsetting what in the past appeared to be an overemphasis on individual piety.[10] That Anselm himself associates faith with individual intellect should not obscure the well-known fact of his having written his works in a communal faith environment (i.e., first at the monastery of Bec and later at Canterbury)[11] long before the time when the close bonds between reason and will, analysis and affection, dialectics and devotion had been weakened by late-medieval nominalism and nearly severed by Enlightenment

---

[8] Jean Leclercq, *The Love of Learning and the Desire for God*, trans. Catharine Misrahi (New York: Fordham University Press, 1982), 277.

[9] More specifically, the intellectual approach focuses on faith as a type of knowing; the fiducial, on faith as personal trust; the performative, on commitment to revolutionary praxis in a historical situation which mediates the Word of God. All three approaches seem complementary and mutually corrective. See Avery Dulles, "The Meaning of Faith in Relationship to Justice," in *The Faith That Does Justice: Examining the Christian Sources for Social Change*, ed. John C. Haughey (New York: Paulist Press, 1977), 14, 23, 34, 39.

[10] See, for example, Oscar Romero, "The Political Dimension of the Faith from the Perspective of the Option for the Poor," in *Liberation Theology: A Documentary History*, ed. Alfred T. Hennelly (Maryknoll, N.Y.: Orbis Books, 1990), 292-303.

[11] R.W. Southern, *Saint Anselm and His Biographer: A Study of Monastic Life and Thought, 1059-1130* (Cambridge: The University Press, 1963), 27-34; 253-55.

[12] Louth, *Discerning the Mystery*, 6-7.

thought.¹² From this perspective, Anselm's seemingly small, inconspicuous textual lapses may very well express some of his deepest assumptions, most of which remain unexamined not for their lack of theological import, but simply because they were so much taken for granted.

More pertinent to the issue at hand is the implication made in Anselm's definition that theology rests on the foundation of faith: "theology without faith" opposes "faith seeking understanding" and is simply a contradiction in terms. This principle of contrariety holds true regardless of whether or not theology, as such, is done from *within* or from *without* one's self-actuation of existence in faith, i.e., "existentially" or "sapientially." Faith is fiducial in the former; intellectual, in the latter. Theology, in turn, is dialogical in the former; a subalternated science, in the latter (i.e., based on principles derived from revelation).¹³ In neither case can faith be suspended, done without, or simply taken for granted. It is a necessary prerequisite for all theological understanding and is precisely what distinguishes the Christian theologian from the historian of religion.¹⁴

Given the above, an interesting parallel arises between faith as a necessary prerequisite for theology and as a fundamental presupposition of all human cognition. Just as theology requires faith to get under way and be continually sustained, human knowing itself cannot take place without what, in effect, amounts to an unqualified "religious" support of its most basic presuppositions. That is to say that theories of rationality simply cannot function without a basic unquestioning adherence to their respective analogical, univocal, and equivocal starting points.¹⁵ While such uncritical allegiances have prompted some to uncover what

---

¹³ For an extended treatment of existential and sapiential theology, see Otto Hermann Pesch, *Die Theologie der Rechtfertigung bei Martin Luther und Thomas von Aquin* (Mainz: Matthias Grunewald, 1967), 935-48.

¹⁴ Principe, "Toward Defining Spirituality," 139-41.

¹⁵ For the relation of such theories to tradition-constituted enquiry, see MacIntyre's discussion of contested rationalities in *Whose Justice? Which Rationality?*, 389-403.

they call "the irrational roots" of human reason,[16] a more appropriate analogue for a proper understanding of such epistemological preconceptions would be the corrective and simultaneous use of the various meanings of faith described above.[17] From this perspective, one may speak of the theological and cognitive senses of faith by granting first the analogous use of the term itself and then the corresponding proportional relation in the nature/supernature distinction.[18] Even their greatest single difference—that one is infused and the other a natural prerequisite of reason—does not disavow a basic continuity existing between such seemingly unrelated spheres of human experience.[19]

II. The Twofold Movement of Seeking

Anselm defines theology not in static terms, but as an investigative action, i.e., "fides *quaerens* intellectum" ("faith *seeking*

---

[16] Thus the revealing insight of William Barrett: "...the rationalism of the Enlightenment will have to recognize that at the very heart of its light there is also a darkness." See *Irrational Man: A Study in Existential Philosophy* (Garden City, N.Y.: Doubleday and Co., 1958), 279. Kenneth Leech's observation seems particularly appropriate in this context: "Writers such as Kuhn and Polanyi have cast doubt on the equation of science with rationality, and it can no longer be said that science involves the expulsion of mystery." See *Experiencing God: Theology as Spirituality* (San Francisco: Harper and Row, 1989), 9.

[17] An analogy can be drawn here with John Henry Newman's notion of liberal education. To exclude one branch of science from a university curriculum would be to impoverish our knowledge of the whole. Likewise, to exclude one of the above understandings of faith from the field of theological inquiry would be to diminish our understanding of the mystery of faith. In other words, the more perspectives utilized in examining the truth , the broader our appreciation of the whole and the relation of the individual part to the whole. See *The Idea of a University* (Westminster, Md.: Christian Classics, Inc., 1973), 45-50.

[18] A developmental or evolutionary approach to the relationship between the natural and the supernatural (e.g., gradual continuity vs. the classical two-tiered model) would effect a similar change in our understanding of the theological and cognitive senses of faith.

[19] See, for example, the correlation among the various stages of cognitive, psychological, moral, and faith development in James W. Fowler, *Stages of Faith: The Psychology of Human Development and the Quest for Meaning* (San Francisco: Harper and Row, 1981), 244-45.

understanding"). To a large degree, the particulars of this action will depend on the believing subject and what he or she understands by "faith." That is to say that the subject's search for understanding will vary according to whether faith is understood in an intellectual, fiducial, or performative sense. The possibility, moreover, of using two or more of these models in creative tension with one another complicates the nature of the theological act even further. Regardless of what one means by "faith," however, any understanding of the act in question must include two important elements: (1) a movement of the subject toward and beyond the subject-informed reality [20] and (2) a movement of the subject toward critical self-reflection. The lack of either of these elements will make the theological act incomplete.

The first element relates the historical influence of philosophy on the theological act. From Cartesian doubt, to empiricist epistemology, to the Kantian categories, one does not have to look very far for evidence in recent centuries pointing to Western philosophy's turn toward the subject.[21] This important hermeneutical shift, with its accompanying "critical problem," has also made its effects known in theology, first in Protestant circles and then among Roman Catholic theologians.[22] The movement in Catholic circles away from a metaphysics-based theology toward one founded on anthropological and epistemological concerns reflects this change in emphasis. Similarly, today's talk of "a linguistic turn" in theology is but a reflection of problems first recognized and formulated by twentieth-century philosophers such as Wittgenstein, Heidegger, and Saussure.[23]

---

[20] In this context, the word "inform" is used in the sense of its Latin root, *informare*, meaning "to give form and shape to."

[21] A brief yet concise treatment of this humanist turn toward the subject appears in Benedict M. Ashley, *Theologies of the Body: Humanist and Christian* (Braintree, Mass.: The Pope John Center, 1985), 204-20.

[22] For the critical problem as it developed in Protestant and Catholic theology, see Ashley, *Theologies of the Body*, 221-26.

[23] For the philosophical origins of this approach, see Richard Rorty, "Introduction: Metaphilosophical Difficulties of Linguistic Philosophy," in *The Linguistic Turn: Recent Essays in Philosophical Method*, ed. Richard Rorty (Chicago: University of Chicago Press, 1967), 1-39. For the linguistic turn in contempo-

The influence of philosophy on theology, however, often incurs an equally strong reaction, all too often, as in the case of the early Barth, rejecting any claim whatsoever of a possible relation between the two.[24] Given the fact that theology today is done in the context of the human subject seeking to understand the meaning of his or her own subject-informed reality, a much milder response seems appropriate. Indeed, the challenge before theology is to move beyond the strictures placed upon it by Western philosophical thought and to see in its own rich tradition the criteria for affirming the very reality of which it finds itself in doubt. Rather than what would amount to a naive return to the subject/object dichotomy of the medieval synthesis (simply taken for granted by Anselm and the later scholastics), such a challenge would reshape Western philosophical thought's emphasis on subject into that of a reality-informed subject, basing itself on the Christian doctrine of creation which views the human person as *imago Dei* (Gn 1:27). From this perspective, the solution of "the critical problem" is resolved in a theological anthropology which has a reality-informed subject informing reality with his or her own natural cognitive structures.[25]

The second element, that of critical self-reflection, insures the integrity of the theological act by its seeking to preserve the continuity between the believer and the believer's search. The seeker, in other words, must be invested in what he or she is looking for, believing in both the content and the method of the

---

rary theology, see The Catholic Theological Society of America, *Proceedings of the Forty-Second Annual Convention (Philadelphia, June 10-13, 1987)*, ed. George Kilcourse (Louisville: The Catholic Theological Society of America, 1987).

[24] As one author puts it: "Karl Barth talks of theology's having escaped from the Egyptian bondage of philosophy..." See John Macquarrie, *Principles of Christian Theology* (London: SCM Press LTD, 1966), 20.

[25] Stated in another way: "The self-appropriation of one's own intellectual and rational self-consciousness begins as a cognitional theory, expands into a metaphysics and an ethics, mounts to a conception and an affirmation of God, only to be confronted with the problem of evil that demands the transformation of the self-reliant intelligence into an *intellectus quaerens fidem*." See Bernard Lonergan, *Insight: A Study of Human Understanding* (San Francisco: Harper and Row, 1958), 731.

search. To allow for detachment or a rift to come between theology and its source in faith renders the theologian's words inauthentic and meaningless in relation to private and, ultimately, even communal life.[26] The element of self-reflection prevents this from happening by challenging the theologian to examine time and time again the personal foundations of his or her faith. Such an examination includes not only a vigorous search into various concepts and rational principles being utilized, but also a close examination of one's own life story. In this respect, theology involves a circular relationship between reason and narrative: the former being dependent on narrative; the latter, on reason.

This mutual interdependence touches the very core of the theological knowledge. That is to say that the believer's search for understanding cannot be separated from the context of his or her own life situation, while faith, however understood, can ponder the depths of its source only against the backdrop of the discernible characteristics of the Christian story: (1) God entered our lives in Christ, (2) gave of himself completely to the point of dying for us, (3) rose to give us life and nourishment, and (4) to become the source of our hope.[27] To separate theology from its underlying narrative structure is to separate the spirit of the Christian message from its material content, thus treating people as if they were disembodied souls and, ultimately, overlooking the incarnational aspect of human existence itself.[28] The point to be made here is that a theological doctrine must remain, at all costs, rooted in and continuous with the narrative Gospel structure from which it came. Gospel narrative, in turn, must be told and retold with special reverence towards the doctrinal elements it was originally meant to affirm.

---

[26] For this reason, Leech finds the gulf between the mystic and the theologian "one of the most worrying aspects of the contemporary religious scene." See *Experiencing God*, 344-45. See also Alan Jones, "Spirituality and Theology," 171; Christian Duquoc, "Theology and Spirituality," *Concilium* 9 (no. 2, 1966): 48.

[27] These themes will be taken up in chap. 2, "The Christ Kernel," 17-31.

[28] For the incarnational basis of all human narrative, see John Navone and Thomas Cooper, *Tellers of the Word* (New York: Le Jacq Publishing, 1981), 107-9, 225.

III. From Understanding to Action

The purpose of theology, according to Anselm's definition, is understanding, the precise nature of which is once again determined by the believing subject's interpretation of the meaning of faith: that of an intellectual nature brings rational understanding; that of a fiducial nature, dialogical relation; that of a performative nature, the transformation of societal structures. Each mode of theological understanding, moreover, corresponds to a different model(s) of revelation: intellectual faith parallels revelation as doctrine; fiducial faith, revelation as inner experience and dialectical presence; transformative faith, revelation as history and new awareness.[29] Each mode of theological understanding also compels the believing subject to action, although obviously in different ways: intellectual understanding challenges the believer to stand behind and defend the truth of his or her convictions; fiducial understanding, to replicate one's relationship with God in one's relationship with one's neighbor; performative understanding, to transform the structures of human existence in such a way that they reveal the presence of the Kingdom. In this respect, the relationship in theology between understanding and action, speculation and practice, theory and praxis must be constituently and effectively continuous. That is to say that faith, in any of the above senses, does not understand itself fully until it is manifested in action.

To speak of all theology as ending in action is thus to recognize, at least implicitly, the ethical orientation of all doctrinal formulations. This recognition bases itself on the closely interrelated nature of reason in its speculative and practical modes of operation and would shy away from any attempt to dichotomize the two.[30] In this respect, Aquinas' understanding of the relation

---

[29] For a short yet precise summary of these models, see Avery Dulles, *Models of Revelation* (Garden City, N.Y.: Doubleday and Co., 1983), 24-30.

[30] To quote Aquinas: "...una et eadem potentia rationis est ratio superior et inferior. Sed distinguuntur, secundum Augustinum, per officia actuum, et secundum diversos habitus: nam superior rationi attribuitur sapientia, inferiori vero scientia" ("... the higher and lower powers of reason are one and the same

between speculative and practical reason comes closer to the mark than, for example, Kant's sharp distinction between pure and practical reason. More importantly, to speak of the close interrelation of theology and action is also to recognize, at least for Christians, the doctrinal orientation of all ethical activity. This orientation, in fact, constitutes the distinctive element of all Christian ethics, which differs from its philosophical counterpart not by way of actual moral norms and content, but by the manner in which these norms are rooted in the Christian mystery. The clearest and, by far, most important example of this circular relationship between doctrine and ethics is the dogma of the Trinity, i.e., the community of divine love seeks to realize itself in human relationships, while every expression of authentic human love in some way reflects the communal life of the Trinity.[31]

To avoid the danger of distortion, theology must closely scrutinize this intimate relation between doctrine and ethics. In the past, doctrinal formulations have all too often been used to justify a wide range of social injustices, ranging anywhere from the burning of witches, to the slave trade, to the social and economic oppression of the poor.[32] To avoid such a misuse of doctrine, criteria must be developed to discern when a particular ethical application of a doctrinal formulation actually represents a deviation from the doctrine's inherent ethical implications. Not to do so would allow doctrine to be manipulated in such a way so

---

power. But they are distinguished, according to Augustine, by virtue of their actions and various habits: wisdom is attributed to higher reason and science to the lower"). See *Summa theologiae*, I. q. 79, a. 9, resp., Leonine ed. (Turin: Marietti, 1952), 390 [Translation mine]. For more on the ethical dimensions of theology, see Haight, *Dynamics of Theology*, 232-35.

[31] On God's self-communication to us through Christ and in the Spirit, see Walter Kasper, *The God of Jesus Christ*, trans. Matthew J. O'Connell (New York: Crossroad, 1984), 128.

[32] These views are respectively expressed in Edward Peters, *Inquisition* (Berkeley: University of California Press, 1988), 40-44; Pierre Dockes, *Medieval Slavery and Liberation*, trans. Arthur Goldhammer (Chicago: University of Chicago Press, 1979), 30-31, 215; and Paulo Friere, "Conscientizing as a Way of Liberating," in *Liberation Theology: A Documentary History*, ed. Alfred T. Hennelly (Maryknoll, N.Y.: Orbis Books, 1990), 10-12.

as to suit the purposes of the powerful. In any case, that theological doctrine has been misused in the past is no reason for theologians to avoid drawing out its authentic ethical significance. It provides, on the contrary, one of the more forceful reasons for doing so.

THE THEOLOGY KERNEL

When interpreted in the above manner, the various elements of Anselm's definition allow for the following description of "The Theology Kernel." It reads thus: based on presuppositions analogous to those supporting the fundamental structures of human cognition, theology involves the believing subject's search for understanding in accordance with the principles of his or her own personal concept of faith; this individual and, by virtue of the cultural context in which the various interpretations of faith take shape, necessarily communal search for truth moves in a direction beyond that of subject-informed reality, on the one hand, and critical self-reflection, on the other; the resulting understanding is fully actualized in ethical action, which must be appropriate to and continuous with the conclusions of authentic doctrinal insight.

Despite the abstract appearance of the above formulation, a number of very practical and concrete issues are at stake. Firstly, by drawing out the analogous relationship between faith and the fundamental presuppositions made in the structures of human cognition, it offers a point even prior to that of conscience around which a dialogue between the believer and non-believer may evolve.[33] Secondly, by recognizing the existence of different models of faith in the life of the Church, it allows for a certain amount of theological pluralism, while at the same time seeking in its formulation to maintain an intrinsic unity in the theological act

---

[33] Establishing a common tradition of rationality within which such a dialogue can take place thus assumes a high priority. On the rationality of traditions, see MacIntyre, *Whose Justice? Which Rationality?*, 349-69.

itself.³⁴ Thirdly, it seeks to preserve the continuity between experience, narrative, and doctrine; in doing so, it challenges the believing subject not to give in to the pressures of rational formalism, but to root theology in the soil of his or her own life experience.³⁵ Fourthly, by emphasizing the importance of understanding the ethical implications of all doctrinal formulations, it brings out the fundamental continuity between practical and speculative reason (hence, between ethics and metaphysics) and provides a basic framework with which to distinguish the distinctive features of Christian ethics.³⁶ Fifthly, it provides a "built-in" theological corrective to the possible misuse of doctrine by insisting on a movement toward critical self-reflection as a constitutive element of the theological search.³⁷ Finally, by describing theology as an act of the believing subject, it reclaims theology for the faithful at large (in a sense each believer is a theologian), while at the same time recognizing the specific contributions of the professional.³⁸ Each

---

³⁴ Dulles points out that, while allowing for pluralism to evolve, the emphasis on the intrinsic unity of theology tries to reduce it to a minimum. In this respect, the goal of theologians is to formulate the most comprehensive unified field theory in theology with as few models as possible. See *Models of the Church* (Garden City, N.Y.: Image Books, 1974), 33.

³⁵ Since symbols mediate spiritual experience and touch the human heart, the most appropriate way to achieve this end would be to raise people's awareness of the symbolic nature of religious language and hence of the Church's theological formulations. See Haight, *Dynamics of Theology*, 152-66.

³⁶ In this respect, an emphasis on the continuity between theory and praxis would constitute an essential element of Catholic moral theology. For the current debate on how moral theology is to be defined, see Bruno Schüller, "Autonomous Ethics Revisited," in *Personalist Morals*, ed. Joseph A. Selling (Leuven: University Press, 1988), 61-70.

³⁷ The purpose of this element of critical self-reflection is to highlight the limited nature of all theological formulations and thus to challenge each new generation of believers to reinterpret their faith in such a way that it will remain continuous with the tradition they have received and yet meaningful in the midst of the exigencies of their present experience. For more on the self-corrective nature of critical reason and its function in theological discourse, see Tracy, *The Analogical Imagination*, 420-21.

³⁸ Considered in this way, there are many levels of theological discourse — from the personal to the popular to the highly specialized — each with its unique contribution to make. Greater attempts must be made to bond these levels more closely together and prevent them from losing contact with each other. What unites them, on whatever level, is that they are being done from within the plurality of believing contexts that constitute the Catholic tradition.

of the above observations represents a specific contribution of "The Theology Kernel" toward a more profound understanding of the nature of theological reflection. The peculiar strength of this principle is that it offers a single synthetic formulation which seeks to emphasize what in recent years has been so greatly overlooked, i.e., the underlying unity of the theological act itself.

THEOLOGY AND RELIGIOUS LIFE

As presented above, the fundamental principle of theology also has particular relevance for religious. Their way of life, more than any other, makes little sense when taken out of the context of a living faith in search of a deeper understanding of its source. More specifically, the religious represents a person whose "faith in search of understanding" has led him or her to embrace a style of living oriented entirely toward the perfection of that understanding. In other words, whatever the model of faith employed, the religious expresses in the vows the eschatological hope of life's ultimate resolution in the beatific vision; the reception of that vision is but another way of saying that the search of faith culminates in the fulfillment of a person's capacity for God.[39] While other states in life (i.e., the lay and priestly) also reflect this same eschatological tendency, the peculiar function of the religious is to make the hope of this vision present in such a way that it makes both others and themselves more aware of this important theological dimension of their own lives.[40] In this respect, religious serve as "a leaven in the world," enabling believers (and often non-believers) to see more clearly within themselves the great importance of their own search for meaning.[41]

---

[39] Jan Walgrave, "Prayer and Mysticism," *Communio* 12 (1985): 277-78.
[40] S. Decloux, "La dimension théologale de la vie religieuse," *Vie consacrée* 57 (1985): 12-15.
[41] "...the religious state of life ...simultaneously *reveals more clearly* to all believers the heavenly goods which are already present in this age" (italics mine). See Vatican Council II, *Lumen gentium*, no. 44 [*CDD*, 176]; English translation: Flannery, *Vatican Council II*, 404.

Religious, moreover, give concrete expression in their lives to the intimate relation between experience, narrative, and doctrine, all three of which relate together to each of the vows. Chastity, poverty, and obedience, in other words, are not meant to be encountered merely as a body of theoretical knowledge or as the detailed telling of someone else's story. Instead, they are intended to be lived and experienced in the depths of a person's being, so much so that the religious identifies with these values, adopts them, and makes them his or her own. From such experience, a "lived" narrative of the vows unfolds, bringing one both intuitively and reflectively to a deeply personal understanding of what it means to be poor, obedient, and chaste.[42] In this respect, religious highlight the continuity between ethics and doctrine, since their own vows challenge them continually to live the theories they espouse. To fail in this regard is to overlook the incarnational nature of both theology and the religious vows themselves.

In this respect, religious who are professionally trained in theology should carry out their work conscious of the specific contribution they can bring to the community of scholars. Rather than hiding behind a thin veneer of univocally argued, "objective" rhetoric, which gives the impression that their work is entirely separable from the lives they lead, they should realize and accept the great extent to which their lives shape the very questions they ask and want answered. Conscious of their own personal investment in these questions, religious theologians can bring a unique dimension to the field of theological inquiry, i.e., the insights gained from faith living the life of the evangelical counsels. This religious dimension of their lives is not something simply to be written up in a prefatory remark to their work or relegated to a footnote. Whether or not it is ever explicitly mentioned (which is not the point here), the vows remain the "looking glass" through which the religious theologian encounters reality, including his or her relation to other theologians, the magisterium, other members

---

[42] On the role of personal experience in the theology of the vows, see Casey, "Toward a Theology of the Vows," 97-98, 106-9, 118-20.

of the Church, those variously incorporated into the Church, and those outside the Church.[43] The religious theologian, in other words, relates to humanity not through the univocal rational principles of ethical formalism, which ultimately separates body from soul just as it divides theory from action and person from vocation, but in the very way in which he or she relates to God, i.e., through an incarnate rationality informed by a life of faith committed to the evangelical counsels. This necessarily analogical dimension of understanding represents the unique contribution of religious to the field of theological study. Not only do their lives make little sense without it, but the lives of others are impoverished for the lack of it. In keeping with the intrinsic variety of God's creation, their particular mode of "faith seeking understanding" has much to offer the other dimensions of creative theological inquiry.

CONCLUSION

When approached hermeneutically, Anselm's definition of theology as "faith seeking understanding" provides an important point of departure for discussing the nature of the theological act. The retrieval initiated by such a discussion places theology squarely within the context of the believing subject's search for truth and the realization of its moral implications. As formulated in this chapter, "The Theology Kernel" represents an attempt to view theology from the perspective of its most universal elements, while at the same time preserving an inclination toward pluralism that results from fundamental differences in the understanding of the nature of faith itself. In doing so, it seeks simultaneously to avoid the contrary tendencies of needless homogeneity and fragmentation.

---

[43] For more on this point, see my reflection on the Congregation for the Doctrine of the Faith's "Instruction on the Ecclesial Vocation of the Theologian" (May 24, 1990) in "Dialogue and Dissent II," *The Furrow* 42 (1991): 303-9.

In maintaining the above tension of extremes, the principle bases itself on a rationality of proper analogical proportions, which enables it to affirm some fundamental continuities between human cognition and faith, the knower and the known, the natural and the supernatural. In stipulating its basis of rational discourse, the principle not only recognizes the limitations of the theological act itself, but also provides the basis for its own self-transcendence. That is to say that the critical self-reflective function of theology encourages "faith in search of understanding" to go beyond its limits, while at the same time remaining continuous with them. The general movement in theology from experience to narrative to doctrine and the subsequent insistence that each form of expression remain rooted in and continuous with what comes before it is but one example of this element of self-transcendence. The orientation of this movement, moreover, is the beatific vision itself which, in bringing to theological discourse an eschatological and mystical point of reference, represents that point toward which experience, narrative, and doctrine will ultimately converge.

In this context, religious have been shown to have a particular contribution to make to the retrieval of theology in the present day. The eschatological nature of their vows offers the world a vision in which the theological act of "faith seeking understanding" is concretized in a life whose experiences, stories, and theories all presuppose a fundamental hope in humanity's mysterious destiny in the divine. The presence of this hope encourages the search of faith to proceed with courage and with care, especially during those times when some of the most basic presuppositions of the theological quest are held in serious doubt.

2

THE CHRIST KERNEL

Is there a fundamental principle of Christology? One of the difficulties in answering this question comes from the tendency on the part of many theologians to overlook the relationship between the internal and external scope of Christology itself. With their formulations focusing either on the meaning of Christ's *inner* divine/human relationships (e.g., one divine person, two natures, hypostatic union) or on his *outer* relationships with the world (e.g., messianic hopes, mission of liberation, suffering servant), their theologies miss the broader Christological significance that a more integrated formulation would have for the Church and its entire sacramental life.[1]

THE DISCIPLINE OF CHRISTOLOGY

While the classical Christological formulations have been faulted for a metaphysical, seemingly introverted, and rather abstract, religious doctrinairism, those of more recent vintage have been accused of turning Christ into the precise opposite, i.e.,

---

[1] Succinct summaries of the problematics of contemporary Christology appear in Walter Kasper, *Jesus the Christ*, trans. V. Green (London: Burns and Oates, 1976), 15-25 and Edward Schillebeeckx, *Jesus: An Experiment in Christology*, trans. Hubert Hoskins (New York: Crossroad, 1985), 575-94.

an extroverted political ideologue.² The truth of the matter is that Christology, as such, is too important a discipline to be left to the uncertain winds of cultural change. The fact that all Christological formulations (as with all theological expressions) are the products of culturally-conditioned linguistic expressions does not excuse the theologian from the task of searching through the tradition of the Church in order to find those common threads which bind together and give shape to the Church's authentic proclamation of Christ.

To find those threads, however, and to understand their historical significance so as to provide a proper context for their meaning in the present, the theologian will often have to examine the Church's historical Christological formulations against the backdrop of ideas they were originally intended to suppress. It should come as no surprise that doctrines such as the virgin birth, Christ's consubstantiality with the Father, and his hypostatic union of two natures, were meant, at least in part, to offset respectively the powerful influences which Docetism, Arianism, and Monophysitism had upon the developing Christian orthodoxy.³ It should also come as no surprise that one of the reasons for the eventual success of the orthodox position was the ability of Church leaders to engender widespread popular support for the edicts of their Councils.⁴ This support found expression in the Church's liturgico-sacramental life which, evolving historically to meet the changing spiritual needs of the people, gave concrete implementation to the Church's theological agenda.

The discipline of Christology, while functioning with its own set of theological purposes (i.e., to understand the meaning

---

[2] For the historical context of such diverse Christological evaluations, see Jaroslav Pelikan, *Jesus Through the Centuries: His Place in the History of Culture* (New Haven: Yale University Press, 1985), 57-70, 206-19.

[3] See Aloys Grillmeier, *Christ in the Christian Tradition: From the Apostolic Age to Chalcedon (451)*, trans. J.S. Bowden (New York: Sheed and Ward, 1965), 91, 193, 479.

[4] It was its superior organization (e.g., "none but the orthodox Christians would have contemplated holding councils") which gave episcopal Christianity a decisive edge on its rivals. See W.H.C. Frend, *The Rise of Christianity* (Philadelphia: Fortress Press, 1984), 283-84.

of Christ and his relationship to the Christ-event), must thus be understood within the context of the whole of theology. In this regard, special emphasis must be given to the related disciplines of Soteriology, Ecclesiology, and Sacramentology. All four — Christ, the Church, the Sacraments, and the doctrine of Salvation — relate to one another in such a way so as to provide a source of continuity to the Catholic theological tradition. Together, they play an important role in the formulation and ongoing cultural espousal of what can be termed "the fundamental principle of Christology."

THE CHRIST KERNEL

The principle itself comprises a process of four related theological movements and may be stated thus: (1) The Word of God entered our world, (2) gave of himself completely, (3) became our nourishment, and (4) the source of our hope. Taken as a whole, these movements represent a single event of both historical and transhistorical significance, occurring, as it were, both in time and out of time, in one age, and in every age, down through the centuries, from now unto eternity.[5] Taken individually, they correspond to different facets of the singular mystery of Christ himself: the first, to his incarnation; the second, to his earthly life and death; the third, to his institution of the Eucharist; the fourth, to his resurrection. A more complete version of the principle would thus read: Christ came to us in his incarnation, gave of himself completely in both his living and his dying, gave us in the Eucharist the nourishment of his own body and blood, and promised us in his resurrection the life of a transformed humanity.

The broad scope of this principle provides Christology with a number of distinct advantages. Questions about Christ's relationship with the world, for example, can be considered alongside

---

[5] The historical/transhistorical distinction is taken from Richard P. McBrien, *Catholicism*, vol. 1 (Oak Grove, Minn.: Winston Press, 1980), 411-12.

of and in relation to those which concern his divine and human makeup. Since each of these categories fall under particular movements of the same Christological process (i.e., incarnation, passion and death, eucharist, or resurrection), they can be answered in part, if not fully resolved, in a way which avoids fragmentation and which preserves both their complementary orientation and underlying theological unity.[6] The principle also puts an end to the hierarchical prejudice which, at various times in the Church's history, has isolated a single movement of the Christological process and hailed it exclusively as the Church's governing theological paradigm. The movements, instead, share a fundamental valuational equivalence, which renders, for example, such statements as the primacy of the Christ's passion vis-à-vis his resurrection or incarnation functionally irrelevant.[7] Each of the four movements, moreover, approach the Christological process from within the concerns of a related theological discipline: movement one encompasses the concerns of classical Christology; movement two, those of ecclesiology; movement three, those of sacramentology; and movement four, those of soteriology. Because of the ease with which it can be grasped, the principle also provides a framework for coordinating spiritual experience with theological doctrine. The result is an increased sense of continuity in the minds of believers between the Church's theory and its spiritual praxis.

MOVEMENT ONE: "THE WORD BECAME FLESH"

The principle's first movement is perhaps best summarized by the Logos theology of John's Gospel: "The Word became flesh

---

[6] For more on the theocentric character of Christology, see Dermot A. Lane, *The Reality of Jesus: An Essay in Christology* (New York: Paulist Press, 1975), 142-46.

[7] An important qualification of this statement arises: while participating in and revealing one and the same mystery, there may exist among these various Christological movements an intrinsic logical priority on the level of knowing and understanding. See, for example, Lane's discussion of the logical priority of the divinity of Jesus to the dogma of the Incarnation in *The Reality of Jesus*, 132-33.

The Christ Kernel

and made his dwelling among us" (Jn 1:14).[8] Rooted in both the Wisdom tradition of the Hebrew Scriptures and the *Logos* doctrine of classical Hellenistic thought, this late first-century statement of antidocetic intent points to a new entrance of God's Word in the world.[9] In Jesus of Nazareth, this Word lived not by virtue of its creative power (as in the rest of creation), but by virtue of its own personal presence. The Word of God entered this world in a new and daring way: it lived among us, as one of us. The Incarnation thus represents a new creative moment in God's providential plan for humanity: God became human so that humanity might become more fully like unto God. God's humanization, in other words, already anticipates humanity's ultimate divinization.

The classical questions of Christology, which concern the relationship between the divine and human in Christ, are nothing more than an attempt to understand more deeply the precise meaning of the Incarnation.[10] The theological formulas used to express this relationship have changed and will continue to change with the growth in our perception of what it means to be human and of what it means to be divine. No formula will ever exhaust the full meaning of the mystery of the Incarnation, not even those of the Councils. For this reason, the Church must always leave open the possibility that a new formulation at a future time may express the mystery more fully. The challenge for modern Christology, therefore, is to state the relationship between the divine and human in Christ in such a way that it will, at one and the same time, remain faithful to past formulations, and

---

[8] Unless otherwise stated, all English translations of the Scriptures in this dissertation are taken from *The New American Bible* (Washington, D.C.: The Confraternity of Christian Doctrine, 1970). All Greek New Testament quotations come from *The Greek New Testament*, 3d ed., eds., Kurt Aland, Matthew Black, Carlo M. Martini, Bruce M. Metzger, and Allen Wikgren (New York: American Bible Society, 1976).

[9] See Helmut Koester, *Introduction to the New Testament*, vol. 2, *History and Literature of Early Christianity* (Philadelphia: Fortress Press, 1982), 188-89; For Christianity's life-and-death struggle with docetic Gnosticism, see Kasper, *Jesus The Christ*, 197-207.

[10] A clear and precise treatment of these classical Christological formulations appears in J.N.D. Kelly, *Early Christian Doctrines*, revised ed. (San Francisco: Harper and Row, 1978), 280-343.

expand our present understanding of the meaning of the Incarnation.[11] Whether or not terms such as "nature," "hypostatic union," even "person" are used has little relevance to the project's ultimate intent. What is important from the standpoint of both tradition and the first movement of the Christological process is that, however expressed, it be maintained that Christ entered this world fully, i.e., that he was fully God as well as fully human.

It should also be pointed out that, even in this first movement, the traditional questions of Christology, which focus on Christ's inner divine/human relationships, touch upon, and, indeed, actually presuppose, his outer relationships with the world. Christ not only became flesh; he also lived among us. It is precisely this "living among us" that enabled the Word in its incarnate state to define for us the ultimate meaning of our humanity.

MOVEMENT TWO: "HE EMPTIED HIMSELF"

The second movement is best summarized by Paul's famous words in Philippians: "... he emptied himself and took the form of a slave" (Ph 2:7). These words from one of the earliest extant Christological hymns describe the extent of Christ's love for humanity and the divine character of his humble self-effacement. Christ's κενῶσις, his utter emptying of self, reveals to humanity the meaning of divine love and provides his followers with a fitting model of Christian service. Christ gave of himself completely: in his birth, in his ministry, in his obedient acceptance of death on a cross. It is the role of servant which thus characterizes the meaning of Christ and of all Christian existence. It represents

---

[11] In the words of Kasper: "The Church cannot regard itself... as a closed system. It must enter on a spiritual exchange and an intellectual discussion with the world. In this, it must on the one hand pay heed to the external prophecy of the world, yet on the other bear witness that in Jesus Christ alone the hopes of mankind have been fulfilled in a unique and insurpassable way; and that he is the great Amen to all promises." See *Jesus the Christ*, 268.

Christ's fundamental posture toward the world and toward all humanity.[12]

This theme of Christ's servanthood has important implications for the Church: Christ's humility serves as a model not just for the individual Christian, but for every level of the Christian community. In one sense, Jesus spent all of his life on earth building community: his gathering of disciples, his openness to sinners, his healing of lepers and outcasts, his challenge to the religious authorities of his day, all represent an attempt to fashion a New Israel from the Old, one that would eventually extend its embrace beyond the strictures of race to all of humanity. Jesus accepted the cross because of his conviction that this act would herald in a new age for the community of Israel. He entered Jerusalem to face certain death, giving up slowly and very painfully his own, very human, will to live. Just as he, for the sake of the human community, emptied himself and took the form of a slave, so too must his Church, for the sake of Christ and the kingdom he sought to establish, empty itself in service to all of humanity. From an ecclesiological perspective, such a statement implies that, whenever the spirit of service is missing in the Church, Christ himself is missing. The Church, in other words, must let go of itself in order to find itself and the kingdom it represents.

This theme of Christ's servanthood also has important implications for the questions in Christology concerned with the relationship between the divine and human in Christ. According to the hymn from Philippians, it was the Word of God which emptied itself, "being born in the likeness of men," and which was "known to be of human estate." In the relationship between the divine and human in Christ, it is thus the divinity of Christ which assumes the role of servant: the Word emptied itself of the powers

---

[12] For Jesus' connection with the servant theme, see Bruce Vawter, *This Man Jesus: An Essay Toward a New Testament Christology* (Garden City, N.Y.: Doubleday and Co., 1973), 72-74; Donald Senior, *A Gospel Portrait of Jesus* (Dayton: Pflaum Press, 1981), 146-52; Oscar Cullmann, *The Christology of the New Testament*, trans. Shirley C. Guthrie and Charles A.M. Hall (Philadelphia: The Westminster Press, 1963), 51-82.

of its divinity and took on the humanity of Jesus.[13] This self-imposed divine limitation stands at the heart of the hypostatic union and anticipates a comprehensible solution to those Christological concerns about the extent of Christ's consciousness and the interplay between his divine and human knowledge.

MOVEMENT THREE: "THIS IS MY BODY"

The third movement is best summarized by the words of Christ's institution of the Eucharist. Of the various accounts, that of Paul preserves what is perhaps the earliest surviving Christian liturgical formula:

> ... the Lord Jesus on the night in which he was betrayed took bread, and after he had given thanks, broke it and said, "This is my body, which is for you. Do this in remembrance of me." In the same way, after supper, he took the cup, saying, "This cup is the new covenant in my

---

[13] There is a difference of opinion among exegetes about whether the Christological hymn in Philippians refers to (1) the humility of the Divine Word in the Incarnation (and hence the development of various "kenotic" Christologies), (2) exclusively to the earthly existence of Christ (thus focusing on Christ's rendering himself powerless while on earth), or (3) a synthesis of both alternatives, i.e., Christ's voluntary giving up of divine glory in the Incarnation *and* a second stage of humiliation involving his whole life on earth of devotion to the Father which culminates in his death on the cross. In this last sense (the one presupposed in the chapter) a fundamental continuity is seen to exist between Christ's divine self-emptying and his earthly life of humility. See Raymond E. Brown, Joseph A. Fitzmyer and Roland E. Murphy, eds. *The Jerome Biblical Commentary*, vol. 2, *The New Testament and Topical Articles* (Englewood Cliffs, N.J.: Prentice-Hall, Inc., 1968), s.v. "The Letter to the Philippians," by Joseph A. Fitzmyer; Idem, *The New Jerome Biblical Commentary*. vol. 2, *The New Testament and Topical Articles* (Englewood Cliffs, N.J.: Prentice-Hall, Inc., 1990), s.v. "The Letter to the Philippians," by Brendan Byrne. For material on the second position, which would disclaim the insights of positions one and three (and thus the way the hymn is used in this chapter), see Jerome Murphy O'Connor, "Christological Anthropology in Ph., II.6-11," *Revue biblique* 83 (1976): 25-50. For a survey of recent exegetical commentary on the hymn, see N.T. Wright, "*Harpagmos* and the Meaning of Philippians 2:5-11," *Journal of Theological Studies* 37 (1986): 321-52.

blood. Do this, whenever you drink it, in remembrance of me." Every time, then, you eat this bread and drink this cup you proclaim the death of the Lord until he comes! (1 Cor 11:23-26).

In his final meal on earth Jesus performed a prophetic action whose symbolism revealed the very heart of his messianic identity. Having gathered his closest disciples around him, Jesus offered bread and wine as the symbols of the New Covenant soon to be ratified by his blood. As such, this sacrament represents both a foreshadowing and a continuation of his sacrificial death. He has given of himself completely, to the point of dying and beyond, to the point of becoming nourishment for others. It is in this manner that Jesus offered his body and blood as food for a redeemed humanity. Whenever the Christian community celebrates the Eucharist, it remembers Christ's death and anticipates with joy his future coming. At the very center of the Church's life and activity, the Eucharist extends to all of humanity and applies throughout all time the effects of Christ's passion, death, and resurrection.[14]

This sacramental extension of Christ's selfless death on the cross emphasizes the κενῶσις which all who eat and drink worthily of the Lord's own body and blood must ultimately undergo. This process of self-effacing love highlights for all Christians the participatory nature of all Eucharistic worship: by breaking bread together, each liturgical community enters more deeply into the mystery of Christ's dying and rising. Nourished by this sacramental food, they are called, in turn, to become spiritually nourishing, life-giving food for others. To celebrate the Eucharist thus requires a commitment to share more deeply in the life of Christ and in the life of one's own believing community. As a result, each Eucharistic community will always be characterized and judged by the quality of its life of service. Perhaps it was for this very reason that, unlike the Synoptic writers, the author of

---

[14] For the centrality of the Eucharist to Christian life and worship, see SCR, *Eucharisticum mysterium*, no. 6 [*CDD*, 544-45]; English translation: Flannery, *Vatican Council II*, 106-7. See also F.X. Durwell, *In the Redeeming Christ*, trans. Rosemary Sheed (New York: Sheed and Ward, 1963), 117-20.

John's Gospel allowed Jesus' ceremonial washing of his disciples' feet (Jn 13:1-17) to take the place of the normal institution narrative.[15]

Christ entered our world, gave himself to us completely, and became our very nourishment. The theme of nourishment has relevance not only for Christ's relationship to the community of believers, but also to the classical questions of Christology. If the Word's posture of service toward the world necessitates a divine limitation which lies at the heart of the hypostatic union and of those questions which concern the human knowledge and consciousness of Jesus, it follows from our consideration of the Eucharist that the divinity in Christ can be understood to limit itself in a way similar to that of nourishment: it relates to humanity on humanity's terms, according to humanity's needs and capacities for growth. From this perspective, Christ's divinity rests at the center of Jesus' being, supplying his humanity with the qualities it needs to fulfill his ministry and messianic vocation. It limits itself, not by cutting itself off from Christ's humanity, but by allowing Jesus' human consciousness to become rooted in and fed by its life-giving ground.

MOVEMENT FOUR: "HE IS RISEN"

The fourth movement is best summarized by Paul's proclamation of Christ's resurrection in 1 Corinthians:

> I handed on to you first of all what I myself received, that Christ died for our sins in accordance with the Scriptures; that he was buried and, in accordance with the Scriptures, rose on the third day; that he was seen by Cephas, then by the Twelve. After that he was seen by five hundred brothers at once, most of whom are still alive, although some have fallen asleep. Next he was seen by James; then by all the apostles. Last of all he was seen by me, as one born out of normal course (1 Cor 15:3-8).

---

[15] For a plausible explanation of the substitution, see Raymond E. Brown, *The Churches the Apostles Left Behind* (New York: Paulist Press, 1984), 88 n. 128.

For Paul, the certitude of faith rests upon the testimony of those who have actually experienced the Risen Lord. Their proclamation forms the basis of what should and should not be believed. If the resurrection had never taken place, they would all be exposed as false witnesses and there would be little cause for hope. If Christ was not raised, then the faith of the Corinthians would be worthless (1 Cor 15:17); if their hope in Christ was limited to this life only, they would be the most pitiable of men (1 Cor 15:19).

In this passage, which is considered by many to be one of the earliest extant accounts of Christ's resurrectional appearance, Paul draws an important connection between the resurrection of Christ and the resurrection of the dead: "If there is no resurrection of the dead, Christ himself has not been raised" (1 Cor 15:13). This association has a great deal of soteriological significance: Christ's resurrection is not an isolated event without any repercussions for humanity. It points, rather, to what we ourselves have in some way already experienced in Christ and hope one day fully to become: transformed, saved, resurrected, wholly ourselves. Without the Resurrection, there is nothing to hope for: faith is worthless; life is meaningless; Christ is dead. With the Resurrection there is everything to hope for, everything to live for, indeed, everything even to die for. The Resurrection verifies the truth of all that has gone before it, i.e., the Incarnation, the Eucharist, Christ's Passion and Death. And it is the testimony of Cephas, the Twelve, James, Paul, and all the others who have experienced the Risen Lord, which verifies and makes credible the meaning of our faith. We hope because others hope on account of what they have seen and come to believe.

During his life on earth, Jesus possessed the fullness of such hope. This awareness of his eschatological destiny was rooted not in the Resurrection (which had not yet taken place) or in the testimony of his disciples (who would never have understood at the time), but in his singular relationship to his own divinity. The Word, who entered our world, gave of himself completely, and became our very nourishment, providing us with hope from the deep eschatological awareness that he found in himself. His, however, was of a selfless nature, concerned not for himself, but for his people, a New Israel under a New Covenant which was to be written in his blood. The very reason why we hope in the resurrection of the dead is because, even before his own resurrection, it was Jesus himself who first hoped for us.[16]

THE IMITATION OF CHRIST

Taken together, these movements provide the variously interconnected aspects of what in this essay has been termed, "the fundamental principle of Christology." The word "principle" has been chosen not to suggest an extrapolation or speculative deduction by an unattached, objective observer, but an internal, practical, and vital source of life. Taken as such, these elements have also been described as a part of a single Christological process rooted not in human contrivance, but in the providence of God and in the wisdom of Christ himself. This "principle," in other words, is rooted in the very heart and being of Jesus Christ, the God-man. It helps to describe not only the relation between the divine and human in Christ, but also his external relationship with the world. It also shows how each of these relationships is related to the other. From this perspective, Christ's identity and vocation are so intricately interwoven that they cannot and, indeed, should not be separated. To do so would result in emphasizing one over the other and this would do damage to the discipline of Christology itself.[17]

---

[16] According to the strict parameters of a high Christology, there was neither faith nor hope in Christ, since each implies an imperfection. Aquinas, for example, points out that instead of faith, Jesus had manifest vision (*aperta visio*) and, instead of hope, full comprehension (*plena comprehensio*). See *Summa theologiae*, I-II, q. 65, a. 5, ad 3m. Only the approach of a low-ascending Christology, which is favored by many contemporary exegetes and theologians, would allow for an element of hope in the earthly Jesus. Neither Christological approach would deny that Jesus himself (regardless of whether or not he himself actually possessed hope) is the source of hope for believing Christians.

[17] In the words of Kasper: "We get closer to the mystery of his [Christ's] person only when we look into that mission. The theological perspective is the only one that does not falsify the person and work of Jesus." See *Jesus the Christ*, 70.

The Christ Kernel

Of equal importance is the connection this principle draws between Christ and the believer's imitation of Christ, the latter being an intrinsic, grace-filled response to the action of Christ in one's own life. In one respect, the fundamental principle of Christology reveals the very meaning and essence of *imitatio Christi*.[18] Just as Christ entered our world and gave of himself completely to the point of becoming nourishment and a source of hope for us, so too are we called, both individually and in community, to enter the various worlds of the people around us and to give ourselves to them in a manner commensurate to that of Christ's sacrificial offering of self, to the point that we too become nourishment for them and a source of life-giving hope. This calling reveals to us the fundamental meaning of our Christian identity. It is accomplished, not by ourselves alone, but by our cooperating with Christ working in us and influencing us by the grace of his Spirit. Imitation, from this perspective, is the human perception of what is for Christ the very process of our own divinization. His vocation, like our own, is concerned with our becoming other christs.[19]

The way in which this process of divinization/imitation is realized will of course depend, to a large degree, upon the particular form of Christian life to which we are called. For married couples, the four movements of the Christological process will manifest themselves in the intimate love which husband and wife are called to share with each other and celebrate with their children. For a single person, they will reveal themselves in that person's relationship to his or her family, friends, and community. For a priest, they will show themselves in his relationship to his bishop, his fellow priests, and the people he is called to serve. For a religious, they will disclose themselves in his or her commitment both to community and to a life dedicated to the vows of

---

[18] For the ambivalent status of this phrase in the history of Christian spirituality, see Gordon S. Wakefield, ed. *The Westminster Dictionary of Christian Spirituality* (Philadelphia: The Westminster Press, 1983), s.v. "Imitation of Christ," by E.J. Tinsley.

[19] Martin R. Tripole, "Suffering with the Humble Christ in Religious Life," *Review for Religious* 40 (1981): 199-200.

chastity, poverty, and obedience. Although the manner in which this process is realized will vary according to the particular state in life embraced, the process itself will always and everywhere remain fundamentally the same: to enter another's world, to give of oneself completely, until one has become for that other a source of nourishment and lasting hope.

It is within the above context that the significance of the religious life for the Church stands out with marked clarity. Called to an individual and communal embrace of the evangelical counsels, religious profess to imitate closely the particular way of life chosen by Christ during his life on earth. A faithful adherence to this lifestyle highlights the radical call to discipleship which Christ himself "propounded to the disciples who followed after him."[20] As such, religious make the life of Christ clearly visible to their contemporaries and represent not a superior way of life, but that very Christological process in which all people, whatever their state in life, are in some way called to share.[21] The meaning of the religious life, therefore, cannot be understood apart from the symbol it offers to married couples, priests, and singles. From this perspective, the role of religious in the Church is to remind others of the various Christological dimensions of their own vocations.

CONCLUSION

The existence of a fundamental principle of Christology brings continuity to those culturally-conditioned linguistic formulas which try to express the meaning of Christ and the Christ-event. Like all theological statements, however, it too is subject to

---

[20] See Vatican Council II, *Lumen gentium* no. 44 [*CDD*, 177, 179-80]; English translation: Flannery, *Vatican Council II*, 404, 406.

[21] In the words of Schneiders: "All Christians must die; and the challenge of each is to transform death into life by transforming what comes as necessity into an act of intimate freedom, the final act of love. Religious, by their choice of consecrated celibacy, raise that Christian choice to striking visibility in the Church." See *New Wineskins*, 129.

historical change. While the four movements developed in this chapter form the basis of the Christological process as it works with regard to the divine and human relations in Christ, with regard to Christ's outer relationship with the world, and with regard to the spirituality of the believing community, it is nearly impossible to conceive of the theological expressions in which each of them is cast as not changing over time in almost direct proportion to the advances in our understanding of language and the nature of theological expression itself. Despite this rather sobering claim, the Christological process continues unabated. It does so because, like the mystery it serves, it is a function of both humanity and divinity, of both time and eternity, of both language and the meaning it conveys. In the final analysis, the fundamental principle of Christology rests in the mystery of Christ himself. Words such as Incarnation, Passion, Eucharist, and Resurrection are not, in and of themselves, essential to the principle that has been described here. But the various facets of the singular mystery they seek to express most certainly are. For this reason, the fundamental principle of Christology receives its validation not from its historically-conditioned theological expression, which is always subject to change, but from Christ himself, who has chosen each movement not only as a part of his own identity and vocation, but also for us, as a part of our very own.

3

THE TRINITARIAN KERNEL

Is there a fundamental principle of Trinitarian theology? It would seem so and it itself is of a triune nature, i.e., three independent yet interrelated postulates coming together to form a single, all-encompassing statement about the nature of God's internal self-relations and external relations with the world.[1] This principle is not to be thought of as a mere intellectual concept: God, the ultimate reality, cannot be confined to our fragile human constructions — not even to our greatest philosophical and linguistic achievements. Rather, it is to be looked upon as the motivating force and life-giving energy of God's very Being. From this perspective, the fundamental principle of Trinitarian theology corresponds to what the Christian tradition itself describes as the inner life of the Divinity itself, i.e., the primal source and eternal expression of authentic communal Love.

THE INTERNAL/EXTERNAL RELATIONS OF LOVE

At the very outset, it will be important to lay to rest some common misconceptions about the scope of Trinitarian theology. The spectrum of this branch of contemporary theology does not,

---

[1] For the unity of the immanent and economic Trinity, see Kasper, *The God of Jesus Christ*, 273-77.

as some would have it, focus only on the relationships within the Godhead,[2] thereby excluding all consideration of these relations in God's economic plan of creation/redemption. To dichotomize God's internal and external relations in such a way undermines the very meaning of the Trinity.[3] To do so would be actually to admit that God does not represent the perfect community of Love. Indeed, such a community could not possibly confine itself to an eternity of unmoved, internal bliss. Love, by its very nature and as an expression of the Good it represents, is self-diffusive.[4] To recognize that the Godhead's internal and external relations are intimately linked (without being equated)[5] is thus to admit both the covenantal nature of the Godhead and the trinitarian nature of human existence. Not to do so runs the risk of relegating the actions of the Triune God to a purely functional form of Deism, whereby the Divinity plays the role of a detached observer of a mechanized cosmos instead of an active participant in human affairs.[6] Such an image of the Godhead would surely represent a diminution of the Christian ideal: God is relieved of the responsibility of caring for the lot of the world; prayer is without purpose;

---

[2] In this chapter, the terms God, Godhead, and Divinity are used interchangeably; they have been employed for stylistic reasons, especially in order to facilitate the use of inclusive language.

[3] Karl Rahner's axiomatic summary is particularly helpful in this regard: "...the Trinity of the economy of salvation *is* the immanent Trinity and vice versa." See "Remarks on the Dogmatic Treatise 'De Trinitate,'" chap. in *Theological Investigations*, vol. 4, *More Recent Writings*, trans. Kevin Smyth (London: Darton, Longman and Todd, 1974), 87.

[4] "*Bonum diffusivum sui.*" This medieval Latin phrase has become axiomatic in describing the love of the Trinity. It has its origins in the sixth-century Neoplatonic writings of Pseudo-Dionysius the Areopagite, *De divinibus nominibus*, 4.1, 4.2, 4.20 [*PG* 3:693-96, 717-22]. See also Dionysius the Areopagite, *On the Divine Names and the Mystical Theology*, 2d ed., trans. C.E. Rolt (New York: Macmillan, 1940; reprint ed., 1951), 86-89, 113-17.

[5] To equate them would open up possibilities for either a pantheistic (i.e. all things are divine) or an emanationist (i.e., all things process from God *by necessity*) interpretation of the visible order, thus erasing the important distinction in Christian theology between the Creator and his creation.

[6] For the impact of Deism on Christian thought, see N. Max Wildiers, *The Theologian and His Universe: Theology and Cosmology from the Middle Ages to the Present* (New York: The Seabury Press, 1982), 153-55.

The Trinitarian Kernel

the poor are rendered helpless in the hands of the powerful. The point to be made here is that Trinitarian theology must admit an integral continuity between the internal and external relations of the Godhead. The source of the Divinity's covenantal relation with humanity, in other words, is to be found within its own internal life of perfect love and social harmony.

THE RELATIONAL GOD

But just what does the classical formulation of Trinitarian theology tell us about the nature of the internal life within the Godhead? What does its theological supposition of a Trinity—three Persons in one God: Father, Son, and Spirit, all consubstantial yet relationally distinct[7] — reveal about the nature of the Godhead as the ultimate source of reality itself? To be sure, one of the greatest contributions of the doctrine of the Trinity to the history of ideas is that it places the concept of "relation" within the very nature of God. The ungenerated Father, the generated Son, and the processing Spirit are distinct from one another by virtue of their differences in relationship, making the Godhead relational in its very essence.[8] But since essence and being are identical in God,[9] the contrary conclusion must also be true: the Divinity is distinct by virtue of its oneness of being and one by virtue of its distinctive relationships. Such is the incomprehensible mystery of

---

[7] For the key magisterial statements on this basic doctrinal insight, see Denz.-Schön., nos. 75 [39], 451 [231], 529 [279], 531 [281], 973 [523], 1130-31 [703-4].

[8] In the words of Kasper: "It was the brilliant insight of the fourth- and fifth-century fathers...that fatherhood, sonship and passive spiration are relational realities, so that the distinctions in God affect not the one divine substance or one divine being but only the relations in God. This insight was later incorporated into official church teaching. It led to the basic trinitarian principle: 'In Deo omnia sunt unum, ubi non obviat relationis oppositio (In God everything is one where there is no opposition of relationship).'" *The God of Jesus Christ*, 280. See also Athanasius, *De synodis* [PG 26:707-12]; Gregory Nazianzus, *Oratio* 29.16 [SC 250:210-13]; Augustine, *De trinitate* 5.5 [CCL 50:210-11; PL 42:913-14]; Denz.-Schön., nos. 528-32 [278-81].

the relational God of the Christian faith, expressed so eloquently in the tradition by the simple term *Trinitas*.

To speak of the Trinity as relational is to emphasize the social character of the Godhead. Doing so, however, runs the risk of projecting one's own culturally-conditioned notions of social behavior onto a utopic metaphysical plane.[10] Such a risk is real and must be constantly kept in check. Regardless of how hard it tries to reach beyond the phenomenal world and capture the numinous, no language (not even the theological) can cut itself loose from its humble origins in human experience.[11]

In the face of this inescapable risk of interpretation, great care must be taken not to relativize (or, even worse, trivialize) the time-honored expressions of the faith. Attentive to this caution, the following statement discloses what, in this essay, has been termed, "The Trinitarian Kernel." It reads thus: The Christian God is a community of Love, one in Being yet three in Person: (1) ungenerated in its Source (i.e., the Father), (2) eternally generated in its Otherness (i.e., the Son), (3) eternally processing in its Oneness (i.e., the Spirit). The relations which differentiate the Persons are united by virtue of the latter's oneness in Being; the oneness in Being which unites the Persons is itself differentiated by virtue of the latter's relations. Unity and multiplicity, therefore, find their resolution in the metaphysical juxtaposition of Being and Relation in the mystery of God's eternal Love. To understand this statement more fully, one may speak of the Triune God as *Ground* (i.e., God, the Father), *Otherness* (i.e., God, the Son), and *Bond* (i.e., God, the Holy Spirit).

---

[9] Thomas Aquinas, *Summa theologiae*, I, q. 3, a. 4, resp. See also, Macquarrie, *Principles of Christian Theology*, 176, 183.

[10] Leech argues that theology is always influenced by the cultural context in which it takes place. For him the important thing is that it not become "captured" by that context. See *Experiencing God*, 384.

[11] Sallie McFague goes so far as to say that "All language about God is human construction and as such perforce 'misses the mark.'" See *Models of God: Theology for an Ecological, Nuclear Age* (Philadelphia: Fortress Press, 1987), 23.

The Trinitarian Kernel

RELATION ONE: "THE FATHER AS GROUND"

Every entity in the universe, from the simplest chemical compound, to the most complex biological organism, to the Divinity itself, has an ultimate source.[12] Classical Trinitarian theology uses the process of human intellection as a means of explaining how God's ultimate source is internal and self-encompassing.[13] God, in other words, does not come from something other than God, but from the Godhead itself. To speak of God as "God coming from God" (and as "Light coming from Light") is to recognize that within God lies the Ground of all reality. One may even choose to speak of this aspect within God in a philosophical way (e.g., in the Aristotelian sense of a Prime Mover or the Neoplatonic notion of the One). Most philosophical formulations, however, fall far short of the richness of the Christian tradition which, basing itself on the Judaic notion of a covenantal God, chose, in the very person of its Founder, to address that Ground as Personal. To be sure, one of the most important arguments in favor of the use of "Father" within the Trinitarian Godhead is that it was Jesus himself who imparted this name to us when he instructed us to call God, "Abba" (i.e., "Father").[14]

To speak of the Father as the Ground of all reality not only recognizes the all-important continuity between the Godhead and creation (ultimately both share the same grounding source),

---

[12] According to the traditional Thomistic framework, existence and essence of the Divinity are identical; it alone can be considered its own ultimate source. All other entities derive their existence by means of participation. See Aquinas, *Summa theologiae*, I, q. 3, a. 4, resp.; I, q. 44, a. 1, resp.

[13] The psychological doctrine of the Trinity is the brainchild of Augustine and determined the course of all later reflection of the Trinity in Latin theology. See *De trinitate*, 14.8; 14.12 [*CCL*, 50A:435-38, 442-44; *PL* 42:1044-45, 1048-49]. The particular point about human intellection as a basis for understanding God's active generative power is found in Aquinas, *Summa theologiae*, I, q. 27, a. 1, resp.; I, q. 27, a. 2, resp.

[14] According to Kasper: "Knowledge of the trinitarian mystery was ...due to verbalized divine revelation and not to a process of deduction." *The God of Jesus Christ*, 276. In this respect, Jesus's appellation of God as "Father" provides a deep insight into both the immanent and economic character of the Godhead.

but also distinguishes between the two (the Divinity grounds itself; creation does not). More importantly, to speak of God as Father and as Ground is already to speak of God in terms of relationship to an Other: every cause is the cause of some *thing;* every father, the parent of a daughter or son; every ground, the sustaining source of that which grows from it. From this perspective, the relationships within the Trinity are already implicit within this very important aspect of the Godhead. And, when referring to relationships in this manner, one cannot help but think of God even under this aspect as Personal. To be sure, that part of the Godhead which is the Cause of all, the Source of all, the Ground of all, indeed, the Father of all, is Personal.

Of course, all which has been said above rests on the assumption that the language used in the analysis of the Trinitarian relations and especially in regard to the Father as Ground is analogous. To speak of God the Father as Ground, and to say that this aspect within the Godhead is itself Personal, embraces as many differences as it does likenesses.[15] God is Personal to an infinite degree, without limitations. Such a reality lies beyond the scope of human experience, which understands the word, "person," as intricately connected to the experience of limitations. Even if the common Thomistic definition of person as "a rational supposite" is accepted, one must admit that "rational" for God is not the same as what it means for human beings ("...my thoughts are not your thoughts," Is 55:8).[16] When referring to God the Father and Ground as "Personal," one must therefore acknowledge the use of proportionate reasoning: just as a newborn infant is a "person" according to the limited capacities of human nature, so too is God the Father a "Person" according to the limitless capaci-

---

[15] For this reason, attributes rooted in human experience can be validly predicated of God only according to the principle of proportionality: $a/b = a'/b'$. It is through this principle that theological language steers clear of the extremes of univocal and equivocal predication.

[16] For Aquinas, the rational creature has only a share (*participatio*) of the Eternal Reason by which it has a natural inclination to its due act and end. See *Summa theologiae*, I-II, q. 91, a. 2, resp. His position stands clear of both an equation of divine and human reason and a complete disjunction between the two.

ties of divine nature. When speaking of God as a Person, perhaps the best way of understanding it for one's own sensibilities is to think of "Personal" as meaning "Suprapersonal" (i.e., beyond the dimensions and scope of human personhood).[17] It is at this point in the discussion where the very delicate question of the relationship between nature and supernature arises. In treating it here, it is important only to point out that the two terms stand necessarily in relation to one another and should not be dichotomized. Although the supernatural is *other* than the natural, it *relates* to humanity in and through human nature.[18] Insofar as it relates to human nature, people experience it as the Ground of their existence. Here is yet another instance where, in the experience of that Ground, a person can address God as "Father."

RELATION TWO: "THE SON AS OTHER"

In contrast to the first postulate of the Trinitarian kernel, which identifies within the Godhead the self-sustaining source and Ground of all reality, the second focuses on the Son as the fullest expression of that source.[19] From all eternity, the ungenerated Father and Ground of all generates the Son as the fullest expression of himself. By its very nature, this expression is other than the Source, i.e., metaphysically one but relationally distinct from the Father. It is precisely this Otherness from the Father which gives the Son his distinctive character within the Godhead: the Father generates; the Son is generated; the Father is the Ground of all

---

[17] For a helpful popular depiction of God's triune nature going beyond the bounds of human personhood, see C.S. Lewis, *Mere Christianity* (New York: Macmillan, 1952), 140-45.

[18] This insight is developed more deeply in Henri de Lubac, *The Mystery of the Supernatural*, trans. Rosemary Sheed (New York: Herder and Herder, 1967), 71-75.

[19] Thus, while the relation of the Father to the Son is one of active generation (*generare*), that of the Son to the Father is one of passive generation (*generari*). See Kasper's treatment of the basic relations in the doctrine of the Trinity in *The God of Jesus Christ*, 279-81.

reality; the Son is the first and highest expression of that Ground; the Father exists eternally; the Son exists as the eternal expression of the Father. Like the Father, the Son is Suprapersonal and possesses the limitless dimensions of the divine nature. Unlike the Father, the Son is not the generating Ground of all, but the Godhead's own self-experience of that Ground. To dwell once more on the analogical dimension of theological language, one might say that just as language serves as an instrument of self-experience in the human dimension, so too is its theological analogue necessary for the experience of self within the Godhead. It is for this reason that classical Trinitarian theology, so strongly influenced in its inception by the Greek philosophical concept of the Divine Logos, has deemed it appropriate to characterize the Son by the appellation of "The Word of God" which, as the fullest expression of the Father's self-experience of being divinely Other, has, in its becoming flesh, been spoken even to the likes of our humbled humanity.[20]

To speak of the Son as Other is to recognize that within the Godhead itself there is not just the capacity, but the reality of loving relationship. The Ground's experience of itself as Other is intensely personal, so much so that the human relationship between a father and his son is what theologians and councils throughout the centuries have used to describe it. While other relationships (such as those between a mother and her daughter or son; or a master and his disciple) might also be used with varying degrees of success, one must recall that, when predicated of God, all human relationships, however intense, fall far short of the ultimate reality they seek to express.[21] For this very reason, it

---

[20] For the use of the *Logos* concept as a means of explaining Christ's divinity, see Pelikan, *Jesus Through the Centuries*, 57-70. See also Jaroslav Pelikan, *The Christian Tradition: A History of the Development of Doctrine*, vol. 1: *The Emergence of the Catholic Tradition (100-600)* (Chicago: University of Chicago Press, 1971): 251-56, 259, 261, 264-65, 276-77, 340, 351.

[21] "When we address God as mother, father, lover, friend, or as judge, healer, liberator, companion, or yet again as sun, ocean, fortress, shield, or even as creator, redeemer, and sustainer, we know that these terms are not descriptions of God. When we speak to God we are most conscious of how inadequate our language is for God, something we more easily forget when we speak about God—that is, when we are doing theology." See McFague, *Models of God*, 181.

might be wise to juxtapose a series of such images which, when taken in conjunction with one another, would capture more fully the reality in question.[22] At the same time, special attention must be given to a tradition which has consistently used the imagery of Father and Son in its Creed, conciliar statements, and liturgical formulations.[23] To be sure, any suggested changes in the current formula must be placed under intense scrutiny.

The relationship between the Father as Ground and the Son as Other, forms the basis of the Trinitarian doctrine of Love. From it, we come to understand how we too are called into loving relationship with each other. From the Ground of all reality there arises an expression of self perceived as Other and respected as such. From such an expression the two are bonded together as one, for the one generating perceives itself not as superior to the one generated, but as participating in a relationship which defines its very being from all eternity. This Bond between the Father as Ground and the Son as Other permeates the Church's doctrine of the Trinity, for the very Bond between Father and Son is what is experienced both within the Godhead and within humanity as Spirit.

RELATION THREE: "THE SPIRIT AS BOND"

The eternal relationship existing between the Father as Ground and the Son as Other is itself experienced within the Godhead as Personal. This Bond is the expression of the mutual Love between the Father and the Son. Although it can be distinguished from them (e.g., even as the Father can be distinguished

---

[22] Such as the approach taken by Avery Dulles in the field of ecclesiology: "Instead of searching for some absolutely best image, it would be advisable to recognize that the manifold images given to us by Scripture and Tradition are mutually complementary." See *Models of the Church*, 36.

[23] "As the creeds of the church amply illustrate, models approach the status of concepts: Father, Son, and Holy Spirit are models of the divine life that inform the tradition's most central concept, the trinity." See McFague, *Models of God*, 34.

from the Son), it cannot be metaphysically separated from them. To admit such a separation would be tantamount to denying the essential oneness of the Godhead, as well as the eternity of the Father and the Son and the authenticity of their Love for one another. For this reason, the Spirit should be looked upon as the Suprapersonal Bond existing from all eternity between the Father and the Son. Unlike the Father, who is the generating Ground of all reality, and the Son, who is the generated expression of that Ground, the Spirit represents the eternally processing Bond existing between them. And not only does it exist between them: from all eternity it reaches out from the Divinity to inspire and dwell within its highest creation.[24]

To speak of the indwelling of the Holy Spirit is to put forth the claim that the Godhead relates to humanity in a manner similar to the way in which it relates within its very Being. That is to say that, although people are created (and, therefore, do not generate or process from the very being of the Divinity), they still are made in such a way that they are able to experience something, however dimly, of the internal life of God.[25] To experience the Spirit is, by its very nature, to share in the loving Bond of the Father as Ground and the Son as Other. This experience in the deepest part of one's being is what molds a person's humbled self into the divinized image of the Godhead. It does so, however, not by some magical inner transformation which keeps people isolated and out of touch with life around them, but by moving them out of themselves into just and responsible relationships with the world.

The Spirit, therefore, is not only the eternal Bond between the Father and Son, but also the principle of Love uniting humanity to the Godhead and humanity to the world. This triple signi-

---

[24] Thus, while the relation of the Father and the Son to the Spirit is one of active spiration (*spirare*), that of the Spirit to the Father and the Son is one of passive spiration (*spirari*). Moreover, since the Good is self-diffusive (see above 34 n. 4) and since there is a fundamental unity between the immanent and economic Trinity (see above 34 nn. 3 and 5), the salvation is effected in us through Christ and in the Spirit. See Kasper, *The God of Jesus Christ*, 277, 279.

[25] According to Aquinas, the desire to see God is a *naturale desiderium* of the human person, *Summa theologiae*, I, q. 12, a. 1, resp. See also de Lubac, *The Mystery of the Supernatural*, 75.

fication of relationships (Father/Son, Godhead/humanity, humanity/world) must be understood according to the principle of proper proportionality: just as the Spirit represents the eternally processing Bond between the Father and the Son, so too is the presence of the Spirit the Bond between the Godhead and humanity, and the resulting Spirit-filled humanity the Bond between humanity and the world. From this perspective, the various dimensions of the Trinitarian life exist not only beyond the phenomenal world in the realm of the numinous, but also in the concrete relationships of people's daily lives.

THE TRINITARIAN DIMENSIONS OF HUMAN SOLIDARITY

From what has been said above, it should come as no surprise to learn that the experience of human solidarity reflects the Trinitarian dimensions of the Father as Ground, the Son as Other, and the Spirit as Bond. To make God present in the world means that humanity has within itself the potential to realize on earth a true reflection of the inner relationships of the Godhead. Whenever humanity realizes these relational dimensions of the Godhead (at whatever level one chooses to look at it — self-experience, friendship, family, community, nation, world), it manifests the internal presence of the Trinitarian God. Whenever humanity fails in this respect, it absents itself from God and subjects itself to the distorted relational dimension of human existence known as sin.[26] From this perspective, the presence and

---

[26] Kasper puts it well: "Here is the decisive point. Christianity sees man not simply as an ensemble of social relations but as a person who, no matter how thoroughly integrated he is into society, possesses an inherent value and dignity and is in turn the source, subject and object of all social institutions. Christianity therefore sees evil as taking the form primarily not of structures and institutions but of sin, which has its origin in the heart of man. The dignity of the person is ultimately based on the transcendence of the person. Human autonomy and theonomy are therefore not related to each other as competitors; they increase in direct, not in inverse proportion." See *The God of Jesus Christ*, 38.

the absence of God exists in the world only in the struggle (or lack thereof) for human solidarity.

To share in this struggle means, first of all, to be willing to recognize the existential Ground common to all humanity. Such a recognition is more than a mere acceptance of superficial similarities in humanity's physical and spiritual makeup. It involves, instead, a recognition of the fact that humanity comes from something beyond, a beyond which sustains it at every moment of its existence and which makes all human beings equal in the sight of God. To accept this common existential Ground from beyond is to embrace the embrace of the Father and to realize that, in sharing this Ground, everyone truly belongs both one to another and to God.

To share in this struggle also means to accept in humanity the reality of Other. This Otherness is unitive, not divisive; it is manifested by humanity's common Ground, which gives it expression and which allows it to be experienced by individuals and groups in their own historical and cultural milieus. The experience of Other brings one ultimately to the experience of self as Other, for to embrace the Other wherever one finds it leads one ultimately to embrace that which is generated by the Ground in the deepest part of the soul. As the expression of this common existential Ground, the human Other defends the dignity of human life, recognizing in the individual a right to exist and to partake of the goodness of the Ground. To accept in humanity the reality of Other is to accept the dignity of each human person and the fundamental bond uniting all human beings. The Son's gift to humanity, therefore, is the reality of Other in the midst of the common Ground it shares.

Finally, solidarity is realized with the experience of humanity as Ground and humanity as Other when it bonds people together in an experience of Spirit. In acknowledging both the fundamental likenesses and differences in people, this experience brings people into communion with one another, a union of lives which forms a whole far greater than the individual entities which make it up. These bonds of human solidarity are the dwelling place of the Spirit in the world: among people whose hearts are united by virtue of their experience of the Ground of humanity

The Trinitarian Kernel

and their own fundamental uniqueness and sense of Otherness from everyone else. The experience of the Spirit in human solidarity represents both the bond which unites humanity within itself and the bond which unites humanity to God. For the perfect community of Love—the Father as Ground, the Son as Other, the Spirit as Bond — never ceases in its striving to make itself present in the experience of authentic human community.

THE TRINITARIAN DIMENSIONS OF RELIGIOUS LIFE

It is within the above context of human solidarity that one is also to understand the Trinitarian dimensions of religious life. Women and men respond to this call and profess the vows of chastity, poverty, and obedience not to remove themselves from their human situation (as if to sever their bonds from humanity) but to embrace it.[27] Although the manner in which this embrace takes place will differ, depending on whether or not one chooses to enter an apostolic or contemplative order, its substance remains the same: to confess by their vows the reality of the Triune Loving God.[28] Through the profession of vows an intimate continuity is affirmed between the Trinitarian relations within the Godhead

---

[27] In the words of the Second Vatican Council: "Let no one think either that their consecrated way of life alienates religious from other men or makes them useless for human society...This sacred council gives its support and praise to men and women, brothers and sisters, who in monasteries or in schools and hospitals or in missions adorn the bride of Christ by the steadfast and humble fidelity of their consecrated lives and give generous service of the most varied kinds to all manner of men." See *Lumen gentium* no. 46 [*CDD*, 179-80]; English translation, Flannery, *Vatican Council II*, 406-7.

[28] The Trinitarian dimension of the religious life is supplied by John Paul II: "By immersing yourselves in the paschal mystery of the Redeemer through the consecration of the religious vows...may there grow deeper in each one of you the joy of belonging exclusively to God, of being a particular inheritance of the most Holy Trinity: Father, Son, and Spirit." See *Redemptionis donum*, no. 8 [*AAS* 76 (1984): 526]; English translation: "*Redemptionis Donum*: An Expression of Love for Religious," 489. See also Vatican Council II, *Lumen gentium*, no. 47 [*CDD*, 180]; English translation: Flannery, *Vatican Council II*, 407.

and the relations of human solidarity. In the vow of poverty, the religious forsakes the possessions of the world in order to affirm the common Ground of humanity shared by all. In the vow of obedience, the religious follows the will of a superior in order to recognize the reality of Other as an expression of that Ground. In the vow of chastity, the religious forsakes the bond of marriage in order to affirm before God an even deeper bond of relation uniting all human beings.

Taken together, the vows help the religious to proclaim the radical import of the Father as Ground, the Son as Other, and the Spirit as Bond. They do this by virtue of their own intrinsic eschatological orientation, pointing to the fullness of that which will never be fully realized in human time. That is to say that, even though human solidarity (even as it is experienced in the religious life) will never be realized in such a way that it fully reflects the inner relations of the Godhead, the religious vows provide the parameters within which these Trinitarian dimensions can be duly fostered. While these Trinitarian dimensions of human solidarity can certainly be nourished in other vocational callings (e.g., single, married, priestly), and in larger communities where these various forms interact, the unique contribution of the religious life lies precisely in the proportionate correspondence each of the vows has to a particular Trinitarian relation: poverty, to the Father as Ground; obedience, to the Son as Other; chastity, to the Spirit as Bond. From this perspective, the religious life can be thought of as leaven present in the world for the precise purpose of raising the consciousness of others to the presence of the Trinity in the forging of their own bonds of human solidarity.[29]

---

[29] For further insights into the Trinitarian dimensions of the religious life, see Fabio Giardini, "Una vita esclusivamente consacrata alla santissima Trinità," *Vita consacrata* 22 (1986): 630-38, 721-32, 817-32; Alfons Deeken, "A Trinitarian Spirituality for Today," *Review for Religious* 31 (1972): 237-46; John J. Markey, "Towards A Trinitarian Model of Religious Life," *Review for Religious* 49 (1990): 22-35.

CONCLUSION

The fundamental principle of Trinitarian theology, as it has been outlined above, seeks to present by means of proportionate analogy a linguistic foundation for the understanding of what must surely be considered the ultimate mystery of the Christian faith, i.e., the nature of the inner self-relations of the Godhead. Such analogical reasoning admits the limitations of the univocal patterns of thought so deeply embedded in the contemporary scientific outlook and wishes to preserve the integrity of the theological statement by recognizing the proportionate degrees of likeness and difference existing between God and creation.[30] While this is not the only way of doing theology (one might, for example, also employ the approaches of negative and symbolic theology), it seems the most appropriate for dealing with the realm of Trinitarian relations. One reason supporting this assumption (which underlies the entire essay) is that the very notion of "relation" is itself a human one, which has in Trinitarian theology been interpolated from human experience and projected onto the metaphysical plane.[31] In doing Trinitarian theology, therefore (and, especially, when speaking about a "Trinitarian Kernel"), one must be careful not to overlook the analogical nature not only of the Persons within the Godhead, but also of the relations they share. Not to do so would run the risk of admitting univocal reasoning into a field where it not only does not belong, but also where it could inflict great harm in its support of a potentially manipulative ideological superstructure.

---

[30] In this respect, the analogy of being becomes "the vehicle by which to construct a legitimate discourse of divine predicates." See Funkenstein, *Theology and the Scientific Imagination*, 52.

[31] Human relationships (both internal self-relation and external societal) are the primary epistemological analogues for the Church's formulations of the nature of the Godhead. That is not to say, of course, that these relations do not exist within the Godhead. The statement merely emphasizes the priority of human experience in the understanding and formulation of religious truth. For more on the relationship between human experience and theological knowledge, see Rosemary Haughton, *The Theology of Experience* (Paramus, N.J.: Newman Press, 1972): 15-18.

In contrast, a fundamental principle of Trinitarian theology which uses analogical reasoning as its base escapes this charge by virtue of a "built-in" theological corrective which emphasizes both the likeness *and* difference existing in the relations between the metaphysical and physical planes. Moreover, while claiming an intimate connection between the inner self-relations within the Godhead and the relations of the Godhead to the world, and while looking to the struggle for human solidarity as the place where these relations are likely to be the most fully realized on earth, it proposes for its substance the undying relations of unconditional Love, which can only be freely given and can never be demanded or taken from anyone by force. From this perspective, to speak of the Father as Ground as the source of all that is shared by the common Ground of humanity, or of the Son as Other as the fundamental expression served in the human experience of Other, or of the Spirit as Bond as the ultimate source of the bonds of human solidarity, seeks not to overlook the great dissimilarities between God and creation, but merely to emphasize the fact that, if similarities are anywhere to exist, they do so wherever there is the experience and realization of authentic committed Love. Such Love, then, is the fullest expression of the fundamental principle of Trinitarian theology ("The Trinitarian Kernel"): (1) it represents the relations within the Godhead as a metaphysical unity ("God is Love"); (2) it is the principle through which God relates to the world (God creates and redeems out of Love); (3) it forms the basis of the bonds of human solidarity (the human vocation is the call to a just and authentic Love of God and neighbor). On each level, this Love exists really but proportionately: in accordance with the different natural and supernatural entities involved. On each level, it is freely given and received to and from the Father as Ground, the Son as Other, and the Spirit as Bond.

4

THE CHURCH KERNEL

Is there a fundamental principle of ecclesiology? Whatever response is made to this question will be valid only to the extent that it relates a systematic reflection on the Church to the whole of theology. Some attempts do not succeed in this regard because they fail to formulate a proper hermeneutical basis for the study of this relationship. Others fall short because they misunderstand the different ways in which theological reflection has operated throughout the history of the Church. Still others waver simply because they disregard the underlying premise of the question itself — that theology is both functionally and constitutively one. Whatever the shortcomings, the failure to integrate ecclesiology with the whole of theology can only result in a fragmented and reductive attitude toward the mystery of the Church and its meaning for the world. To offset this rather questionable tendency in contemporary theology, the following pages will set forth the theological principle known as, "The Church Kernel."

THE CHURCH'S HERMENEUTICAL AWARENESS

Perhaps the best way to begin is by raising the epistemological question: Just what can be known about the Church? Generally speaking, the answer boils down to one of three possibilities — something, everything, or nothing. Each response discloses a different basis of rational discourse which, in the history of philosophical and theological thought, spans a diverse gamut ranging respectively from Thomistic analogy, to Scotist univocity, to Nominalist equivocation.[1] Each response, moreover, is mutually exclusive and cannot accommodate itself to either of the others without compromising its own internal logic. Hence, the prospect of analogical equivocation, or of equivocal univocity, or of univocal proportionality is about as likely as that of there being such a thing as a "square-circle" or the possibility of the omnipotent Godhead creating a rock which it could not lift. From this perspective, the formulation of any theological principle will vary greatly depending on the presuppositions it makes about the nature of rational discourse. In nearly all cases, these presuppositions are based on irreducible values which, in the final analysis, are themselves the result of fundamental cognitive preconceptions.[2]

From the perspective of ecclesiology, to be conscious of these preconceptions would mean that the Church has incorporated within itself the hermeneutical basis for its own self-critique. That is to say that the Church would realize that it has, from its inception, been involved in a hermeneutical circle which defines it, gives it life and meaning, and from which it cannot escape.[3] To

---

[1] For the differences in these approaches, see Etienne Gilson, *History of Christian Philosophy in the Middle Ages* (London: Sheed and Ward, 1955), 372, 463-64, 494-97.

[2] In the words of Alasdair MacIntyre: "...our education in and about philosophy has by and large presupposed what is in fact not true, that there are standards of rationality, adequate for the evaluation of rival answers to such questions, equally available, at least in principle, to all persons, whatever tradition they may happen to find themselves in and whether or not they inhabit any tradition." See *Whose Justice? Which Rationality?*, 393.

[3] Generally speaking, the hermeneutical circle describes how, "in the process of understanding and interpretation, part and whole are related in a circular way: in order to understand the whole, it is necessary to understand the parts, while to understand the parts it is necessary to have some comprehension of the whole." See David Couzens Hoy, *The Critical Circle: Literature, History, and Philosophical Hermeneutics* (Berkeley: University of California Press, 1978), vii. When applied to ecclesiology, it means that a deeper understanding of the rational preconceptions upon which the Church's theological formulations are based will bring insight into the meaning of the particular aspect of Christian belief under consideration and, hence, a fuller understanding of the nature of the whole of theology — and vice versa.

be sure, the greater awareness the Church has of the preconceptions guiding it, the freer and more truly itself does it become. In contrast, the lesser its awareness of them (for whatever reason), the more do its chances diminish of actualizing within itself and in the world the potential of its divine mandate.

THE QUESTION OF MODELS

With the above precautions in mind, it will do well to consider briefly what has probably become the most popular way of thinking about the Church in the post-Vatican II era — that of models. This approach, perfected and popularized by Avery Dulles, suggests that the mystery of Church is such that it cannot be reduced to a definition or confined to a single topos.[4] Instead, a series of images are used to deepen one's theoretical understanding of the reality in question. These "models," which describe the Church as institution, mystical communion, sacrament, herald, and servant, do not exhaust the reality of the Church and are, in fact, interdependent. Since one model usually plays a dominant role in an individual's outlook toward the Church, the approach is particularly helpful in understanding the differences between members of the same family, parish, diocese, or religious congregation. Most importantly, this approach safeguards the transcendent element within the Church by its insistence upon the interplay of models and the ultimate indefinability of the ecclesial reality.[5]

The use of models, originally the domain of the physical and social sciences, was first applied to the fields of philosophy and theology by such thinkers as Max Black, Frederick Ferré, and I.T.

---

[4] "Much harm is done by imperialistically seeking to impose some one model as the definitive one." See Dulles, *Models of the Church*, 36.

[5] "... the Church, like other theological realities, is a mystery. Mysteries are realities of which we cannot speak directly. If we wish to talk about them at all we must draw on analogies afforded by our experience of the world." See Dulles, *Models of the Church*, 13-14.

Ramsey.⁶ The fundamental insight of this approach is the claim that there exists "a logical gap" between the model and the reality it seeks to express. While this "gap" (or "isomorphic correspondence") can never be fully overcome, the use of other models, each with its own respective "gap," allows the reality to be experienced from a number of epistemological perspectives at alternating points in time. The result is the construction of "a logical web" of insights which, when taken in its totality, reveals more of the reality than any single model in itself. From this perspective, one may conclude that pluralism of insight never exhausts the intrinsic unity of the real, while mystery always takes precedence over any or all attempts to express it.⁷

As fresh and innovative as this new theological approach may seem, especially with its more recent adaptation to the interests of ecclesiology, one should not overlook the ways in which it stands in marked continuity with a number of other of the Church's time-honored hermeneutical traditions. One need only to point to the combined effect of the Areopagite's affirmative (positive, kataphatic) and disclaiming (negative, apophatic) theologies, or to the quadruple sense of Scripture in medieval allegoresis (literal, allegorical, tropological, anagogical), or even to Aquinas' use of proper proportionality in his discussion of the Divine Names, to find comparable instances from the past which distinguish mystery from its linguistic expression and which nevertheless propose a plurality of such expressions as a means of deeper insight.⁸ The point to be made here is that, if it is true that

---

⁶ Max Black, *Models and Metaphors*; Frederick Ferré, *Language, Logic and God* (New York: Harper and Row, 1961); I.T. Ramsey, *Christian Discourse* (London: Oxford University Press, 1964); Idem, *Religious Language: An Empirical Placing of Theological Phrases* (New York: Macmillan, 1967). See also Robert M. Scharlemann, "Theological Models and Their Construction," 68.

⁷ "In order to offset the defects of individual models, the theologian, like the physicist, employs a combination of irreducibly distinct models. Phenomena not intelligible in terms of one model may be readily explicable when another model is used. Admitting the inevitability of such a pluralism of models, theology usually seeks to reduce this pluralism to a minimum. The human mind, in its quest for explanations, necessarily seeks unity." See Dulles, *Models of the Church*, 32-33.

⁸ For the Pseudo-Dionysius' positive and negative approach to theology, see Gilson, *History of Christian Philosophy in the Middle Ages*, 81-85; for an explana-

The Church Kernel

models have only recently been applied to understanding the mystery of the Church, it is also true that some of the most basic insights supporting this approach exist well within the mainstream of the Church's theological tradition. It is within the context of this tradition that I now propose to look beyond the models suggested by Dulles.

A LOOK BEYOND THE MODELS

The question to be asked is this: Do models actually reveal a part of the mystery they seek to express, or do they minimize the significance of the logical gap existing between them and that mystery to such an extent that they manifest, in fact, nothing other than a synthetic "supermodel," which may, or may not, bear any resemblance to the reality itself? Is there, in other words, a model behind the model? Or is there a direct correspondence between the model and the mystery itself? The answer to these questions depends not so much on the model itself which, after all, is nothing other than a product of the mind, but on one's attitude toward the logical gap it helps to create. This attitude, in turn, depends a great deal on the presuppositions one makes about the nature of rational discourse: accentuating the gap (as the early Barth would have had it) leads to equivocation; minimizing it (as Leibniz would have insisted), ends in univocity; a balance between the two (the approach of Aquinas), proceeds by proportional thinking.[9] To be

---

tion of the quadruple sense of Scripture, see Henri de Dubac, *Exégèse médiévale: les quatre sens de l'écriture* vol. 2 (Aubier: Editions Montaigne, 1959), 643-56; for Aquinas' use of proper proportionality, see Etienne Gilson, *The Philosophy of St. Thomas Aquinas*, trans. Edward Bullough (New York: Dorset Press, 1948), 108-111.

[9] Barth started his theological career with an insistence of the total otherness of God and the inability of human reason to penetrate his mystery (an extreme application of Ockham's principle of parsimony). He described the *analogia entis* as "the invention of the AntiChrist." See *The Epistle to the Romans*, trans. C. Hoskyns (London: Oxford University Press, 1933), 28; Idem, *Church Dogmatics*, 2d ed., vol. 1/1, *The Doctrine of the Word of God*, trans. G.W. Bromiley (Edinburgh: T. and T. Clark, 1975), xiii. Leibniz begins with the Scotist position that human reason must be able to define *exactly* the basic notions of being (i.e.,

sure, what one sees when looking beyond the models is itself a function of these same rational preconceptions: the equivocal maximizer sees no relation whatsoever; the univocal minimizer, the mystery itself; the balanced proportional thinker, a reference to some *tertium quid*. Once again, it is clear that the formulation of a fundamental principle of ecclesiology depends very much on the preconceptual stance one takes toward the nature of rational discourse. At the same time, one still must ask which of the three possibilities (equivocation, univocity, proper proportionality) is most appropriate for the theological task at hand.

This essay embraces proper proportionality as the best rational basis from which to construct a systematic theological reflection on the Church. Despite the obvious limitations involved, it accepts this preconceptual stance as the only conceivable way of steering clear of the imbalances inherent in the other two outlooks, i.e., that of the equivocal propensity for the meaningless, and univocity's tendency toward human/divine interchangeability. Indeed, to the extent that it seeks to state something about the Church without actually defining it, the typical presentation of Church models (as proposed by Dulles, for example) already presupposes the approach of proportional thinking suggested above. This suggests that a model (or logical web of models) does not give expression to the mystery itself, but to an analogical relationship which both of them share.[10]

---

goodness, wisdom, justice, etc). He surpassed Scotus, however, by interpreting the "univocity of being" in terms of infinitesimal calculation. In his mind, human reason extends itself to infinity in the same way that the model of a rising curve approximates infinitesimally the infinite point "x." See J. Jalabert, *Le dieu de Leibniz* (Paris: Éditions du Cerf,1960), 139. Aquinas used the analogy of proportions (i.e., $a/b=a'/b'$) as a means of making kataphatic statements about the nature of God. In his mind, human reason lacks the intuitive simplicity of God's understanding and must proceed by way of notional distinctions (*distinctio rationis*). This way of proceeding is only a remote shadow of God's knowledge in its unified form. See Gilson, *The Philosophy of St. Thomas Aquinas*, 108-111.

[10] Dulles himself admits, but does not expound in the way suggested here, the role of analogy in the use of theological models. See *Models of the Church*, 27-28, 32, 33-34, 42, 57, 168-69, 193, 210. For a systematic presentation of the role of analogy in contemporary theology, see Tracy, *The Analogical Imagination*, 405-45.

THE CHURCH KERNEL

The purpose of a fundamental principle of ecclesiology is to help elucidate the nature of such a relationship. Probably the best way to explain this principle is by examining the Church in relation to its origin and end in the vision of God. Such an approach looks beyond the Church's origin in the apostolic experience of the Christ-event by concentrating on the purpose behind the event itself. From this perspective, the Church has its origin not in the coming of the Spirit to the early followers of Jesus, or in their experience of the Risen Lord, or in the reality of the Risen Lord himself, but in the divine purpose which brought all of this about, i.e., the *visio Dei*. These words (literally, "the vision of God") can be understood in either of two ways, depending on whether or not one takes the Latin word *Dei* for a possessive or objective genitive. The former would refer to the Godhead's *own* vision, which in turn could be subdivided into its *internal* vision of Trinitarian self-relations and its *external* vision of its creation. The latter would refer to the beatific vision, i.e., a person's ultimate union with God in the afterlife. Properly speaking, the Church has its origin in God's external vision of creation and its end in that process of divinization which ultimately leads to the beatific vision. It goes without saying that this entire description rests on the principles of proper proportionality and the analogy between divine and human vision. From this description, it should also be clear that a part of the divine mystery, the Godhead's own internal vision, remains largely its own domain, seemingly beyond the grasp of created intelligence.[11]

One of the benefits of looking at the Church as beginning and ending in the *visio Dei* is that it places ecclesiology in the context of the whole of theology. The outcome, in fact, is not unlike the

---

[11] In the view of Aquinas, although natural reason cannot see the divine *essence* by its own powers (*Summa theologiae*, I, q. 12, a. 4, resp.), it can come to a knowledge of God's existence and his attributes by arguing from his effects in creation to the cause (*Summa theologiae*, I, q. 12, a. 12, resp.). Since grace is necessary for the human intellect to see the divine essence, it would seem that human beings possess an obediential potency for the beatific vision.

Neoplatonic schema of *exitus/reditus* around which Aquinas structures his *Summa theologiae*: the *Prima pars* representing the going out of all things from God; the *Secunda pars* and *Tertia pars* signaling their eventual return.[12] From the perspective of ecclesiology, one would say that the Church emerges from the external *visio Dei* and ends in the *visio Dei* of divinized humanity. Even though the various subject/object demarcations of each of these uses of *visio Dei* must remain intact, when examined in relation to one another, they give a remarkable description of the proportionate relations which God and humanity will ultimately share. That is to say that, in addition to its internal, Trinitarian gaze, the Godhead gazes externally upon the fullness of divinized humanity; the latter, in turn, will gaze to the limits of its capacity upon the eternally gazing God (i.e., into the seemingly impenetrable confines of the Trinitarian relations themselves). Furthermore, insofar as the internal and external relations of the Godhead should be neither unduly dichotomized nor rashly equated, one could also make a case for the continual, albeit proportional, extent of divinized humanity's outward gaze with God upon the whole of creation. Such is the extent to which divinized humanity shares in the intimate life of the Trinity.[13]

When explaining the significance of the Trinity for the life of the Church (and, hence, for "The Church Kernel"), one may also utilize the principles of scholastic causality. In this respect, each of Aristotle's four causes takes on a particular ecclesiological dimension: the *material* corresponds to all those people, living and dead, who, in varying degrees, are incorporated into the believing community; the *formal* pertains to the Spirit of God who, as the life-giving soul of this community, not only gives it shape, but also inspires it to cooperate in the process of humanity's divinization;

---

[12] M.-D. Chenu, *The Scope of the Summa*, trans. R. E. Brennan and A.-M. Landry (Washington, D.C.: The Thomist Press, 1958), 15-25.

[13] "The 'beatific vision' ...is an intimate participation in the vision the Son has of the Father in the bosom of the Trinity. Revelation, by making us know in his Son, the personal and trinitarian God, the creating and saving God, the God 'who was made man to make us God,' has changed everything." See de Lubac, *The Mystery of the Supernatural*, 299. See also Leech, *Experiencing God*, 383-84.

the *efficient* refers to Christ who, as the head of this mystical body, continually directs the gaze of this community toward that of his Father, whom he called, "Abba"; the *final* has to do with the *visio Dei* itself which, as explained above, involves the Godhead: (1) contemplating the Church within itself from all eternity, (2) gazing upon it externally as an integral part of its creation, and (3) receiving the gaze of the community of believers — an act which, ultimately, ends in the most intimate of spiritual unions (i.e., the beatific vision).[14] From this perspective, the question of causality has a great deal to do with the proper explication of the fundamental principle of ecclesiology. As will become evident, each of the principle's key elements not only interrelate, but also correspond, both individually and as a group, to a specific schema of rational causality.

When treating the Church from the perspective of its origin and end in the *visio Dei*, one must eventually look beyond the strict confines of causality and investigate the manner in which the promise of this truth has been preserved throughout the historical and transhistorical continuum of time and eternity. The movement involved here extends from the purposefulness of God's internal vision, to the transhistorical significance of the Christ event, from the narrative proclamation of the apostles and early followers of Jesus, to the dogmatic formulations of the evolving Church, and, finally, to the mystical union inherent in the beatific vision itself. This movement (from purpose to event to story to dogma to union) should be understood not in a linear but in a circular fashion. That is to say that God's purpose foresees humanity's transformation by the divinity, while that very transformed humanity embraces the divine purpose which begot it.

---

[14] Although the use of Aristotelian causality to explain theological realities was a common enough practice among the schoolmen (mainly on account of the various entries of Aristotle to the West during the twelfth and thirteenth centuries and the subsequent attempt on the part of such scholastics as Albert Magnus and Thomas Aquinas to draw a synthesis of Christian theology on the basis of peripatetic thought), I am not aware of any classification such as the one outlined above. For an explanation of the fundamental insights of Aristotelian causality, see Joseph Owens, *An Elementary Christian Metaphysics*, 2d ed. (Houston: Center for Thomistic Studies, 1985), 236-37.

The Gospel narratives and the Church's dogmas, in turn, are intricately related to each other and to the Christ event, while the latter both constitutes and is, in part, constituted by the former. This circular movement makes it clear that the divine purpose is expressed through a continuum of interrelated values. To be sure, the danger for ecclesiology occurs precisely when any one of these elements is placed above the rest and cut off from its contextual surroundings.[15]

From what has been said thus far, the fundamental principle of ecclesiology (i.e., "The Church Kernel") may be summarized thus: The Church consists of the community of believers, living and dead, who, by virtue of their origin and end in the mind of the Father, interpret (i.e., contemplate, celebrate, formulate, proclaim, and serve) through Christ and in the Spirit, the mystery of their own communal life and the gift of humanity's divinization. Upon this statement a number of important observations follow: (1) it is not a definition (the ecclesial reality cannot be circumscribed in an absolute manner); (2) it represents a broad synthesis of the previous models involved (in various ways, each of the five — institution, mystical communion, sacrament, herald, servant — will find it compatible with its own perspective); (3) it accentuates the relationship between these models and the mystery that is the Church (and so remains true to the prerequisites of proportional analogy); (4) it provides for itself a "built-in" hermeneutical corrective (allowing for theological reflection to reinterpret the meaning of Church in changing historical circumstances); (5) it relates ecclesiology to the whole of theology (while maintaining its identity as a discipline in its own right). When taken together with the preliminary remarks given earlier, these observations demonstrate the manner in which the fundamental principle of ecclesiology as developed in this essay can be used as a basis for a systematic theological reflection within the Church. In this

---

[15] See Louth's discussion of the "dissociation of sensibility" in contemporary theology and his proposal of "a return to allegory" as a way of reintegrating spiritual experience, Church doctrine, and the Gospel narrative. *Discerning the Mystery*, 1-16, 96-131.

The Church Kernel

respect, they highlight the universality of "The Church Kernel" and the extent to which it can be applied to all aspects of ecclesial life.

THE ROLE OF RELIGIOUS IN THE CHURCH

Of particular concern is the way in which this fundamental principle of ecclesiology pertains to religious. As in the lay and priestly states, their way of life contains the essential elements of "The Church Kernel" (i.e., a life in community oriented toward the Trinity). The ecclesial element is explicit: religious make their vows to God, through Christ, in the Spirit, and before the believing community. What is distinctive about religious life, however, is the way in which the vows heighten the special significance of the *visio Dei* for all the members of the believing community. In their chastity, religious proclaim God not only as the love of their life, but also as the source and end of their own divinization. In their poverty, they recognize that they possess nothing (least of all their creatureliness) which does not ultimately come from the mind of God. In their obedience to their superiors, they affirm that the purpose of their life lies hidden in the will of their Creator, often beyond the scope of their own understanding. When taken together, the vows show a sensitivity to the *visio Dei* in both its possessive and objective aspects (e.g., the *exitus/reditus* of Aquinas). That is to say that they take into account God's external gaze upon humanity, as well as humanity's ultimate gazing into the mysteries of the Godhead itself. In this respect, the religious life highlights for the rest of the Church both the transcendent and eschatological elements of the one salvific process.[16]

Religious are thus called to help others recognize more

---

[16] "We have spoken of the witness of the religious to Christ as transcendental and eschatological, meaning that he is a living reminder to man that, good as this world is, it can never satisfy the heart of man (transcendental); and that man has not here on this good earth a lasting city (eschatological)." See John Powell, *The Mystery of the Church* (Milwaukee: The Bruce Publishing Co., 1967), 214-15.

clearly the gaze of God upon their lives and the gaze of God to which they themselves are called. Their way of life serves as a leaven within the Church, raising the consciousness of those around them to a deeper recognition: firstly, of God's action in the world; secondly, of that other world to which all of humanity has been called. Religious, in other words, embrace the fundamental principle of ecclesiology ("The Church Kernel") as the fundamental principle of their lives. God, for them, is encountered in the midst of "the community of believers, living and dead, who, by virtue of their origin and end in the mind of the Father, interpret (i.e., contemplate, celebrate, formulate, proclaim, and serve) through Christ and in the Spirit, the mystery of their own communal life and the gift of humanity's divinization."[17] By means of this total, unconditional embrace of God and humanity, they challenge others to examine their own vocations more deeply and to discover the particular way in which they themselves participate in the mystery of the *visio Dei*.[18]

In this regard, the religious life serves a hermeneutical function in the life of the Church. The vowed life of a religious community benefits the entire believing community by calling it to be ever more conscious of the covenant it shares with its Creator. From this perspective, the religious community is itself a living model of what the entire Church is called to become. This call is specified not so much in terms of its concrete mode of living (which obviously will change depending upon whether or not one is called to the single, married, or priestly way of life), but in the quality of its life of faithfulness to the Lord. In this hermeneutical

---

[17] See above 58.

[18] In the words of the Second Vatican Council: "All the members of the Church should unflaggingly fulfill the duties of their Christian calling. The profession of the evangelical counsels shines before them as a sign which can and should effectively inspire them to do so. For the People of God has here no lasting city but seeks the city which is to come, and the religious state of life, in bestowing greater freedom from the cares of earthly existence on those who follow it, simultaneously reveals more clearly to all believers the heavenly goods which are already present in this age." See *Lumen gentium*, no. 44 [*CDD*, 176-77]; English translation: Flannery, *Vatican Council II*, 404.

role, religious confront the Church with the call to discipleship which, although experienced and proclaimed in different ways throughout the Church's long history, possesses the common thread of genuine fidelity to the person of Christ and is extended to all who pass under the *visio Dei*. The religious life, in other words, calls the Church (at all levels) to live a life of authenticity. By presenting this challenge to the Church, religious, as members of the Church, are themselves challenged to live a life of continual conversion.[19] In this way, they are able to arrive at a deeper understanding of their own lives and the significance it has for them individually, for their respective religious communities, and for the life of the Church.[20]

RELIGIOUS AND MARY

To the extent that they give witness to the significance of the *visio Dei* for the community of believers and serve a hermeneutical function within the Church by calling all of its members (including themselves) to a deeper life of conversion, religious share a special relationship with Mary, the Mother of their Lord. She it was who, "full of grace" and "filled with the Spirit," first proclaimed the greatness of the Lord from the depths of her soul in the midst of a doubting and uncertain world. Fully receptive to the God of her ancestors, she experienced the life of this God taking shape within her and gave birth to a son whom she and her spiritual descendants would, for generations to come, hail as their Messiah and Lord. As the first of humanity to experience the

---

[19] For the mutual call to conversion within the Church and its particular significance for religious, see John R. Sheets, "The Call to the Renewal of Religious Life," *Review for Religious* 43 (1984): 179-80. On the pedagogy of personal conversion, see Paul Griéger, "La conversione personale," *Vita consacrata* 22 (1986): 361-66.

[20] The ecclesiological dimension of the religious life is further developed in Yves Congar, "La vie religieuse vue dans l'Église selon Vatican II," *Vie consacrée* 43 (1971): 65-88; Albert Chapelle, "La vie religieuse dans le mystère de l'Église," *Vie consacrée* 51 (1979): 104-118.

fullness of Redemption, she experiences now what still remains the fundamental hope of her spiritual progeny, i.e., the beatific vision itself. Indeed, Mary, who received the gaze of God's vision in the conception and bearing of her son, now embraces that vision with her own gazing into the mystery of the Godhead.

It is for these reasons that Mary can be thought of as the Mother of the Church. As the first of humanity to experience the fullness of the process of divinization and the movement of *exitus/reditus*, going out and return to God, she stands at the heart of the community of believers, calling them all, whatever their state, to a life of authentic faith in Christ. In doing so, she also performs a hermeneutical function in the Church. That is to say that, like religious who, in this regard, seek only to emulate her, she challenges others to understand more deeply the way in which they themselves are called to live out their lives under the gaze of God's vision. This hermeneutical function of Mary goes to the very heart of her being. As virgin *and* mother, she constantly challenges the believing community to maintain a balanced self-understanding which recognizes the need for doctrine *and* experience, both of which should be seen not only as interrelating, but also as coming under the more encompassing influence of the *visio Dei* in all its aspects.[21]

CONCLUSION

Using proper proportionality for its rational basis, the fundamental principle of ecclesiology developed in this chapter (i.e, "The Church Kernel") combines hermeneutical self-awareness with the theological embrace of the *visio Dei* to provide a contextual understanding of the nature of the Church's own mystery. In doing so, it not only steers clear of the extremities of univocal and equivocal thought, but also places the discipline of ecclesiology itself within the context of the whole of theology. Such an ap-

---

[21] Mary's hermeneutical function for the Church as virgin and mother is developed more fully in chap. 14, "The Marian Kernel," 201-14.

proach to the mystery of the Church moves beyond the use of "models" so prevalent in today's theology, not by refuting their worth, but by recognizing that the "logical gap" created by them (and inherent in all theological language) actually refers to a shared relationship of proportion between the models' primary analogues and the one mystery they seek to express. In this respect, the principle outlined in this essay takes an important hermeneutical look back toward the Church's own theological tradition, many of whose authors (e.g., Augustine, Pseudo-Dionysius, Aquinas) recognize a creative tension between the contrary approaches of positive and negative theology.

In the final analysis, "The Church Kernel" describes the mystery of the universal ecclesial community by referring it again and again to the fundamental mystery of all of reality, i.e., the Divine Godhead. This relationship of *mystery-to-mystery* provides the believing community with not only an important transcendent point of reference (*visio Dei*) from which it can formulate those structures of symbol and rational thought necessary for its own self-understanding (e.g. in the liturgy; through positive theology), but also a critical hermeneutical consciousness to help it see the limitations of the very models it constructs (e.g., through analogical thought, negative theology).

In this regard, religious play an important role in the life of the Church. Along with Mary, the mother of Jesus, their lives within the Church presuppose the radical embrace of the Father, through the person of Christ, in the Spirit. From this perspective, their vows of chastity, poverty, and obedience cannot be thought of apart from a life centered around the Trinity, and, hence, oriented toward the *visio Dei*.[22] To the extent that they enable themselves and others to become more conscious of this funda-

---

[22] In the words of John Paul II: "Religious profession creates *a new bond between the person and the one and triune God in Jesus Christ*. This bond develops on the foundation of the original bond that is contained in the sacrament of baptism... and is a fuller expression of it." See *Redemptionis donum*, no. 7 [*AAS* 76 (1984): 522]; English translation: "*Redemptionis Donum*: An Expression of Love for Religious," 487 [italics mine]. See also Godfried Danneels, "Le don de la rédemption," *Vie consacrée* 56 (1984): 271-74.

mental orientation (and option) to which all of humanity is called, and to the extent that they help themselves and others to shed those structures of human action, attitude, and thought which render their lives inauthentic before their Creator, they can be thought to embrace the fundamental principle of ecclesiology ("The Church Kernel") as the fundamental principle of their own lives and the lives of those around them. In this respect, their lives represent the challenge of the mystery of God to the mystery of the Church, that of God's humanization to the realization of the human desideratum, that of divinity to the potential of divinity in all of humanity.

5

THE FALL KERNEL

Is there a fundamental principle of the theology of original sin? The answer to this question depends not only on the way in which the truths of the doctrine are distinguished from the details of its classical Augustinian formulation, but also on the way in which the theologian relates these insights to those of a sound Christian anthropology. Of further importance is the wider connection such refinements have to recent shifts in the categorizations of personal and social sin. The impact of such shifts calls for proportional changes in the Church's doctrine of the Fall.

THE CLASSICAL FORMULATION

The doctrine's classical expression comes from Augustine of Hippo (354-430), who uses it to offset the two main tenets of Pelagian environmentalism: (1) that sin is learned through imitation, and (2) that a person can earn salvation without grace and on his or her own merits.[1] To do so, Augustine develops the notion of

---

[1] For the historical background to the Pelagian controvery, see Frend, *The Rise of Christianity*, 673-80. For a full doctrinal exposition of the controversy, see J. Tixeront, *History of Dogmas*, vol. 2, *From St. Athanasius to St. Augustine (318-430)*, trans. H.L.B. (Westminster, Md.: Christian Classics, 1984), 432-505. See also Alfred Vanneste, *The Dogma of Original Sin*, trans. Edward P. Callens (Louvain: Nauwelaerts, 1971), 57-92.

a seminal nature, according to which all of human nature is germinally contained (as in a seed) in humanity's first parents.[2] From this perspective, the fall of Adam is not a mere personal sin, but one affecting the entire human race. Adam's disobedience, in other words, results in humanity's own inner disobedience to self, the horrible effects of which include ignorance, death, the hardship of human labor, and inordinate concupiscence (i.e., lust).[3] For Augustine, the latter is always concomitant with sexual union and is responsible for transmitting both the sin and its effects from one generation to the next.[4]

Even from this brief summary of Augustine's classical formulation a number of important insights emerge: (1) he presupposes the historicity of the literal sense of the Genesis story; (2) he emphasizes the hereditary aspects of Adam's sin by means of a mixture of genetic and nature metaphors; (3) he considers the Fall a cataclysmic event which brings about an anthropological shift in human nature (i.e., the weakening of human reason and will); (4) he uses the term "sin" in an analogous fashion with the notion of personal sin serving as its primary epistemological analogue.[5] Taken together, these observations lend further support to the hermeneutical distinction between the formulation of the Augustinian doctrine and the theological reality it seeks to express. In pointing out the historical and philosophical assumptions of the former, they contribute to the formation of the condition for the possibility of the latter's theological reformulation.

It should also be noted that, while Augustine's is considered the classical formulation of the doctrine of original sin, it is in no way the only one. When opposing Gnostic dualism with his own doctrine of recapitulation, Irenaeus of Lyons (c. 180) speaks of the fall of Adam as a slight fall from childlike innocence, almost to be expected in the light of humanity's overall movement toward the divine.[6] In similar fashion, Eastern fathers such as Athanasius

---

[2] *De civitate Dei*, 13.14 [*CSEL* 40/2:34; *PL* 41:386-87].
[3] *De civitate Dei*, 14.15 [*CSEL* 40/2:34-37; *PL* 41:408-9].
[4] *De nuptiis et concupiscentia*, 1.19 [*CSEL* 42:233-35; *PL* 44:425-26].
[5] For a concise presentation of the classical Augustinian doctrine, see Kelly, *Early Christian Doctrines*, 361-66.
[6] *Adversus haereses*, 4.37.1; 4.38.1-3 [*SC* 100/2:919-23; *PG* 7:1099-1109].

The Fall Kernel

(295-373)[7] and Gregory of Nyssa (c. 395)[8] stress the soteriological impact of Christ's incarnation as the basis for humanity's deification. In doing so, they view humanity's initial failure to come to terms with its own creaturely limitations in the wider context of a single creative and redemptive process. Although the classical formulation of the doctrine of original sin is clearly a Western category, shaped by Western concerns, and mainly by Western minds, the question arises as to whether or not its most fundamental concerns are consistent with these seemingly less influential but, nonetheless, equally valid formulations of the Church's theological tradition.

The answer to this question is a simple and unqualified, "yes." Once differentiated from their historical choice of language, style, and form, all orthodox formulations portraying humanity's lack of creaturely innocence (known only in the West as "original sin") — be it Augustine's or the more positive emphases of Irenaeus and the Eastern fathers — affirm: (1) that humanity shares in the fundamental goodness of creation and has been created in the image and likeness of God; (2) that a person enters this world in need of redemptive healing and elevation;[9] (3) that this redemption cannot be achieved through human effort alone; and (4) that redemption begins in each person decisively through Christ's grace received at baptism.[10] These four elements of the

---

[7] *De incarnatione*, 54.3 [*SC* 199:458-59; *PG* 25:191-92].

[8] *De opificio hominis*, 16 [*SC* 6:151-61; *PG* 44:178-88].

[9] Aquinas distinguishes the redemption of fallen humanity in terms of a twofold movement of healing (i.e., from the effects of original sin) and elevation (i.e., to participate in the divine nature). See *Summa theologiae*, I-II, q. 109, a. 2, resp.; a. 4. resp. The second element of this movement of redemptive grace (that of "elevation") corresponds exactly to the concept of "divinization" developed by the Greek fathers.

[10] Nos. 2-4 appear in an earlier reflection on the fundamental truths of original sin. See Dennis J. Billy, "Traducianism as a Theological Model in the Problem of Ensoulment," *The Irish Theological Quarterly* 55 (1989): 31. No. 1 has been added to emphasize the way in which the doctrine of original sin affirms the goodness of creation against Manichean dualism. In this respect, Augustine's formulation of the doctrine can be understood as an attempt "...to adopt and maintain a position somewhere between Manichaeism and Pelagianism." See Gabriel Daly, "Theological Models in the Doctrine of Original Sin," *The Heythrop Journal* 13 (1972): 128.

traditional formulations must be included in any new expression of the Catholic doctrine of the Fall. All other considerations (e.g., the particular models employed; the historical interpretation of the Genesis story) are of a secondary and nonessential nature.

Two key observations flow from these basic components of the doctrine's theological tradition. Firstly, the causal order, where original sin precedes personal sin (i.e., the latter arises, at least in part, from the weakening effects of the former on human reason and will) must not be confused with the epistemological order, where personal sin has precedence (i.e., an individual first comes to know and understand the reality of sin as something intensely personal). Secondly, the traditional formulations overlook the more modern concept of social sin, or at least remove it from practical, conscious reach by submerging it deep within the philosophical notion of nature.[11] Such comments point to the need of rooting even these essential elements of the doctrine's tradition in a more comprehensive theory of Christian anthropology.

THE LEVELS OF CHRISTIAN ANTHROPOLOGY

Another way of stating the difficulty is that, while the traditional formulations of the doctrine of original sin address the anthropological levels of the human universal (i.e., *natura humana*) and the human individual (i.e, *persona humana*), today's Christian anthropology places an added emphasis on the human social (i.e., *societas humana*). Although some attempts have been made to reinterpret the doctrine in the context of the latter (e.g., Piet Schoonenberg's, "the sin of the world"),[12] it seems more appropri-

---

[11] These tensions have arisen, in part, from the general methodological shift from metaphysical to phenomenological categories that features in most contemporary theologies. See Macquarrie, *Principles of Christian Theology*, 29-34.

[12] Piet Schoonenberg, *Man and Sin: A Theological View*, trans. Joseph Donceel (Notre Dame: University of Notre Dame Press, 1965), 98-123; Idem, "Original Sin and Man's Situation" in *The Mystery of Sin and Forgiveness*, ed. Michael J. Taylor (Staten Island, N.Y.: Alba House, 1971), 243-52.

The Fall Kernel

ate to keep each of the various anthropological categories distinct. A more preferable response would be to make a corresponding adjustment in the Church's classification of sin that would deal with humanity's experience of moral evil on the societal level. In such a case, personal sin would still remain the primary epistemological analogue for the concept of "sin," but some of the tension inherent in the causal relationship between original and personal sin would be shifted to the relationship of circular causality between personal and social sin. In this respect, a reciprocal relationship would be seen to exist between a person's contribution to moral evil in society, on the one hand, and society's inducement to personal sin, on the other.

When taken together, the above insights suggest the need for taking a closer look at the connection between Augustine's classical formula of the doctrine of original sin and the teaching it was designed to negate, i.e., Pelagian environmentalism.[13] The point in question here is whether or not the latter can be adjusted in such a way so as to address the anthropological level of the societal and, in doing so, be moved from a confrontative to a complementary relationship with the Augustinian formulation. Because the teaching's heterodox tendencies stem not so much from an unwillingness to acknowledge the reality of sin in human life, but from a failure to distinguish between the anthropological levels of the human universal and the human social, a positive evaluation to this mode of inquiry seems probable. In failing to make this subtle, albeit important distinction, the teaching effects a mixture of anthropological levels which results in a serious confusion in its theological doctrine. That is to say that Pelagius ends up attributing to the anthropological level of the human universal what, in

---

[13] "'Propagation' is specifically intended to be antithetical to 'imitation,' while 'generation' acts as a foil to 'regeneration,' a fact which limits and defines the linguistic function of both words. 'Imitation,' as Pelagius had employed it, conveyed an environmental, purely extrinsic, conception of the origin of sin. The orthodox response was 'propagation,' which was intended to state the inherent, antecedent, sinfulness of man even before he had been exposed to bad example and has actually begun to sin personally." See Daly, "Theological Models in the Doctrine of Original Sin," 124.

fact, should really have been attributed to that of the societal. While Augustine is surely justified in his confrontation and ultimate condemnation of Pelagius' teaching, the question arises as to whether or not his approach (i.e., the classical formulation of the doctrine of original sin) is the only valid theological response. Just as valid would be the approach of distinguishing the particular anthropological level addressed by each: in the case of Augustine, the human universal; in the case of Pelagius, the societal. Of course, the historical doctrine of Pelagian environmentalism remains a far cry from what contemporary theologians describe as the reality of "social sin."[14] In many ways, its focus remains on the individual who, learning the meaning of moral evil through his or her contact with the environment, is still the central focus of the doctrine's understanding of sin. At the same time, one cannot help but think that, despite the limitations of the theological language of his day, Pelagius is trying to come to terms with the intricate relationship of the individual with his or her social environment, a relationship which ultimately must be dealt with in terms of circularity and which also necessarily involves the anthropological levels of human society and the human person.[15]

The point to be made from the above discussion is that the threefold anthropological levels of the human universal, the societal, and the personal shift the relationship between Augustinian and Pelagian thought from confrontation to complementarity. Such a shift takes place only by strongly em-

---

[14] In today's usage, social sin refers to the way in which patterns of injustice have become institutionalized in the very structures of human society. For a description of "the profound primary evil of social sin" as understood by contemporary liberation theologians, see Alfred T. Hennelly, "The Red-Hot Issue: Liberation Theology," in *Liberation Theology: A Documentary History*, ed. Alfred T. Hennelly (Maryknoll, N.Y.: Orbis Books, 1990), 511.

[15] The relation of circularity in Pelagian thought consists in the twofold belief that (1) moral reform is necessary to effect a change in society, and (2) individuals sin by imitating the very socio-cultural environment in which they find themselves and desire to reform. While Pelagius emphasized the capacity of individuals to rise above the environmental circumstances of sin (i.e., human nature unaided by grace), it was widely considered a "heroic ideal" that only a few could achieve. See Frend, *The Rise of Christianity*, 674.

phasizing both the analogous nature of the concept of "sin" and each of the three anthropological levels described above. In maintaining these analogies, there emerges from the tradition the historical bases for the fundamental principle of the theology of original sin.

THE FALL KERNEL

An acceptable formulation of this principle would read as follows: The Church's doctrine of original sin is an analogous concept which, basing itself on the notion of personal sin as its primary epistemological analogue and addressing the anthropological level of the human universal, conveys four essential truths of the Christian tradition: (1) the fundamental goodness of all creation with humanity being created in the image and likeness of God; (2) the need for humanity's redemption (i.e., healing and divinization); (3) the weakness of creaturely limitation; and (4) the need for the grace of Christ which comes through baptism. When taken as such, the doctrine's full significance comes to light only when its proportional relations are viewed in the context of two other anthropological levels: that of the societal and that of the personal. That is to say that the analogous nature of the Church's teaching on sin presupposes a certain relationship of circularity, in which a shift in the understanding of sin dealt with on one anthropological level necessitates a proportional shift in the understanding of the concept of sin on the others.

The above principle has important ramifications for the theology of original sin. Changes in the categorizations regarding personal sin (e.g., from the mortal/venial sin distinction to those of fundamental option/serious sin/less serious sin)[16] and in the understanding of social sin (e.g., the notion of structural evil and

---

[16] See, for example, the schema suggested by Kevin O'Shea, "The Reality of Sin: A Theological and Pastoral Critique," in *The Mystery of Sin and Forgiveness*, ed. Michael J. Taylor (Staten Island, N.Y.: Alba House, 1971), 107-8.

the ideological oppression of the poor)[17] demand similar shifts in the formulation of the doctrine of original sin. That is to say that not only must the classical formulation be relieved of its unnecessary secondary characteristics (i.e., the historical approach to Genesis; the Augustinian concept of seminal nature), but the presupposition of a causal relationship between original sin and human anthropology (i.e., original sin *causing* an anthropological shift in human nature) must also be called into question. To use a simple analogy: just as theology in recent decades has moved from what may be termed a high-descending to a low-ascending Christology, so too the Christian understanding of sin has moved from a high-descending (original sin to personal sin) to a low-ascending mode (personal sin to social sin to original sin).[18] In other words, rather than simply accepting the doctrinal assumption of a causal movement starting, at least in part, in human nature and ending in the personal sin of human choice, contemporary theology starts with the recognition of a person's fundamental option in life, draws an analogous relation to the options of moral good and evil made by society and as evidenced in its structures, and then comes to recognize a more universal tendency operative in all of humanity. In this restructuring of theology's approach to the doctrine of original sin, the notion of personal sin still remains the primary epistemological analogue; what has been replaced is a linear sense of the historical causality with one of reciprocal anthropological influence. The doctrine of original sin, in other words, is "original" not in the sense that it represents the historical sin committed by our first parents, but in

---

[17] See the discussion on the structural dimensions of sin in Marciano Vidal, *Moral de actitudes*, 5th ed., vol. 1, *Moral fundamental* (Madrid: P.S. Editorial, 1981), 572-91. See also, Idem, "Structural Sin: A New Category in Moral Theology?" in *History and Conscience: Studies in Honour of Sean O'Riordan, C.SS.R.*, eds. Raphael Gallagher and Brendan McConvery (Dublin: Gill and Macmillan, 1989), 181-98.

[18] For a concise description of the difference between a high-descending and a low-ascending Christology, see Lane, *The Reality of Jesus*, 13-18. The application of this methodological approach to the doctrine of original sin underscores the intrinsic unity of the whole of theology and constitutes an original contribution of this work.

that it describes humanity's fundamental weakness on that anthropological level which relates to the universal roots of human existence.[19]

ORIGINAL SIN AND RELIGIOUS

As described above, the fundamental principle of original sin ("The Fall Kernel") has special significance for religious. Each of their vows affirms one or more of the essential elements of the doctrine's theological tradition: (1) in their vow of chastity, they give witness to their faith in the existence of a beyond and offer significant protest against a society whose human and sexual relationships are all too often damaged by sin;[20] (2) in their vow of poverty, they forsake possessions in order to make the threefold assertion of the world's created goodness, humanity's divine resemblance, and its experience of the need of redemption; (3) in their vow of obedience, they recognize their need for others and their incapacity to recognize and carry out the will of God by themselves. While other callings in life (i.e., lay and priestly) also reflect these same elements, a life dedicated to the evangelical counsels discloses them in a radical and uncompromising manner. That Church tradition has so often referred to religious profession as an individual's "second baptism" and to the religious life in general as "the angelic life" (*vita angelica*)[21] manifests

---

[19] This is the approach taken in Vatican Council II, *Gaudium et spes*, no. 13 [*CDD*, 697-98]; English translation: Flannery, *Vatican Council II*, 914. According to Daly: "...there is Vatican II's *homo in seipso divisus*. This phenomenological approach chimes with a psychology-conscious age, is rooted in the seventh chapter of Romans, and can be directly related to traditional teaching on concupiscence. In view of its scriptural and conciliar roots, there is a strong case for making it the control model." See "Theological Models in the Doctrine of Original Sin," 138.

[20] Edmund Hill, *Being Human: A Biblical Perspective* (London: Geoffrey Chapman, 1984), 166-67.

[21] John Bugge, *Virginitas: An Essay in the History of a Medieval Ideal*, International Archives of the History of Ideas, no. 17 (The Hague: Martinus Nijhoff, 1975), 30-35.

this close association to a heightened consciousness of sin, the life of conversion, and the reception of Christ's redemptive grace.

It is also quite evident that the religious vows bear meaning on each of the three anthropological levels dealt with in the preceding paragraphs. The vows of chastity, poverty, and obedience pertain not only to the human person (in the sense that an individual makes these vows and is bound by them), but also to human society (in the sense that these vows are taken in the context of religious community life and the larger life of the Church), and to the human universal (in the sense that they point to a general need in all of humanity, i.e., redemption by Christ). In this respect, one of the functions of the religious life is to keep these various anthropological levels visibly distinct in the eyes of the Church and all of its variously incorporated members, while at the same time recognizing their fundamentally interconnected nature.[22] These relations would apply to all levels of theology and, as has been demonstrated above, in a particular way to the doctrine of original sin.

By affirming each of the essential elements of the four fundamental components of this teaching, while at the same time helping to maintain the various anthropological levels involved, the religious life may be seen as a concrete way in which the Church gives witness to both the analogous nature of sin (i.e., personal, social, original) and the relationship of circularity which all of these levels share.[23] This is so because, on each of these levels, moral evil is experienced not as an abstract theological notion, but as a recognized existential lack in personal, social, and universal human perfection. To the extent that the religious life gives witness to this experience on each of these levels, it serves as a

---

[22] In doing so, it focuses on the solidarity that all human beings share by virtue of their fundamental human dignity, thereby warning against any human ideology that either exalts the individual to an exaggerated degree (as in liberal Western capitalism) or submerges his or her welfare completely to that of the state (as in communism).

[23] "Simply to say that 'sin' in the term 'original sin' is an analogue borrowed from personal sin is itself to recognize that we are using 'fiduciary' language." See Daly, "Theological Models in the Doctrine of Original Sin," 137.

leaven for both itself, for other states of life within the Church, and for the world as a whole, and calls for a continual conversion on not just one, but on the multidimensional levels of human experience. In this respect, religious have an integral role to play in the Church's teaching and proclamation of "The Fall Kernel."

CONCLUSION

This essay has offered a historical, linguistic, and anthropological analysis of the Church's theology of original sin. In doing so, it has emphasized the importance of viewing the classical Augustinian formulation of the doctrine in the context of those concepts it was originally intended to negate (i.e., Pelagian environmentalism), while at the same time being aware of those essential elements of Church teaching it was intended to affirm. The latter can be distilled from the Church's teaching by finding the common characteristics which the classical Augustinian formulation shares with other approaches rooted in the Church's theological tradition (i.e., Irenaeus' theory of recapitulation, the theory of divinization of the Eastern Church).

In addition to a simple knowledge of these elements, recent shifts in the approaches taken in other theological disciplines (e.g., from a high-descending to a low-rising Christology) call for comparable changes in emphasis in the Church's theology of original sin. Of prime importance is a renewed emphasis on personal sin as the primary epistemological analogue for the Church's understanding of the various meanings of sin.[24] In this respect, the doctrine of original sin cannot be understood (as if in a vacuum) apart from the Church's understanding of moral evil as

---

[24] For a recent magisterial document that emphasizes "personal sin" as the primary experiential category for sin, see SCDF, *Instructio de libertate christiana et liberatione* no. 75 [*AAS* 79 (1987): 588]; English translation: "Instruction on Christian Freedom and Liberation" in *Liberation Theology: A Documentary History*, ed. Alfred T. Hennelly (Maryknoll, N.Y.: Orbis Books, 1990), 485. For a critique of this position, see Hennelly, "The Red-Hot Issue: Liberation Theology," 511.

it exists on both the personal and societal levels. Sin, by its very nature, is encountered not as an isolated idea or as a disembodied principle, but as an experienced lack on each of humanity's three anthropological levels: the personal, the societal, and the universal. The latter alone comprises the theological domain of the Church's doctrine of original sin and should not be confused with either of the preceding two.

Religious play an important role in the Church's clarification of original sin not only because their vows are specifically ordained to the doctrine's essential elements, but also because the proper integration of their individual, communal, and universal lifestyles are meant to reflect the unity of the anthropological factors involved in the doctrine's proposed reformulation. In this respect, religious manifest to the world the analogical nature of the Church's doctrine of sin and thus give concrete expression to the multidimensional aspects of humanity's experience of moral evil in the postmodern world. From this perspective, religious are called to provide the world with a balanced picture of its participation in the reality of moral evil. They do so not only by disclosing (and without confusing) the analogical nature of sin's personal, societal, and universal aspects, but also by enabling both others and themselves to accept the responsibility for their failures at each appropriate anthropological level.

6

THE GRACE KERNEL

Is there a fundamental principle of the Church's teaching on grace? The answer to this question depends on how one understands the relationship between: (1) the classical categories of grace as they have been accepted and modified in the ongoing theological tradition of the Church and (2) the conditions for the possibility of the reception of grace as they exist in the spiritual lives of individual Christians and are reflected in the various communities to which they belong. Such a relationship reflects both the objective and subjective dimensions of the reality of grace (i.e., as something freely-given and received) and is obviously related to the whole of theology.

RETRIEVING THE DISTINCTIONS OF GRACE

It is not uncommon these days to refer to as "classical" the well-known scholastic divisions of grace as developed by Aquinas,[1] adopted by Trent[2] and expanded by the post-Tridentine manualist tradition.[3] The designation is a rather dubious one, since it expresses a certain ambivalance towards what many

---

[1] *Summa theologiae*, I-II, q. 111, aa. 1-5.
[2] *Decretum de justificatione*, Denz.-Schön., nos. 1520-83 [792a-843].
[3] Comprehensive in scope and exhaustive in detail, these manuals developed the Church's theological language in a thoroughly systematic fashion. See Ashley, *Theologies of the Body*, 183-4. In developing this language, however, they were

perceive, on the one hand, as an extremely coherent and systematic approach to some of the standard problems of Western theology and, on the other hand, as a body of thought poorly adept at dealing with the intellectual and spiritual needs of the postmodern world.[4]

This ambivalence increases after hearing about the way in which Thomas' late scholastic interpreters "reified" the meaning of grace through their many subtle distinctions and apparent lack of concern for the conscious dimensions of a person's spiritual growth.[5] It has also led to an implicit devaluation of the scholastic synthesis itself which, in the light of later developments (i.e., sixteenth-century Protestant fideism and eighteenth-century Enlightened rationalism), contributed substantially to the stability of the Catholic faith during extended periods of theological turbulence and intellectual reductionism.[6] Perhaps there is also a touch

---

not immune from intense (and sometimes bitter) theological controversies (e.g., the Molina/Báñez debate). See Hubert Jedin and John Dolan, eds., *The History of the Church* (New York: The Seabury Press, 1980), vol. 5, *Reformation and Counter Reformation*, by Erwin Iserloh, Joseph Glazik and Hubert Jedin, 542-45.

[4] This ambivalence toward the classical scholastic divisions of grace is symptomatic of a more deeply rooted tension in the Western religious psyche. When reflecting on the nature of "the religious classic" in general, Tracy states that "the 'dialectic' of the eighteenth-century Enlightenment has given rise to a cultural configuration of profound ambiguity." In his opinion: "both Enlightenment models of rationality and traditionalist models of heteronomy tend to destroy our ability to interpret the claims of the classics by interpreting all claims through the restrictive lenses of techniques developed by autonomous and heteronomous interpreters." See *The Analogical Imagination*, 196. For the difference between the modern and postmodern approaches to theology, see George Aichele, Jr., "Literary Fantasy and Postmodern Theology," *Journal of the American Academy of Religion* 59 (1991): 329.

[5] For the broad contours of this abstract pattern of reification, see the historical development of the manualist positions in A. Vacant, E. Mangenot and E. Amann, eds., *Dictionnaire de théologie catholique* (Paris: Librairie Letourzey et Ané, 1924), s.v. "Grace," by J. Van der Meersch.

[6] More research needs to be done on the relationship between the stability of Church doctrine during this period (i.e., the post-Tridentine/pre-Vatican II era) and its adversarial position toward the world (as exemplified in its reaction to Modernism). One wonders to what extent a stable synthesis is possible in a Church that now seeks to enter into dialogue with the world in a non-triumphalistic manner. For important background to the Modernism

of envy involved: Thomas and his later interpreters (both magisterial and manualist) achieved for Catholic theology in their respective historical epochs what today's theologians have yet to accomplish for their own. i.e., a coherent, systematic exposition and synthesis of the most fundamental elements of the Catholic faith.

What is becoming more and more evident, however, is that it is not so much the distinctions of scholastic theology that have become irrelevant, but rather a number of preconceptions upon which they are only partly based (e.g., the two-tiered relationship between nature and grace; a naive trust in the theological capabilities of scholastic dialectic; a subtle mistrust of emotions). If this be so, then what is called for is not so much a complete overhaul of the scholastic system of classification, but a reorientation of its many useful distinctions toward the fundamental concerns of the present theological arena. In this respect, the scholastic discussion of the elevating power of habitual grace and the obediential potency in human nature necessary for its reception can be studied in the light of more recent theological insights into the relational boundaries shared by the natural and the supernatural.[7] Further efforts could also be made into the hermeneutical limits of the scholastic method itself,[8] while attempts at comparing the nature of the rational discourse behind the scholastic classification and that of, for example, contemporary depth psychology might end in a more complementary understanding of the objective and

---

controversy, see Hubert Jedin and John Dolan, eds. *History of the Church*, vol. 9, *The Church in the Industrial Age*, by Roger Aubert et al., trans. Margit Resch (New York: The Seabury Press, 1981), 420-80.

[7] See, for example, Rahner's discussion of obediential potency in light of the supernatural existential in "Concerning the Relationship Between Nature and Grace," chap. in *Theological Investigations*, vol. 1, *God, Christ, Mary and Grace*, trans. Cornelius Ernst (London: Darton, Longman and Todd, 1974), 315-17.

[8] Two of the more interesting studies in this regard are Brian Stock, *The Implications of Literacy: Written Language and Models of Interpretation in the Eleventh and Twelfth Centuries* (Princeton: Princeton University Press, 1983), which places the scholastic method of the time in the context of rituals of developing textual communities, and Alexander Murray, *Reason and Society in the Middle Ages* (Oxford: Clarendon Press, 1978), which focuses on the rise of reason in the Western world as a functioning social commodity.

subjective orientations of the communication of divine grace.[9] The point being made here is that the classical distinctions in the scholastic treatment of grace can be maintained only if they are reinterpreted through the most fundamental preconceptions of postmodern thought. Distinctions such as "created" and "uncreated," "internal" and "external," "actual" and "sanctifying" grace are significant if for no other reason than that they convey a sense of continuity with the past and serve as heuristic devices within which the contours of an individual's or group's theological spirituality may grow in its present lived experience and theological explication. Such an act of retrieval is the task set before those theologians today who, intrigued by the intellectual accomplishments of the Church's theological past, find themselves looking back at it through the fragmented lenses of post-Enlightenment thought.[10] Beset with a subliminal and, at times, overwhelming experience of what many now refer to as the sense of "nostalgic desire,"[11] they are to search through the Church's theological tradition and reinterpret it for their contemporaries in

---

[9] According to Carl Jung: "dogma, like mythology, in general, expresses the quintessence of inner experience and thus formulates the operative principles of... the collective unconscious." See *The Collected Works of Carl Jung*, Bollingen Series, no. 20, 2nd ed, ed. Sir Herbert Read, et. al., trans. R.F.C. Hull, vol. 18, *The Symbolic Life* (Princeton: Princeton University Press, 1970), 707. Despite his well-known distrust of institutional religion, Jung's insights into dogma as an extended system of symbols, which connect with the unconscious and mediate a personal experience of grace, would be a promising point of departure for such a discussion. For more on Jung's view of dogma, see Wallace B. Clift, *Jung and Christianity: The Challenge of Reconciliation* (New York: Crossroad, 1982), 93-103.

[10] One of the strongest statements to this effect comes from Louth: "...we have seen in the sciences and their success the manifestation of the self-confidence of the Enlightenment's search for objective truth through the employment of a method, and I have suggested that far from the humanities needing to develop any similar techniques, they have their own approach to knowledge which is betrayed if they seek to ape the sciences. I have argued too that theology is, not surprisingly, a part of the older way of attaining knowledge and that it betrays itself if it seeks to become 'scientific' by any attempt to fashion an objective method." See *Discerning the Mystery*, 132.

[11] The term "nostalgic desire" (*Sehnsucht*) was coined by M. Horkheimer, *Die Sehnsucht nach dem ganz Anderen* (Hamburg: Furche-Verlag, 1970), 88. It first arose in the context of the postmodernist discussion of theodicy and the problem of evil.

such a way that it becomes relevant for them while also remaining continuous with its own historical horizon. To do so requires a highly attuned and sensitive theological imagination, precisely what many of Thomas' late scholastic interpreters lacked.

REVISING THE LANGUAGE OF GRACE

If the scholastic system of classification tended eventually to reify the reality of grace in the lives of believers, the fluid and rather poorly focused terminology often found in contemporary theology has surely contributed to its oversubjectivization. Each of these currents of thought has something to offer: grace is neither a thing to be measured and meted out, nor a mere projection of the deepest yearnings of the human heart; it has certain objective, subjective, even communal aspects to it. For postmodern spirituality, these aspects can best be expressed in terms of divine and human encounter. It presupposes: (1) a meeting of distinct persons or groups, (2) a personal and, hence, social sharing of self, and (3) a mutual indwelling.[12]

(1) To say that grace involves a meeting of distinct persons or groups is to recognize, quite simply, that all talk in the Christian tradition about the natural and the supernatural, the divine and the human, the gift and the reception of grace, is superfluous if the personal and communal realities behind these concepts are utterly incapable of communicating with each other. The fact that God, human beings, and the social realities of which they form a part (e.g., the Trinity, the Church, the family, the religious order)

---

[12] These categories take what is considered the best of human interpersonal experience (i.e., a respect for a person's otherness, the risk of encounter, the intimacy of friendship) as the primary epistemological analogue for the discussion of grace as a divine and human encounter. From a metaphysical standpoint, these elements exist in the fullest degree possible in the life of the Trinity. It is precisely because they are applicable on both ends of the theological spectrum — both anthropologically and metaphysically — that these categories have been selected as a fitting framework within which the mystery of God's grace can be further probed and understood.

are personal only in an analogous sense does not render the condition of their possible encounter impossible. Human beings and their social groups are distinct from the Triune God, and in this sense the classical depiction of the difference between nature and supernature has something to offer contemporary theology. At the same time, what has been overlooked all too often even in this traditional distinction is that human beings and their various social institutions ultimately have their origins in God and thus must be considered not only apart from, but also in conjunction with their Creator. One might even go so far as to say that the very notion of the supernatural is implied in the limitations of creaturely existence. Human beings and human society in general have a natural capacity for the reception of grace and, in this respect, the relationship between the natural and the supernatural — even as it stands in the traditional formulation — is much closer than has been previously thought.[13] This close connection between God and creation affirms, at one and the same time, both the distinct and objective otherness of their beings and the condition for the possibility of their subjective interaction. To speak of grace as a meeting of the divine and human other preserves both aspects of this connection.

(2) As a personal and, hence, intrinsically social sharing of self, grace represents a movement on the part of God towards the human person and society and a corresponding movement on their part towards God. That is not to say that one is necessarily dependent on the other: the human person is rarely (if ever) conscious of the intimate workings of God's grace in his or her life; nor is the movement of God's grace predetermined by a person's interior dispositions or a particular culture's societal infrastruc-

---

[13] From a Thomistic standpoint: "...'the analogy of being,' if really grounded philosophically in Thomas' own original metaphysical insight into the radical dialectical otherness of *esse*, can prove a genuine philosophical analogy to the theological 'analogy of grace' grounded in the Christian religious experience of the radical giftedness and all-pervasiveness of grace." See Tracy, *The Analogical Imagination*, 414. See also Rahner, "Some Implications of the Scholastic Concept of Uncreated Grace," chap. in *Theological Investigations*, vol. 1, *God, Christ, Mary and Grace*, trans. Cornelius Ernst (London: Darton, Longman and Todd, 1974), 346; Rahner, "Concerning the Relationship Between Nature and Grace," 317.

ture. God remains utterly free to dispense with his gift of self whenever and wherever he wills, while the human person or the society to which he or she belongs is always free to cooperate with or to reject that gift. In choosing the former, a person or social group participates in the divine and human sharing of self. In choosing the latter, a person or social group fails to render a commensurate response. To speak of grace as a divine and human sharing of self is significant not only because it highlights the communicative nature of humanity's relationship to the divine, but also because it preserves, once again, both an objective and a subjective aspect in the relationship. To share with another person or group requires a risk of entering another's world, where one is faced with uncertainties beyond one's immediate control. This is true for both ends of the divine and human encounter: in giving us free will, God has chosen to put a part of his created world outside his immediate control;[14] similarly, a person or group will never know for sure just where a genuine response to God's grace will lead.

(3) The sharing of self between God and humanity culminates in the mutual indwelling of selves. The relationship between the divine and the human becomes such that the divine can be seen to dwell within the human and the human within the divine. To speak of God indwelling in a person or social institution is but another way of speaking of the human person or society dwelling within God: the two realities are nothing more than two sides of the same coin. This is sometimes forgotten in the classical distinctions which tend to emphasize the indwelling of the divine in the sphere of the human (often to the exclusion of the social dimension of human existence). And this is one area in which the traditional categories need to be modified by the postmodern concern for relationality. Indeed, the very concept of God dwelling within the human person is a shallow, two-dimensional construct in need of

---

[14] The phrase, "outside his immediate control" refers to the Godhead's voluntary self-limitation ("self-discipline," one might add) which is the condition for the possibility of humanity's exercise of *liberum arbitrium*. It in no way denies God's providential plan of salvation, God's permissive will in all things, or the working of divine grace in the human heart.

correction by a complementary concept of the human indwelling of the divine in all its various aspects, i.e., the physical, the psychological, the spiritual, and the social.[15] The classical formulation of the soteriological principle affirms both of these aspects: God became human so that humanity might become divine. The nature of this indwelling, which in the classical terminology is referred to as sanctifying grace, is such that God's presence in the person and the person's presence in God become one and the same, i.e., the human person is a temple of the Holy Spirit in the same way that a child, at baptism, is initiated into the Kingdom of God. The effects of this mutual indwelling differ by virtue of the varying levels of personhood involved: in a human person or group, the effect is sanctification (i.e., divinization); in God, the effect is the *gloria Dei* itself.

THE GRACE KERNEL

Given the above insights, the fundamental principle of the Church's teaching on grace ("The Grace Kernel") emerges as the analogous relationship of divine and human encounter (with the latter referring either to individual persons or to entire groups) whereby an authentic meeting of distinct personalities manifests itself in a mutual and free sharing of selves, thus culminating in the reciprocal effect of divine and human indwelling. The nature of this encounter is such that there exists an objective *and* a subjective element for each of the members involved: for the human, the former refers to the distinct personal otherness of the

---

[15] Unlike some of his later interpreters (e.g., the manualists), who tended to "reify" the notion of grace and thereby miss some of the fuller implications of the mystery of God's love, Aquinas maintains a dynamic understanding of the divine and human encounter. In his mind, charity is not only love of God but also "a certain friendship with God" that implies "a certain mutual return of love, together with mutual communion" (*Summa theologiae*, I-II, q. 65, a. 5, resp.). In this respect, Thomas' emphasis on relationality presents postmodern thought with a familiar vantage point from which to view the mystery of the divine-and-human encounter.

The Grace Kernel

divine giver, while the latter points to the human capacity for the reception of the gift; for God, the former refers to the distinct personal otherness of the human receiver (especially in relation to its creaturely status), while the latter refers to the infinite capacity of God to first sustain and then elevate creation for his own greater glory. While such an encounter can be but momentary and orientated toward a particular circumstance or occasion, it reaches its fullest expression when it culminates in an ongoing habitation of the divine in the human and the human in the divine. In this respect, grace represents the bond of love existing between God and humanity not by virtue of their relationship of Creator and creature, but because of their free and mutual giving of self.[16] It is for this reason that, in the relationship between God and humanity, grace is closely associated with the gift of the Spirit.

Given the above formulation, a number of observations arise:

(1) This description of grace as a divine and human encounter involving a threefold process of meeting, sharing, and indwelling does not replace the classical scholastic distinctions, but complements them by providing today's Christians with more relevant and understandable terms as a point of departure. While the unifying point between both approaches to the mystery of grace is the provision for both objective and subjective aspects involved in the gift and reception of grace, the description of grace in terms of encounter brings this distinction more to the fore and discourages any further tendency to reify grace or to think of it as a measurable, verifiable quantity. In this respect, it highlights the personal element involved in the gift and reception of grace and thus looks upon grace as a bond resulting from a mutual sharing of life, friendship, and love.

(2) In the above classification, the scholastic distinctions would be transformed as follows: (a) "uncreated grace" is the divinity in its distinct personal otherness; "created grace," the

---

[16] In the words of Paul J. Wadell: "In making us another self to God, charity does not abolish differences between God and ourselves, it works for the union of hearts that is every friendship's perfection." See *Friendship and the Moral Life* (Notre Dame: University of Notre Dame Press, 1989), 138-39.

Godhead as it pours itself out to humankind; (b) "internal grace" is God dwelling within individual and corporate humanity; "external grace," the divinity as it expresses to and shares itself with humankind through some external, benevolent deed; (c) *"gratia gratis data"* (i.e., "grace freely given") is the Godhead expressing itself to another through some human instrument (e.g., a prophet or priest); *"gratia gratum faciens"* (i.e., the grace of sanctification), God's direct communication of self for the sake of humanity's salvation; (d) "habitual or sanctifying grace" is the ongoing mutual relationship of human and divine indwelling; "actual grace," the interior help given by God in particular circumstances; (e) the various distinctions of actual grace would also hold — the grace of "illumination" enlightens the mind ; that of "inspiration," the will; "prevenient grace" precedes a deliberate act of will; "subsequent grace" accompanies the deliberative act; "sufficient grace" bestows the power to accomplish a particular action ; "efficacious grace" assists in its accomplishment.[17]

(3) There are certain worthwhile distinctions which the scholastic tradition expresses in a better way than that which is proposed above. One such example is the distinction between "the grace of God" (i.e., grace given by God to the angels and to humanity's first parents before the Fall) and "the grace of Christ" (i.e., the elevating and healing grace of Christ's redemptive action).[18] The importance of such a distinction is that it highlights, on the one hand, the freedom of God's self-communication to his creatures regardless of whether or not they have ever been affected by sin and, on the other, his determination to offer himself to his creatures in spite of their turning away. It is also a helpful distinction in helping one come to understand the difference between God's creative and redemptive outpouring of self upon creation.

(4) The proposed classification surpasses the scholastic distinctions in its concern for the social aspects of the divine-human

---

[17] A concise description of these classical categories of grace is found in Ott, *Fundamentals of Catholic Dogma*, 220-22.
[18] Ibid., 221.

encounter and also in its insistence that, as a result of this free, mutual indwelling, there is a certain way in which one can say that the Godhead benefits from its radical offering of self, i.e., its own greater glory. To be sure, this is what the manualists would call the primary final cause of the gift of God's grace. The eternal salvation of humanity would be considered by them as only a secondary final cause.[19] The proposed classification's emphasis on the social aspect of the divine and human encounter highlights the social dimensions not only of the human person (i.e., having corporeal, psychological, spiritual, and social needs and orientations), but also that of the Godhead itself (i.e., the Three Persons of the Trinity: Father, Son, and Spirit). In this respect, it proposes the doctrine of humanity created in the image of God as the analogical basis for the communication of grace and is thus much more comprehensive than the scholastic tradition in its understanding of the relationship between the human and divine.

(5) The limitations of both the scholastic classification and that described in terms of divine and human encounter must also be affirmed. Both are human constructs designed to make some sense out of the mysterious movement of God in the life of the human person and in human society. In no way do they claim to exhaust all the ways in which God may interact with people. Nor should any attempt be made to identify the distinctions themselves with the reality they seek to express. In this respect, any language of grace — be it that of the scholastics or the one proposed above — makes sense only if it is understood as fundamentally analogous in nature, expressing at one and the same time both a likeness and difference with the theological mystery involved.[20]

(6) While no claim is being made that one particular language of grace is better than the other, allowance must be made for the appropriateness of one language over another in certain

---

[19] For a typical manualist presentation of the causes of grace, see Ibid., 220.

[20] For more on the analogy and its relationship to the doctrine of grace, see Eric Mascall, *Existence and Analogy* (London: Longmans, Green, 1949); Idem, "The Doctrine of Analogy," *Cross Currents* 1 (1951): 38-57.

circumstances. That is to say that, while the scholastic language and the one proposed above are complementary in nature and hence should normally be used in conjunction with one another, a stronger emphasis may be given to one over another in the case of particular extenuating circumstances. The coherent and organized nature of the scholastic language would thus lend itself more to theological analysis and speculation than the relational approach. The latter, in turn, would be more suited to situations involving theological reflection, preaching, and group sharing.

(7) The above formulation proposes a different theological model of grace, while all the time recognizing and insisting upon the intrinsic worth of the tradition from which it comes. In effect, what is proposed is bipolar dialectic in the language of grace which enables the mystery to be expressed more fully, if for no other reason than that the weaknesses of one language can be compensated for by the strengths of the other. This approach to the mystery of grace invites still other ways of expressing the mystery in the hope that a logical web of conflicting and complementary models might render the mystery more comprehensible in changing historical circumstances. However many languages might eventually be developed, the manualist and relational languages expressed above would be foundational touchstones to be consulted, confronted, and studied at every turn.[21]

---

[21] Even the approach of complementary models has certain limitations. It takes the mystery in question (in this instance, the mystery of "grace") as a function of *ratio*, i.e., as something mysterious to reason, but which can be further explained with the right "mix" of theological language. One should not overlook Rahner's insightful remark: "...may there not be a more primordial unity of spirit, whatever its name, prior to the division into the 'faculties' of *ratio* and *voluntas*? — an authentically scholastic question (cf. St. Thomas, *Summa theologiae*, I, q. 16, a. 4) — and may not this primordial unity be the reality to which the mystery is directed and related? In other words, perhaps the will and its freedom have the same essential relation to the mystery as *ratio*, and the mystery to them, when they are considered in their original state of unity with the *ratio*. Would it be then correct to assume that mystery and mysterious truth are one and the same thing?" See "The Concept of Mystery in Catholic Theology," chap. in *Theological Investigations*, vol. 4, *More Recent Writings*, trans. Kevin Smyth (London: Darton, Longman and Todd, 1974), 38.

The Grace Kernel

GRACE AND RELIGIOUS

What do religious have to offer in the above considerations? Without a doubt, the theology of the religious life has undergone immense changes since Vatican II. Religious have been asked to develop a new way of expressing their lifelong dedication to the following of Christ through the evangelical counsels.[22] Influenced by categories borrowed from the psychological and sociological sciences, this new language tries to make the vows meaningful for those who, even today, are still called to follow the life-style that Christ himself chose when he walked the earth. While seeking to do so, it also has endeavored to remain in touch with the Church's traditional theological language, but in such a way so as to integrate it with an individual's present self-understanding in the contemporary world. As followers of Christ and recipients of his selfless, redemptive love, religious can look upon part of their vocation in today's Church as translators of the riches of the Church's theological tradition. The area of grace would be but one of the many areas where they would be able to communicate to others the meaning of the Church's teaching as it exists in both its classical and contemporary settings.

To place Jesus at the center of one's life forms a part of the universal call to salvation and is thus something which all men, women, and children are asked to heed, regardless of their state in life. The religious life, however, emphasizes a person's individual and social relationship to the person of Christ in a very concrete and structured way. Each of the vows has meaning only from the perspective of the religious' individual and communal relationship of divine and human encounter. In their vow of chastity, religious forego the goods of marriage in order to reap the benefits of a life directed totally and immediately, without distraction, to their relationship with the Lord.[23] In their vow of poverty, they seek to free themselves from inordinate attachments to material

---

[22] The principles for the up-to-date renewal of religious life are clearly laid out in Vatican Council II, *Perfectae caritatis*, no. 2 [*CDD*, 335-36]; English translation: Flannery, *Vatican Council II*, 612-13.

[23] Ibid., no. 12 [*CDD*, 343-44]; English translation: Flannery, *Vatican Council II*, 617-18.

things in order to make room in their lives for the only attachment that ultimately matters, i.e., their relationship to Christ.[24] In their vow of obedience, they seek to empty themselves of all self-centeredness by accepting the discerning will of their superiors as the will of Christ for them in their lives.[25] The vows, in short, retain their significance only to the extent that Christ is the origin, the sustaining force, and the terminus of the person who lives them out. Without Christ, the vows are an empty burden of needless and fruitless obligations. With Christ, the vows point beyond themselves to the intimate relationship between the divine and human that exists in the here and now in this particular community of individuals and which will reach its fulfillment in the life to come.

When seen from the perspective of grace, the contemporary theology of the vows fits in nicely with the threefold movement of divine and human encounter. That is to say that the vows become for the individual religious and the particular community to which he or she belongs the medium through which Christ is personally met, mutually shared, and made continually present within. This threefold movement is important not only for the individual, but for the entire religious community. Just as there is a social element to the human individual, so too is there is a personal element (i.e., an orientation towards the individual) in every social group. This mutual self-orientation is reflected in the Trinitarian doctrine of the Christian God and points to an even further effect of God's gift of redemptive grace. That is to say that in a grace-filled community not only does God dwell within the individual and group and the individual and group dwell in God, but both the individual and the group to which he or she belongs dwell mutually within each other.[26] To the extent that this is

---

[24] Ibid., no. 13 [*CDD*, 344-45]; English translation: Flannery, *Vatican Council II*, 618-19.

[25] Ibid., no. 14 [*CDD*, 345-47]; English translation: Flannery, *Vatican Council II*, 619-20.

[26] This mutual indwelling or "grace-filled reciprocity" is the characteristic goal or terminus of all sound Christian relationships: within the Godhead itself, between God and humanity (both communal and individual), among the relations of individuals. See Wadell, *Friendship and the Moral Life*, 122-24, 130-33.

accomplished in a particular community it can be said that God's reign is being realized on earth through the outpouring in the human heart of life in the Spirit.

Religious are asked to view their relationship with Christ — their meeting him in the day to day circumstances of life, their sharing with him of their innermost thoughts and secrets, their dwelling within and resting in him at all times and especially in life's most difficult moments — in and through their faithful dedication to the vows.[27] This commitment is not meant to be something on the periphery of their lives (as if it were merely accidental, to be put aside or disregarded whenever convenient), but the medium through which they encounter the very person of God. In this respect, the vows, regardless of the various distinctions involved, have always been closely tied to the continuing life of grace for a select group of people in the Church who seek with all their hearts to live and to love as closely and as concretely as possible along the path that was chosen by Christ himself.[28]

CONCLUSION

In its attempt to formulate a fundamental principle of the Church's teaching on grace ("The Grace Kernel"), this chapter has proposed a classification which complements the classical scholastic distinctions and makes them more approachable from within the perspective of the contemporary intellectual mindset. Its description of grace as the relationship of divine and human encounter, manifesting itself in a threefold expression of a meeting of others, a sharing of selves, and a mutual personal indwelling, purports not to replace the insights of the scholastic tradition, but to provide contemporary Christians with the means of correcting the weaknesses of the traditional approach while, at the same

---

[27] See Vatican Council II, *Lumen gentium*, nos. 43-44 [*CDD*, 174-77]; English translation: Flannery, *Vatican Council II*, 402-5.

[28] For more on grace and the religious life, see Jean Galot, "L'azione di grazie nella vita consacrata," *Vita consacrata* 24 (1988): 705-18, 785-97.

time, being able to utilize its greatest strengths. The result is an interesting balance of theological models which express the mystery of God's grace in a variety of perceptive, challenging, sometimes conflicting, ways. An interesting effect of this approach is the fundamental insight it has into the unity of theology, not merely as it exists in each succeeding historical epoch, but as it extends throughout the centuries and manifests itself in competing world views. The basis for this claim is the approach's insight into the analogical nature of theological language itself. Because such language can never fully express the mystery it seeks to express, the insights of any particular era can attain only a relative validity. They are open to correction by insights yet uncovered, forgotten in the past or, for whatever reason, deemed irrelevant. It is for this reason that the discipline of historical theology is being studied with renewed interest: not merely because it deals with the development of theology in history, but because it helps theologians retrieve models from the past whose relevance, although modified for their contemporary concerns, continues even into the present.[29]

Down through the centuries, religious have had to adapt their understanding of the vows to the developing theology of their times. They have done so, while at the same time trying to remain faithful to the various traditions from which they came and also seeking to provide a sense of continuity to those who will follow after them. Such experience makes religious especially suited as translators of the Church's theological tradition for the contemporary world. With respect to the Church's teaching on grace, it means that they can manifest through their faithful dedication to the vows the mystery of what it means to be in a personal relationship with Christ and, from that relationship, expound with renewed vigor the various distinctions about the nature of grace which flow from it. In doing so, religious offer themselves as a testimony to the presence of Christ in their private and communal lives and highlight the vows as the particular

---

[29] See, for example, Tracy's discussion of "the great twentieth-century retrievals of Thomas's own analogical vision." In *The Analogical Imagination*, 413-14.

means given them in which and through which this encounter with Christ is to be realized.

In the final analysis, the fundamental principle of the Church's teaching on grace ("The Grace Kernel") offers a language that is itself subject to further change and development. What is important is not the particular terms involved — be they "grace" or "encounter, "uncreated" or "other," "habitual" or "indwelling" — but the way in which the terms themselves complement each other in their attempt to express the nature of the relationship between the human and the divine in all of its rich and multifaceted aspects. In this respect, the discussion of grace within the Church may proceed not only within the bounds of some very clear and well thought-out theological controls, but also without any fear that its long and fruitful tradition will be forgotten, supplanted, or simply ignored by whatever theological innovations may appear on the horizon.

7

THE REDEMPTION KERNEL

Is there a fundamental principle of soteriology? The answer to this question depends on how one understands the relationship between the eternal component of the salvific act itself (i.e., the Christ event) and its various linguistic manifestations in time. More specifically, it has to do with the way in which theologians relate history to the eternal, the human to the divine, conceptual thought to the reality it seeks to express. If it exists at all, the principle should demarcate clearly the continuities and discontinuities between the various historical manifestations of redemption theory. In doing so, it should also provide a sound hermeneutical basis for determining those elements of a single formulation which constitute an integral part of the Church's theological tradition.

THE PROBLEM OF DEVELOPMENT

At the outset, it will do well to consider one of the recurrent difficulties in nearly all forms of theological study, one which becomes even more apparent in the time-bound complexities of redemption theory, i.e, the problem of development.[1] The ques-

---

[1] For the origins of the theory and for a concise survey of its recent Catholic and Protestant versions, see Peter Toon, *The Development of Doctrine in the Church* (Grand Rapids: William B. Eerdmans, 1979), 1-35, 75-103.

tion arises: how is the theologian to contextualize a particular theological doctrine historically? That is to say, how is he or she to maintain the eternal significance of one culturally-conditioned theological formulation, while at the same time relating it to other formulations of past, prior, even contemporary historical epochs? And how can one do so without becoming vulnerable to the charge of historical relativism?

To answer these questions, theologians have employed three very different approaches: (1) ahistorical dogmatism, (2) developmental rationalism, and (3) contextual historical consciousness. The first, characterized by a complete lack of regard for the historical conditioning of theology, identifies the theological concept with the mystery it seeks to express and thus disallows the possibility of change by way of alternative formulation. In doing so, it emphasizes the kataphatic element of theological language to the detriment of its apophatic counterpart.[2] The second, in contrast, admits the possibility of reformulation, but in a rationally-linear fashion in which doctrinal development is seen as a teleological function of necessary historical change. In this way, theology is reduced to a dialectical progression of causally-related ideas.[3] The third bases theological reformulation not on the as-

---

[2] In making this claim, a distinction between two types of kataphatic theology must be drawn: one based on proportionate analogical reasoning ; the other, on univocal thought. The former maintains the linguistic gap by way of proportional relationships between the particular expression employed in a theological formulation and the mystery it seeks to express (i.e., $a/b=a'/b'$). The latter identifies the two in such a way that the finite expression is actually considered the perfect expression of the infinite. The approach of ahistorical dogmatism pertains strictly to the latter type. Analogical kataphatic theology, in contrast, is more easily (but not necessarily) aligned with the approach of contextual historical consciousness.

[3] Behind this claim of a linear historical progression of increasingly refined theological expressions lies a naive "Enlightened" presupposition about the inevitability of human progress. Historical theologians who take this approach give no sense that "the historico-theological pie could be sliced up another way." See, for example, my criticism of John Mahoney's presentation of the development of the Church's penitential practice in "The Penitentials and 'The Making of Moral Theology,'" *Louvain Studies* 14 (1989): 142-51. A slightly more nuanced (and more acceptable) version of this approach is the "organic" or "epigenetic" model. Guided by the Spirit, Church doctrine in this instance is thought to develop according to a preprogrammed code (as an oak develops

The Redemption Kernel

sumption of the progress of ideas, but on that of the continuing, albeit limited, capacity of language to shape theological mysteries to the historically-conditioned contours of human consciousness. The emphasis here is first to contextualize and then to analyze particular formulations with a view toward determining their specific contribution to the theological mystery under consideration.[4]

The constants in each of these approaches vary considerably: the first upholds the definitive nature of the theological concept; the second, the unfolding, indeed, evolutionary nature of doctrinal development itself; the third, the capacity of language to articulate, yet never to exhaust that which ultimately surpasses all description. Each approach also conveys a different attitude towards theological change: in the first, it is non-existent; in the second, it is a foregone rational conclusion; in the third, it is linguistically and historically dependent on the interminable nature of the divine mysteries. If the first approach is insensitive to the historical dimensions of a theological formulation, the second reduces those dimensions to the level of a rational idea (i.e., the Enlightenment's notion of ongoing progress), while the third sees those dimensions as the inescapable context of human self-transcendence. The last approach, the one utilized in this essay, escapes the charges of historical relativism by its use of analogical reasoning as a means of avoiding the epistemological break which otherwise empties the events of time of all transcendent value.[5]

---

from an acorn) that was entirely present in the original deposit of divine revelation. For a detailed exposition of this approach, see John Henry Newman, *On the Development of Christian Doctrine*, with a Foreword by Ian Ker, Notre Dame Series in the Great Books (Notre Dame: University of Notre Dame Press, 1989). See also Karl Adam, *The Spirit of Catholicism* (London: Sheed and Ward, 1929; 8th reprint ed., 1969), 153-61.

[4] This approach takes not historical progression (of neither the "linear" nor "organic" type) as its formal point of departure, but the limited and historically-conditioned character of linguistic (and hence theological) expression. For a treatment of the doctrine of redemption according to these lines, see Macquarrie, *Principles of Christian Theology*, 280-93.

[5] See above 96 n. 2.

THEORIES OF REDEMPTION

The above insights weigh heavily in any discussion of redemption theory, of which there have been four significant formulations in the history of Christian thought: (1) ransom, (2) satisfaction, (3) subjective atonement, and (4) liberation. The first three models have been aptly explained and documented by Gustaf Aulén in his monumental work on the subject entitled *Christus Victor* (1931).[6] The last is a more recent contribution from the work of political theologians and the theologians of liberation.[7]

(1) Considered the classical expression of the patristic and early medieval periods, redemption as ransom views the human person as an insignificant player in the cosmic battle between God and the heavenly hierarchy, on the one hand, and Satan and the forces of Hell, on the other. Expressed in the universalizing language of legend and myth, it reckons Christ's incarnation and death on the cross as a necessary ransom for humanity's release from the snares of death, the latter seen as a right won by Satan as a consequence of Adam's sin.[8]

(2) First formulated by Anselm of Canterbury in the *Cur Deus homo* (c. 1098),[9] redemption as satisfaction views Christ's willful

---

[6] Gustaf Aulén, *Christus Victor: An Historical Study of the Three Main Types of the Idea of the Atonement*, trans. A.G. Herbert, with a Foreword by Jaroslav Pelikan (New York: Macmillan, 1931; reprint ed., 1969). Much of Aulén's work appears to be based on J. Rivière, *Le dogme de la rédemption: essai d'étude historique*, 2d ed. (Paris: Librairie Victor Lecoffre, 1905). For more recent treatments of the doctrine of the atonement, see Richard Swinburne, *Responsibility and Atonement* (Oxford: Clarendon Press, 1989); Colin E. Gunton, *The Actuality of Atonement: A Study of Metaphor, Rationality and the Christian Tradition* (London: T. and T. Clark, 1989); Paul S. Fiddes, *Past Event and Present Salvation: The Christian Idea of Atonement* (London: Darton, Longman and Todd, 1989).

[7] See, for example, Gustavo Gutiérrez, "Toward a Theology of Liberation" in *Liberation Theology: A Documentary History*, ed. Alfred T. Hennelly (Maryknoll, N.Y.: Orbis Books, 1990), 62-76.

[8] For the mythical dimensions of the ransom model, see Joseph Campbell, *The Masks of God: Creative Mythology* (New York: The Viking Press, 1968; 2d reprint ed., New York: Penguin Books, 1978), 17-18. For its historical context, see R.W. Southern, *The Making of the Middle Ages* (New Haven: Yale University Press, 1953), 234-35.

[9] *Anselmi opera omnia*, 2:68-69.

The Redemption Kernel

incarnation, suffering, and death as a free expression of the divine love needed to satisfy the demands of divine justice which humanity itself could not appease. Based on the legal structures and language of feudal vassalage, it turns redemption theory away from that of a cosmic drama between God and Satan and focuses, instead, upon the actual relationship between a just and loving God, on the one hand, and a sinful human race, on the other. In this respect, Satan moves to the background of redemption theory, while divinity and humanity confront each other face-to-face.[10]

(3) A fundamental response of Enlightenment thought to the Christian religion, redemption as subjective atonement attempted to remove all anthropomorphisms from the Christian concept of God. A number of theologians from this period (mainly Protestant) insisted that God could not possibly be propitiated by means of a sin offering: divine punishment was ameliorative instead of retributive; nothing could ever possibly change the goodwill of the omnipotent, immutable God.[11] The result of their insights was not only a relativization of the concept of sin, but also a strong emphasis on humanity's potential — both individually and societally — to lead the moral life. Such was the highly humanistic and overly optimistic redemptive outlook of what Leibniz concluded was "the best of all possible worlds."[12]

(4) The tragic relationship in the twentieth century between the ideologies of power — Fascism, Marxism, Capitalism — and large-scale exploitation of human life has led theologians in recent decades to develop yet another theory, i.e., redemption as libera-

---

[10] Southern, *The Making of the Middle Ages*, 236. For a comprehensive treatment of Anselm's satisfaction model, see Jasper Hopkins, *A Companion to the Study of St. Anselm* (Minneapolis: University of Minnesota Press, 1972), 187-212.

[11] The earliest formulation of the subjective model is attributed to Peter Abelard. For pertinent texts, see Peter Abelard, *Commentaria in epistolam Pauli ad Romanos* [CCCM 11:115-118]. Looked upon with suspicion in its day, but never completely silenced, it eventually came into prominence with the work of eighteenth and nineteenth century theologians of the Enlightenment. See Aulén, *Christus Victor*, 133-142.

[12] G.W. Leibniz, *Essai de théodicée sur la bonté de Dieu, la liberté de l'homme et l'origine du mal*, chap. in *Opera philosophica*, ed. J.J. Erdmann (Berlin: G. Eichleri, 1840), 566 [no. 201].

tion. Rooted in an eschatology which seeks the realization of the Kingdom in the present world, this approach locates evil primarily in corrupt societal structures designed to oppress the poor for the advantage of a privileged elite. In this respect, redemption refers to the realization of human solidarity through the universal call to justice.[13]

This is not the place to develop the subtleties existing within each of the redemptive theories summarized above. The relationship of the ransom model to Mk 10:45 and Mt 20:28, Aquinas' refinement of Anselm's satisfaction theory, Luther's reaction against the overly juridic emphasis of satisfaction and his subsequent reinstatement of the ransom approach, Catholicism's deep suspicion of the idea of subjective atonement, and its guarded magisterial reaction to the theologies of liberation, have all been documented elsewhere and need not be repeated.[14] What does need to be developed, however, is precisely what has been missing in nearly all recent discussions of redemption theory, i.e., the specific contribution of each of these models to the Church's actual understanding of the mystery of Redemption.

---

[13] In the words of one of liberation theology's most powerful spokesmen: "An intimate relationship exists between the kingdom and the elimination of poverty and misery. The kingdom comes to suppress injustice." See Gutiérrez, "Toward a Theology of Liberation," 73.

[14] For the concept of ransom in the Jewish Scriptures and in early Christianity, see Frances M. Young, *Sacrifice and the Death of Christ*, with a Foreword by Maurice Wiles (Philadelphia: The Westminster Press, 1975), 36, 57, 67, 78, 80. For Aquinas' refinement of Anselm's satisfaction model, see *Summa theologiae*, III, q. 1, a. 2 resp.; III, q. 46. aa. 1-3. For Luther's understanding of redemption, see Aulén, *Christus Victor*, 101-22. For a description of early Catholic suspicions of subjective atonement (i.e., Bernard of Clairvaux vs. Abelard), see Rivière, *Le dogme de la rédemption*, 333-442. For the guarded reaction of the magisterium toward liberation theology, see the SCDF, *Instructio de quibusdam rationibus "Theologiae Liberationis"* [*AAS* 76 (1984): 876-909]; English translation: "Instruction on Certain Aspects of the 'Theology of Liberation'" in *Liberation Theology: A Documentary History*, ed. Alfred T. Hennelly (Maryknoll, N.Y.: Orbis Books, 1990), 393-414; Idem, *Instructio de libertate christiana et liberatione*, [*AAS* 79 (1987): 554-99]; English translation: "Instruction on Christian Freedom and Liberation," 461-97.

THE REDEMPTION KERNEL

These contributions come to the fore when the theories themselves are examined in the light of the specific relationship(s) addressed by each. The ransom model, for example, employs mythic language within a largely Neoplatonic framework in order to express the cosmic relations between the forces of Good and Evil.[15] The satisfaction model, in turn, utilizes legal language and the Anselmian notion of necessary reasons in order to describe the significance of humanity's relationship to the divine.[16] The subjective model uses the optimism of Enlightened rationalism to discuss the internal dimensions of the moral life.[17] The liberation model employs the concepts of contemporary political analysis to accentuate the importance of just social structures.[18] Each theory focuses on a different type of relationship: ransom, on "the cosmic"; satisfaction, on "the divine and human"; the subjective, on "the inner personal"; and liberation on "the societal." In their respective positions, these relations also describe the realities of: (1) divine-human unrelation, (2) divine-human relation, (3) human self-relation, and (4) human social relation. In this respect, each makes a specific contribution to our understanding of redemption theory.

(1) To speak of redemption in terms of "divine-human unrelation" is to place the concerns of humanity not at the center, but merely on the periphery of God's providential plan.[19] Here, humanity sees itself in creaturely solidarity with the entire uni-

---

[15] Campbell, *The Masks of God: Creative Mythology*, 117-18.

[16] Aulén, *Christus Victor*, 90.

[17] Ibid., 135.

[18] Gutiérrez, "Toward a Theology of Liberation," 76. See also the criticism of liberation theologians' use of Marxist analysis appearing in SCDF, *Instructio de quibusdam rationibus "Theologiae Liberationis,"* [*AAS* 76 (1984): 890-94]; English translation: "Instruction on Certain Aspects of the 'Theology of Liberation,'" 401-3.

[19] A similar focus is found in some of the proponents of "creation theology." See, for example, Kevin Treston, "Living in a Unitary Age," in *Creation Spirituality and the Dreamtime*, ed. Catherine Hammond (Newtown, N.S.W.: Millennium Books, 1991), 51-71.

verse, not as the center of God's undivided attention. In doing so, it recognizes that the scope of the redemption extends far beyond its own need for salvific grace, including elements far beyond its own comprehension. In this respect, humanity understands that the struggle against evil is not a mere anthropocentric concern and cannot focus solely on its own potential for sin.

(2) To speak of redemption in terms of "divine-human relation" is to focus on the way in which humanity actually does figure in as the center of God's providential plan. Created in God's image and called to walk with him in paradise, humanity recognizes the extent to which sin has disrupted its relationship with God and understands that its hope rests only in the salvific love of Christ. In this respect, the soteriological principle that "God became human so that humanity might become divine"[20] is of fundamental significance: humanity's divinization is contingent on God's humanization; in this all-embracive redemptive moment, God meets man and woman face-to-face.

(3) To speak of redemption in terms of "human self-relation" is to emphasize the effects of this process of divinization on the individual and to call attention to the way in which each person participates in God's providential plan. Cooperation with this plan becomes the sign of whether or not a person can actually be considered the master of his or her own actions. In this respect, redemption manifests itself as an inner conversion towards the standards of a just and moral life. Grace, in other words, is experienced in a highly personal, subjective manner; received internally, it moves the person to lead a virtuous life out of sheer love for God.

(4) To speak of redemption in terms of "human social relation" is to recognize the societal character of human existence and to believe in the potential of a divinely-inspired humanity to transform not only individuals, but even the political and economic structures by which they live. In this respect, redemption is understood as taking place not through the promise of an "other

---

[20] See Athanasius, *De incarnatione*, 54.3 [SC 199:458-59; PG 25:191-92]; Gregory of Nyssa, *De opificio hominis*, 16 [SC 6:151-61; PG 44:178-88].

worldly" reward or in the eschatological reality of some past or future age, but within the parameters of humanity's ongoing earthly existence. From this perspective, redemption occurs in humanity's liberation of the oppressed by means of its continuing search for social justice.

These relations are to be thought of as complementary movements of the one redemptive mystery. When taken as such, they underscore the limited capacity of any language (be it mythic, juridic, subjective, political) or any philosophy (be it Neoplatonic, scholastic, Cartesian, or Marxist) or any historical epoch (be it the patristic, medieval, Enlightened, or postmodern) to capture completely the reality it seeks to express. In this regard, it would be fair to say that, while obviously falling short of providing a complete description of the redemptive mystery as a whole, each theory does succeed in highlighting at least one of the doctrine's essential salvific relations. From this perspective, the doctrine of the Redemption can be thought of as containing facets of the cosmic, the divine and human, the subjective, and the social. To deny any one of these important components would impoverish the significance of the mystery and be unfaithful to the doctrine's theological tradition.[21]

At this point, a more comprehensive formulation of a fundamental principle of soteriology ("The Redemption Kernel") can be formulated. It reads as follows: Redemption concerns the manifestation of the divine in the person of Christ under four interrelated aspects: (1) divine-human unrelation, through which humanity finds its place in the universal macrocosm of its divine Creator, (2) divine-human relation, through which humanity recognizes in the suffering of Christ the salvific love of a personal God, (3) human self-relation, through which a person's experience of that love manifests itself in inner conversion to a life of virtue, and (4) human social relation, through which humanity

---

[21] In this respect, the development of doctrine is not a linear historical progression, where one theological model emerges from and incorporates previous formulations, but an interlocking web of penetrating insights into the nature of a mystery which no single historically-conditioned linguistic formulation can ever exhaust.

struggles to realize the presence of the Kingdom within the historical structures of its present earthly existence. Each of these aspects reveals an essential facet of the singular mystery of the Christ event, the particular significance of which is variously interpreted according to the changing needs and theological comprehension of the times.

The operative hermeneutical principle in the above description rests on the assumption that, while the mystery of the Redemption remains constant for all time and is always inclusive of the four relational components outlined above, particular theological formulations will vary according to the predominant linguistic, philosophical, and cultural needs of the historical epoch in question. Any particular period will tend to emphasize one relational component, sometimes to the exclusion of the others: the patristic period emphasized the cosmic element; the high middle ages, that of the human-divine encounter; the Enlightenment, the subjective; the postmodern, that of political and societal liberation. As expressed above, "The Redemption Kernel" is sufficiently malleable to adapt to changing theological and philosophical perceptions while, at the same time, acquitting itself of the charges of historical relativism. It does so by giving proportional emphasis to both the kataphatic and apophatic aspects of theological language and by employing a complementary approach to the various historical attempts at giving the mystery of the Redemption some kind of doctrinal formulation.

REDEMPTION AND RELIGIOUS

The fundamental principle of soteriology has special significance for religious. Their personal and communal dedication to the evangelical counsels manifests a special concern for each of these redemptive relations: in their chastity, they forsake progeny and sexual intimacy in order to express more deeply their belief in the existence of a beyond; in their poverty, they remove themselves from the structures of oppression and align themselves freely with the needs of the poor; in their obedience, they give witness to the divine and human encounter in their lives and recognize in faith the will of the divine in that of their religious superior. Taken as a whole, their lives represent a call to continual personal and communal conversion, which is to serve as a leaven for both others and themselves in their struggle to live the demands of Gospel love.[22]

This is not to say that religious are uninfluenced by the various emphases a particular historical formulation may place on one or more of the above redemptive relations.[23] Nor does it imply that religious give a necessarily better witness to these redemptive relations than any other state of life (i.e., lay or priestly). What it does imply, however, is a certain amount of malleability in the structural foundations of religious life itself, which enable it to adapt to the changing emphases within the fundamental principle of soteriology and to reinterpret itself in such a way it can speak to the discernible needs of the time. In this respect, religious life changes shape, form, and practice according to the perceived shifts in emphasis given the fundamental principle of soteriology itself. Religious life, in other words, is a function and manifestation of the historically-operative relations of the one redemptive kernel.

One particular strength of viewing religious life in light of the fundamental principle of soteriology is the way in which it clarifies the relationship between the active and contemplative lives. As manifestations of "The Redemption Kernel," each form of religious life gives witness through vowed life in community to each of the four essential redemptive relations (i.e., divine-human unrelation, divine-human relation, human self-relation, and hu-

---

[22] For religious and the call to conversion, see John Paul II, "La vita religiosa si comprende essenzialmente nella dimensione ecclesiale," no. 2 [*IGP* 6/2:578-79].

[23] Perhaps the clearest example of this is the way the tenth-century *oratio continua* piety of Cluny espoused the "cosmic battle" motif of the ransom model. Cluniac choir monks looked upon themselves as "soldiers for Christ" waging through their continuous liturgical services a cosmic struggle against the powers of Satan. For tenth-century Cluniac customs, see Barbara Rosenwein, *Rhinoceros Bound: Cluny in the Tenth Century* (Philadelphia: University of Pennsylvania Press, 1982), 94. For the origins of the monk considered as *miles Christi* and its relationship to *Christus victor*, see Bugge, *Virginitas*, 47-58.

man social relation). The difference between them is the added emphasis each gives to one or another relation: the contemplative life would tend to stress a combination of the cosmic, divine and human, and subjective relations; the active life would embrace the latter two, but move away from an emphasis on the cosmic (i.e., divine-human unrelation) in order to concentrate more on the social dimensions of the redemptive mystery. In contrast, mendicant spiritualities which, according to Aquinas, represent a dynamic balance between contemplative prayer and apostolic action,[24] arose in the Church just a little more than a century after Anselm's formulation of the satisfaction model. Through their strict adherence to the ideal of evangelical poverty, they exhibit in their spiritual lives some of the implications that a redemptive theory focusing on "divine-human relation" would entail.[25] Such insights show that the active and contemplative forms of religious life are united by virtue of their common dedication to the life of the vows, the very nature of which is to manifest the four redemptive relations of "The Redemption Kernel"; their differences, in turn, lie in the particular relation(s) to which they give added stress.[26]

---

[24] "Contemplata aliis tradere." See Aquinas, *Summa theologiae* II-II, q. 188, a. 6, resp.; Mary Ann Fatula, *"Contemplata Aliis Tradere*: Spirituality and Thomas Aquinas, the Preacher," *Spirituality Today* 43 (1991): 24-26.

[25] Evangelical poverty as a means of conforming oneself to the life of Christ (*imitatio Christi*) affirms humanity's participation in the Christ event and is very amenable to a theory of redemption that focuses specifically on the divine-human relation. The connection between Anselm's satisfaction model and the rise of the movements of evangelical poverty has yet to be studied in detail. Such a study would complement the more recent economic and sociological approach to these movements. See, for example, Lester K. Little, *Religious Poverty and the Profit Economy in Medieval Europe* (Ithaca: Cornell University Press, 1978), 113-69.

[26] For more on the soteriological dimensions of the religious life, see Jean Galot, "Redenzione e vita religiosa," *Vita consacrata* 13 (1977): 129-44, 193-204, 257-68, 321-28, 419-36.

CONCLUSION

As formulated in this chapter, the fundamental principle of soteriology ("The Redemption Kernel") offers a historical analysis and a theological synthesis of the four major redemptive theories in the Church's tradition. It shows that the specific contribution of each theory centers on a particular relation which expresses an essential facet of the one redemptive mystery. While one relation may be emphasized in a certain historical epoch (sometimes to the exclusion of others), the mystery of the Redemption itself necessarily includes all four. That is not to say that these relations dispel all hope of further theological insight. Recognizing the inherent limitations of all human language, the theologian must always be open to the possibility of new formulations.

Closely linked to the historical manifestation of "The Redemption Kernel" is the ongoing tendency of religious life to adapt itself to the prevalent redemptive relation of its day. In doing so, religious life has demonstrated itself to be open to historical change, while at the same time remaining true to the essential requirements of the redemptive mystery manifested in the vows. To the extent that religious have been open to grace and have dedicated themselves to the evangelical counsels, they have been successful in keeping alive the essential redemptive relations of the Christ event. In this respect, they have remained faithful to the Church's theological tradition and give witness to the extension of the Christ event in both time and eternity. The extent to which one or more of these redemptive relations are emphasized more than the others reveals some of the basic differences between the active and contemplative lives. In this respect, the fundamental principle of soteriology ("The Redemption Kernel") brings to light not only the fundamental unity of religious life, but also the differences between its various forms.

In the final analysis, "The Redemption Kernel" offers humanity four fundamental components of relation and unrelation which confront each individual with the meaning of his or her place before God, society, the self, and the universe. To overlook any one of these relations would diminish the significance of the mystery of the Redemption and deprive both individuals and groups of some of the basic insights necessary for understanding their place in the Christian configuration of reality. In this respect, the mystery itself is preeminently human in its concern for the various levels of a person's existence (i.e., the transcendent, the internal, the social, the universal). To the extent that religious bring these various redemptive levels to consciousness and enable others to encounter these levels in their own lives of faith, they tap the deep human roots of the Church's own vocation and render a valuable service to humanity.

8

THE RESURRECTION KERNEL

Is there a fundamental principle of the Resurrection? The answer to this question depends on the way in which one understands the relationship of history to the reality of the Risen Christ. This relationship, in turn, depends on the stance one takes towards the possibility of a transhistorical event and the type of impact it would have on the continuities and discontinuities of historical change. However understood, the impact itself would have vast ramifications for the whole of theology.

RESURRECTION: DISTINGUISHING THE IDEA FROM THE REALITY

At the outset, it may be helpful to distinguish between resurrection (1) as a particular item in the history of ideas and (2) as the reality experienced among the earliest followers of Christ. The former may be separated from the viewpoint of faith, compared with other ideas about the nature of the afterlife, and evaluated on a rational basis for its various strengths and weaknesses as a viable explanation of the nature of life after death.[1] The latter, as a transhistorical event with historical consequences, is

---

[1] Such is the approach taken in Philip P. Wiener, ed., *Dictionary of the History of Ideas* (New York: Charles Scribner's Sons, 1973), s.v. "Death and Immortality," by Jacques Choron.

intricately bound to the faith of the primitive Christian community and cannot be studied in such a detached, analytical manner.[2] Any effort to formulate a fundamental principle of the Resurrection must be careful to take both sides of this distinction into account.

(A) The Idea of Resurrection. A well-grounded discussion of an idea should begin with an attempt to identify its most distinctive characteristics. With respect to its general meaning, one could accurately describe the term, "resurrection," as: a belief common among Christians that, at some point after death, an individual is transformed by the power of God on every level of his or her anthropological makeup — the corporeal, the psychological, the spiritual, and the social — and thus raised to a higher level of human existence in a way that always remains in fundamental continuity with his or her historical, earthly life.[3]

The most distinctive marks in this short yet exact account of the idea of resurrection include: (1) personal life after death, (2) in a transformed state, (3) embracing all the anthropological factors of human existence, and (4) in a way continuous with an individual's concrete, earthly life.[4] Each of these elements is essential to the idea of resurrection as it is used in this essay and as it exists in the major Christian traditions.

These characteristics also set the idea of resurrection apart from the related idea of bodily resuscitation (e.g., the raising of Lazarus, Jn 11:44), as well as from the other major philosophical

---

[2] "The resurrection was something real, although transhistorical, for Jesus; but it was something real and historical from the side of the disciples, so profoundly were they affected by it and by the appearances." See Richard McBrien, *Catholicism*, 1:433. For a balanced exegetical presentation of the problem of the bodily resurrection of Jesus, see Raymond E. Brown, *The Virginal Conception and the Bodily Resurrection of Jesus* (New York: Paulist Press, 1973), 69-129. For different Christological responses to the Easter Event, see Lane, *The Reality of Jesus*, 76-81. For appropriate reflections drawn from systematic theology, see Karl Rahner, "Jesus' Resurrection," chap. in *Theological Investigations*, vol. 17, *Jesus, Man, and the Church*, trans. Margaret Kohl (London: Darton, Longman and Todd, 1981), 16-23.

[3] Philip P. Wiener, gen. ed., *Dictionary of the History of Ideas*, (New York: Charles Scribner's Sons, 1973), s.v. "Death and Immortality," by Jacques Choron.

[4] See the discussion on the transformed body in Ashley, *Theologies of the Body*, 585-95.

The Resurrection Kernel

and religious explanations of the nature of life in the hereafter (e.g., the immortality of the soul, reincarnation, Nirvana). When these are compared, the idea of resurrection distinguishes itself: (1) from bodily resuscitation, in its emphasis on a transformed existence in life after death; (2) from the immortality of the soul, in its inclusion of all of humanity's anthropological factors in the nature of that existence; (3) from reincarnation, in its rupture of the cycle of time and its insistence on the fundamental continuity of life in the hereafter with a person's earthly existence; and (4) from Nirvana, in its avowal that final beatitude does not involve the extinction of individual consciousness. The greatest strength of the idea of resurrection is that, of all of the ideas about the nature of life after death, it alone safeguards the inviolate dignity of each human being on every level of his or her existence.[5] That is to say that it alone keeps human nature eternally intact while, at the same time, saving the individual from ultimate personal extinction. Its greatest weakness is that, in representing the fulfillment of one of the deepest and most profound hopes of the human heart, it seems almost too good to be true, an attractive but highly unlikely possibility. For this reason, of all the ideas of life in the hereafter, resurrection is the one most difficult to accept on the simple basis of faith.

(B) The Reality of the Resurrection. Rooted in the hopes of Jewish apocalypticism during the centuries just prior to the appearance of Christ, and promulgated during Jesus' own lifetime by the devout religious group known as the Pharisees, the idea of resurrection developed to its present form as a result of theological reflection on the nature of the Christ event, most especially in the primitive Christian community's interpretation of the meaning of the apostolic experience of the Risen Lord.[6] This reflection

---

[5] For this reason, the Church must take care in its dialogue with non-Christian religions not to accommodate the idea of resurrection to conceptions of the afterlife that do not embrace the dignity of the human person in his or her totality. This basic ethical implication of the idea of the resurrection is not subject to compromise and is to be strictly maintained.

[6] For late Jewish ideas about the afterlife and the distinctiveness of the early Christian proclamation, see Schillebeeckx, *Jesus: An Experiment in Christology*, 518-25.

is intimately tied to the trust that community placed in the validity of the apostolic witness and to the experience of faith upon which it rested. It is also the context within which one may speak of the resurrection not as an idea, but as a reality and a hope.

What precisely happened on that first Easter morning remains shrouded by the eschatological character of the event itself and by the subjective awareness of the earliest followers of Jesus. That awareness probably ran the gamut of several emotional states — from depression and fear, to suspicion and isolation, to incipient faith and the lingering yearning for the retrieval of lost expectations — and most likely varied in each of the persons involved. That is not to say that the event has no basis outside the experience of Jesus' followers, but only that there is no way to determine what it is with any historical accuracy. The Easter event, in other words, touches history, but extends far beyond it. Probably the most important consequence of this unique eschatological/historical encounter is the faith experience of Jesus' immediate followers that provided the original impetus for the rise and spread of the earliest Christian communities.[7] The faith of the Church universal rests upon the foundation of these earliest apostolic witnesses.

A distinction must now be made between the faith of those who witnessed the Easter event personally and those whose faith relies on the testimony of the apostles. The proclamation of the Church rests upon the eyewitness accounts of the apostles, i.e., on those who made the startling claim to have experienced for themselves the reality of the Risen Lord. Their experience of faith remains qualitatively different from that of the believer in the pew, for they claim to have experienced a reality outside of themselves, rooted in the objective order, distinct from their own subjectivity, and identified with the person of their Master, Jesus of Nazareth. Without the unprecedented boldness and resiliency of these claims, the Christian project would have nothing distinc-

---

[7] According to Brown: "...while the risen Jesus stood outside the bounds of space and time, by his appearances he touched the lives of men who were in space and time, men who were in history. The interaction between the eschatological and the historical should not be lost sight of." See *The Virginal Conception and the Bodily Resurrection of Jesus*, 126.

tive in its message and possibly might never have gotten off the ground.[8]

These apostolic claims emerge from one of two possibilities: the experience of the Risen Christ was *with* or *without* a basis in the person of Jesus in the external order. That is to say that the experience of the apostles corresponds to a reality outside of themselves or remains entirely subjective in all respects. If the former is true, then the further question must be asked regarding the nature of this basis in the external order. If the latter be true, then the only conclusion to be drawn is that the apostles suffered from self-delusion, that their testimony is false, as is the religion to which it gave rise. The fact that neither of these possibilities can be proven highlights the underlying quality of faith inherent in the conclusions of both the believer and non-believer alike.

Still more can be said about the position of the believer. If the apostolic experience of the Risen Christ *does* have an external basis in the person of Jesus, then this affirmation, when combined with the idea of resurrection developed earlier in this essay, necessarily points to an event of singular historical significance, indeed, an event which could be measured by the instruments of historical observation only by its effects (e.g., a missing body) and which, for this reason, must be placed in a category unique to itself and understood as a transhistorical event with historical consequences. This is so precisely because the Risen Christ, existing in a transformed state but in a way continuous with his earthly life, does not lead "a historical existence" in the way in which the phrase is commonly used. That is to say that space and time no longer set the limits for his physical existence. In his resurrected state, Christ is the Alpha and the Omega, a singular dimension unique unto himself, who recapitulates, both now and forever, all of creation within himself, into the love of the Father and the joy of their Spirit.[9]

---

[8] On "apostolicity" as an identifying mark of the Church, see Macquarrie, *Principles of Christian Theology*, 367-72.

[9] Despite this vast, encompassing vision of the redemptive value of the Easter event, the possibility that some people will exercise their human freedom in such a way so as to refuse God's gift of salvation will always remain. Unless, of course, one embraces the rather tenuous doctrine of Origenist ἀποκατάστασις (i.e., the ultimate restoration to God of all created beings — even devils),

THE RESURRECTION KERNEL

From all that has been said, a sound formulation of the fundamental principle of the Resurrection ("The Resurrection Kernel") would consist in the affirmation of faith that the idea of resurrection has become a reality in the Risen Christ. This reality is rooted in the transhistorical nature of the Christ event, the historical consequences of which linger even to this day in the ongoing proclamation of the Church. Based on the testimony of its apostolic forebears, the Church has, in its ministry down through the centuries, kept alive for humanity the fervent hope that the deepest yearnings of the human heart will one day be fully realized.[10] That is to say that the transformation wrought by God in Christ promises to extend itself to all who are incorporated into his Body, the Church. In this respect, a sharing in the life of the Risen Lord may be looked upon as the ultimate destiny of all of humankind and will be impeded only by a stubborn private or corporate persistence in the life of sin.

Given the above formulation, a number of important observations arise:

(1) To affirm that an idea has become a reality is to utilize the well-known philosophical distinction between the internal (i.e., subjective) and external (i.e., objective) orders. The limitations of this distinction are well known, and care must be taken not to stretch the analogy beyond its avowed usefulness. Indeed, special care must be taken not to project the concerns of the so-called critical problem back to a time before its significance was entirely known.[11]

Christ's recapitulation of all of creation must be understood in this qualified sense. See Ashley, *Theologies of the Body*, 610-20.

[10] "The formulations of that faith have changed and will change, but the existential attitude which constitutes the core of the faith has remained constant. So the inner meaning, if we may so speak, of the apostolicity of the Church is its constancy in the faith of the apostles." See Macquarrie, *Principles of Christian Theology*, 368.

[11] Related distinctions include: (1) that between apostolic experience of the Risen Lord and the various linguistic expressions of this experience, and (2) what the evangelists "meant" by their words and how those words are "understood" or "received" in the various interpretative traditions (Protestant and Catholic) of

The Resurrection Kernel

(2) God the Father is the primary agent in bringing about this realization in Christ. Since idea and reality are intimately connected in the Divinity's vision of itself, the Resurrection of Christ may be viewed as a Providential movement on the part of the Father to bring the plan of redemption in accord with the working of the Divine Mind, i.e., the Logos. In this respect, Christ's Resurrection is that event which, touching upon history but transcending time, initiates the ultimate return of all created things back to God.[12]

(3) This view of Christ's Resurrection also sheds light upon the development in the early Church of the doctrine of the Incarnation. If in Christ's Resurrection flesh has been divinized and lifted up into the reality of the Word, it is easy to see how early Christians would come to believe that, at some point prior to this momentous occasion, the Word itself had descended into the reality of human flesh and had become a human person. Putting aside for the moment, the various intricacies involved in discussing the Christological controversies in the early centuries of the Church, it seems quite appropriate to say that the doctrines of Christ's Incarnation and Resurrection form two aspects of a single salvific event which, if one were to borrow the Neoplatonic *exitus/reditus* structure adopted by Aquinas, represents the *recreation* of all things going out of (*exitus*) and going back (*reditus*) to God. It is in this sense that all things are recapitulated in Christ, the New Adam (Rm 5:15).[13]

(4) As described above, the Resurrection is not merely the

---

which they form a part. See Raymond E. Brown, *The Critical Meaning of the Bible* (New York: Paulist Press, 1981), 35-37; Schillebeeckx, *Jesus: An Experiment in Christology*, 392-97.

[12] According to Kasper: "Jesus' Resurrection is not only God's decisive eschatological act, but his eschatological revelation of himself; here it is finally and unsurpassably revealed, who God is... In raising Jesus from the dead God proved his faithfulness in love and thus finally identified himself with Jesus and his work." See *Jesus the Christ*, 145.

[13] "We need scarcely point out that Aquinas was not the first theologian to locate the mystery of the Incarnation and the role of Christ within the general economy of salvation. Any Christian thinker who made use of the Platonic scheme would be led, quite naturally, to suppose Christ as the way or means of man's journey back to God." See Chenu, *The Scope of the Summa*, 33.

state of Christ's postmortem existence, but an intricate part of the whole process of Redemption. If Christ's *exitus* from the Father reaches its furthest extension in his passion and death on the cross (described in the Creed as his descent into hell), his *reditus* is ushered in by the events of Easter morning, and his Spirit is the principle by which all things continue to be gathered into his body and thus into the presence of the Father.[14]

(5) As a transhistorical event with historical consequences, the Resurrection of Christ exists outside of but in relation to the realm of historical inquiry. In this regard, it lies beyond the realm of scientific investigation and can be affirmed only through faith in the testimony of those claiming to have actually experienced Jesus after his death. That is not to say that the apostles did not experience something outside of themselves (i.e., in the external order), but only that the basis for their experience cannot be verified.

(6) Indeed, probably the only historical consequence of measurable scientific value would have been the disappearance of Jesus' body at the actual moment of his Resurrection. Since the precise whereabouts of the body was a point of contention even in the initial aftermath of the Easter proclamation (Mt 28:13), one must conclude that, although its disappearance at this time could have been verified, if not scientifically, then at least through impartial eyewitness accounts, it obviously was not.[15]

(7) On all other points, a detached observer may not have been able to separate the subjective experience of the apostles from the reality of the Risen Christ. There may, in other words, have been no way of determining whether or not they were actually experiencing anything beyond their own intensified inner awareness. The singularity of this experience would be expected if a transhistorical event were to occur and be experienced in its historical consequences.[16]

---

[14] For more on Jesus' resurrection as a redemptive event, see Kasper, *Jesus the Christ*, 154-59; Schillebeeckx, *Jesus: An Experiment in Christology*, 523-25.

[15] For details about Jesus' burial and for the evolution of the empty tomb narratives, see Brown, *The Virginal Conception and Bodily Resurrection of Jesus*, 113-25.

[16] Macquarrie, *Principles of Christian Theology*, 265-66.

The Resurrection Kernel

(8) To the extent that it is not based on direct experience but on the testimony of others, the faith of the subsequent Christian believers is qualitatively different from the faith of the apostles. Not only does it rest on the conviction of those who claimed to have had an actual experience of the Risen Lord, but, in one respect, it is even a purer experience of faith: "Blest are they who have not seen and have believed" (Jn 20:29).[17]

(9) Belief in the Risen Christ keeps alive in people the hope that, after death, their lives will not end, but merely be changed. Because of Christ's Resurrection, they look forward to a transformed existence in the hereafter, one in continuity with their own lives on earth. Sustained by a believer's prayerful response to the contemporary challenges of Christian discipleship, this hope forms the basis upon which life in the Resurrection is anticipated even in the present.[18]

(10) Through their participation in the ministry and life of the Church, people receive a foretaste of this transformed existence, especially when they partake of the sacraments around the table of the Lord. At Emmaus, Jesus' disciples recognized him in the breaking of the bread (Lk 24:30).[19] Today, Christians seek the same when they gather in churches throughout the world to celebrate the Eucharist.[20] This is especially true for those who

---

[17] Despite this important qualitative difference, both the faith of the apostles and that of the individual believer are similar in that they both undergo a parallel process of development and deepening maturity. See Lane, *The Reality of Jesus*, 151-53.

[18] For more on the relationship between Jesus' resurrection and Christian hope, see Kasper, *Jesus the Christ*, 155-56.

[19] "We need not maintain that Jesus consecrated the Eucharist; Eucharistic formulas, however, were absorbed into the story as it was retold in liturgical gatherings." See Raymond E. Brown, Joseph A. Fitzmyer and Roland E. Murphy, eds. *The Jerome Biblical Commentary*, vol. 2, *The New Testament and Topical Articles* (Englewood Cliffs, N.J.: Prentice-Hall, Inc., 1968), s.v. "The Gospel According to Luke," by Carroll Stuhlmueller.

[20] According the Schillebeeckx: "...the memory of Jesus' life and especially the Last Supper must have played a vital role in the process of their [the apostles'] conversion to faith in Jesus as the Christ, the one imbued to the full with God's Spirit." See *Jesus: An Experiment in Christology*, 312. For Christians, the celebration of the Eucharist plays a similar role in their ever-deepening understanding and recognition of the presence of the Lord Jesus in their midst.

dedicate their lives to Christ through the following of the evangelical counsels.

RELIGIOUS AND THE RESURRECTION

In their vows of chastity, poverty, and obedience, religious strive to center their lives upon the reality of the Risen Christ. They seek to do so by virtue of their firm conviction that they are called to share in the life of the Resurrection by making the *idea* of the vows a *lived reality* in their day-to-day existence.[21] Christ, who exhibited both before and after his Resurrection a life dedicated to the Father through the eschatological signs of the evangelical counsels, asks religious to do the same. The strength to do so comes from Christ and is mediated by his Spirit through his Church and its ministry of the sacraments. While such dedication is never fully realized in the present, religious are called to imitate Christ throughout their entire lives. It is for this reason that, at the end of their earthly lives, they hope to share in the fullness of his transformed existence.

In their vowed life in common, religious pledge to give themselves over entirely to the life of the Risen Lord. In their vow of chastity, they promise to forego the goods of marriage, children, and sexual pleasure, thereby accepting Christ's Gospel declaration that there will be neither husband nor wife in the life to come (Lk 20:35) and that, even in the realm of relationships, all who abide in him will live a transformed existence. In their vow of poverty, they seek both physical and spiritual detachment from material goods, doing so not out of a suspicion about the fundamental goodness of creation, but from the conviction that it too will undergo a transformation in the fullness of Christ's kingdom. In their vow of obedience, they promise to accept the will of their superiors as a manifestation of God's plan for their lives, thus hoping to establish within themselves a continual movement of

---

[21] Note Powell's reflections on the meaning of the vows in the light of the Easter event, in *The Mystery of the Church*, 211-13.

accord between their own wills and that of their Risen Lord. Finally, in their communal existence, they hold each other accountable for the way of life they have chosen and seek to reflect in their mutual relations that dignity and care appropriate to those who are called to be members of Christ's body. By means of their individual and communal dedication to the evangelical counsels, it is clear that religious seek, even in this present life, a deeper share in the life of the Resurrection.[22]

Through their vowed life in community, religious thus provide a faithful witness for themselves, the rest of the Church, and the entire world that the idea of resurrection has not only been made a reality in Christ but that it is striving, at this very moment, to be realized in the lives of those who believe. In this respect, their witness affirms the movement of Christ's Spirit in the life of the Church and provides a foretaste of the life to come. That is not to say that religious embody this charismatic dimension of the Church better or more faithfully than any of the other vocations within the Church (e.g., the married, single, and priestly calls), but only that their way of life is especially suited to it. Of its very nature, the religious life forms a part of the charismatic dimension of the Church.[23] Indeed, to the extent that religious communities do not manifest to both others and themselves the gentle yet challenging presence of the Spirit, they fall short of the explicit nature of their call to center their lives entirely around the reality of the Risen Christ. He it was who first imparted the Holy Spirit to his body, the Church. He it is who continues to do so even to the present day.

Through their faithfulness to the vows, lived in community and in the Spirit, religious seek mainly to nourish their relationship with the Risen Christ. This personal relationship to the Lord

---

[22] "The vows of a religious are meant to express the attitude of a resurrected person. They are the expression not only of the death to sin but of complete belonging to God in Christ." See Powell, *The Mystery of the Church*, 211.

[23] "The state of life, then, which is constituted by the profession of the evangelical counsels, while not entering into the hierarchical structure of the Church, belongs undeniably to her life and holiness." See Vatican Council II, *Lumen gentium*, no. 44 [*CDD*, 177]; English translation: Flannery, *Vatican Council II*, 405.

motivates all of their activity for the establishment of God's kingdom; it is also what draws others to follow their particular way of life. Indeed, the care with which they tend this relationship is itself a sign that the reality of Christ's Resurrection is meant for all to share and experience in all its fullness. In this respect, religious must be ever conscious that their vowed life in common has little meaning if it is separated from life in the Spirit of the Risen Christ and seen as an end in itself. To be sure, there is nothing sadder in the life of the Church than to see individual religious and, at times, entire communities lose sight of the meaning of their vocation. When people of such great promise and potential compromise themselves and begin to believe that the Spirit is no longer active in their lives and that things will never change for the better, when men and women, who are called to be signs of hope, begin to believe in the voices of hopelessness, then the time is ripe for a prophet to arise within their midst to summon them to live in hope the life to which they have been called. At the same time, there is nothing more joyful in the life of the Church than to see men and women who, out of love for their Lord, renounce the very things for which most actually strive during their sojourn on earth. To live in poverty, without children or spouse, and without full personal liberty provides others with the constantly needed reminder that the fullness of riches, family life, and freedom is ultimately found only in one's relationship to him whom the apostles acclaimed to be truly Risen.

CONCLUSION

This chapter has sought to outline the basic, underlying principle of the Christian doctrine of the Resurrection. It has done so, on the one hand, by describing in as precise detail as possible the meaning of the idea of resurrection as understood in the Church's teaching and, on the other hand, by looking into some of the fundamental presuppositions regarding the Resurrection of Christ as experienced by his earliest followers. Bringing these two currents of inquiry together, the fundamental principle of the

The Resurrection Kernel

Resurrection ("The Resurrection Kernel") was described as the affirmation of faith that the idea of resurrection has become a reality in the Risen Christ. Seen as a transhistorical event with historical consequences, the acclaimed Resurrection of Jesus of Nazareth lies, for all practical purposes, beyond the scope of scientific verification and remains intimately tied to the internal, subjective event of faith to which it gave life. That is not to say that Jesus' Resurrection has no ground in the external order, but only that it ultimately lies beyond the scope of controlled observation. In this respect, the faith experience of those who experienced the Risen Lord is qualitatively different from that of those whose faith rests upon their testimony. Blessed precisely because they believe without seeing, today's believers share in the hope of their own transformed existence which, through their experience of the Spirit in the Church community of the faithful, may be experienced even now in quiet anticipation of the fullness of a reality yet to come. They bring their hearts' deepest yearning for the fullest presence of the Risen Christ to the table of the Lord, where they are blessed with a glimpse of his continued presence in their Eucharistic breaking of the bread.

Through their communal dedication to the evangelical counsels, religious affirm their faith that the idea of resurrection has in Christ indeed become a reality. Their life of chastity, poverty, and obedience gives expression to their faith in the new creation which has been wrought in Christ and to their hope that they too will share in the transformation of all things in Christ. In centering their lives entirely on Christ, religious seek to live in his Spirit in a way that will anticipate the fullness of this transformation even in this present life. In doing so, they serve as a leaven for both themselves and others who seek the presence of the Lord in their midst and keep alive the hope of Christ's promise to be with his Church even unto the end of time (Mt 28:20). In this respect, religious participate in the charismatic dimension of the Church by their attempt to cooperate with and to further along the Spirit's ultimate recapitulation of all things into the body of the Risen Christ.

In the final analysis, the fundamental principle of the Resurrection ("The Resurrection Kernel") emphasizes the fact that the idea that has become a reality in Christ is not only just a state of existence, but also a movement in the economic process of God's redemptive plan (*exitus/reditus*). In this respect, life in the Risen Christ means that one is participating in this process and will ultimately share in the fruits of Christ's kingship. It also breathes new life into the significance of the soteriological principle that God became man (i.e., Incarnation) in order that humanity might become divine (i.e., share in the life of the Risen Lord).[24] If nothing else, the fundamental principle of the Resurrection highlights the importance that a rigorous understanding of this doctrine would have for the whole of theology. Like the body of the Risen Lord, this sacred science, as also the Church it seeks to serve, should not continue to exist in a separate or fragmented state.

---

[24] Among the Church fathers, the soteriological principle is expressed most clearly in Athanasius of Alexandria (*De incarnatione*, 54.3 [*SC* 199:458-59; *PG* 25:191-92]) and Gregory of Nyssa, (*De opificio hominis*, 16 [*SC* 6:151-61; *PG* 44:178-88]). As expressed in this chapter, the Resurrection Kernel underscores the intimate link between Jesus' Resurrection and the process of human divinization, the principle's stated goal.

9

THE SACRAMENTAL KERNEL

Is there a fundamental principle of sacramental theology? The answer to this question depends on the way in which theologians develop the relationship of the sacraments to those theological disciplines pertaining to the Church (i.e., ecclesiology), the person of Christ (i.e., Christology), and the Godhead itself (i.e., Trinitarian theology). A break in continuity in any of these disciplines pays a disservice not only to the richness of the Church's sacramental tradition, but also to the underlying twofold movement of the *visio Dei* itself, i.e., the divine encounter of the human and the corresponding human encounter of the divine. To disregard either one of these aspects in the discussion of sacramental theology is to totally misconstrue the meaning of the Church's theological treasure.

THE SACRAMENTAL GOD

At various times in the history of Christian thought, the importance of the sacraments has been de-emphasized in one of two ways: (1) by considering them only incidental to the mystery of redemption, the effects of which, it is supposed, come to an individual exclusively and without mediation from his or her faith in Christ, or (2) by thinking of them as merely an intermediary (and, hence, temporary) means, whose very reason for being will come to an end in the life to come.¹ In neither case is the meaning of the word, μυστηριον (the Greek equivalent to the Latin, *sacramentum* — meaning, "mystery") given its fullest and proper weight. That is to say that the sacraments, at their deepest and most significant level, must be thought of as revealing something of the mystery of God's very essence.²

To speak of a sacramental divinity brings to the fore a number of important theological questions. How, for example, can such a concept be rectified with the traditional association the sacraments have with the material world? How is it possible for a sacramental God to manifest himself beyond the fullness of his own completed act? What is the nature of the relationship between the sacramental God, the sacramental nature of Christ, his Church, and the individual sacraments themselves?

To be answered properly, such questions must be understood in the context of the fundamental element uniting the concept of sacramentality with that of divinity, i.e., the personal encounter of genuine selfless love. That is to say that the notion of sacramentality is not inexorably tied to the world of matter, since the latter becomes necessary only when the former enters the realm of concrete human experience. The term, "sacrament," moreover, relates to humanity in a variety of ways, as is evident by its frequent and analogous use in reference to Christ and his Church (i.e., Christ as "the sacrament of God"; the Church as "the

---

[1] One of the clearest examples of these reductionist tendencies is found in the Sacramentarian controversy of the early Protestant reform. The incidentalist interpretation was held by Ulrich Zwingli (1484-1531), who thought of the sacraments as mere signs and seals of divine grace already given; the intermediary approach was defended by Martin Luther (1483-1546), who considered them the temporal means by which God freely imparts his grace. See Harold J. Grimm, *The Reformation Era: 1500-1650*, 2d ed. (New York: Macmillan, 1973), 156-59.

[2] If it is true that "all beings are by their nature symbolic, because they necessarily 'express' themselves to attain their own nature," it follows analogously that the sacraments, as symbolic expressions of God's saving action in Christ, express something of the very mystery of the Godhead. See Karl Rahner, "The Theology of Symbol," in *Theological Investigations*, vol. 4, trans. K. Smyth (London: Darton, Longman and Todd, 1974), 224.

The Sacramental Kernel

sacrament of Christ").[3] Similarly, while the individual sacraments may be considered the primary epistemological analogues of the concept of sacramentality (insofar as they convey to us our first understanding of the meaning of the term), and while Christ and his Church may be, respectively, the primordial sacramental referents of creation and human existence (insofar as the former mediate the reality of the divine to the latter), what is so often overlooked by many of today's theologians is that the ultimate sacramental expression of divine love is rooted in the very mystery of the Trinity itself.[4] There, love exists beyond the bounds of the material and manifests itself in an eternal unity of generating Source, generated Word, and processing Spirit. It is this Triune Godhead which, containing within itself the fundamental requisites of authentic personal encounter (i.e., outward selfless expression and genuine reciprocating response), forms the underlying basis of all other sacramental realities, including those of Christ and his Church.[5]

Sacramentality, then, is essentially an analogous concept moving downward in ontological significance from the Godhead, to Christ, the Church, and the sacraments, and upward epistemologically in reverse order. This downward and upward move-

---

[3] For these and other analogous uses of the term "sacrament," see Michael Schmaus, *Dogma*, vol. 5, *The Church as Sacrament* (London: Sheed and Ward, 1975), 1-19. For more detailed studies, see Edward Schillebeeckx, *Christ the Sacrament of the Encounter with God*, with a Foreword by Cornelius Ernst (New York: Sheed and Ward, 1963) and Colman E. O'Neill, *Meeting Christ in the Sacraments*, revised ed. Romanus Cessario (New York: Alba House, 1991).

[4] This important Trinitarian aspect of sacramental theology is overlooked by such well-known authors as Bernard Cooke, *Sacraments and Sacramentality* (Mystic, Conn.: Twenty-Third Publications, 1983) and Monika Hellwig, *The Meaning of the Sacraments* (Dayton: Pflaum Press, 1972). It is covered only by way of prefatory remarks in Schmaus, *The Church as Sacrament*, 3-5. Schillebeeckx treats the sacramental aspects of the Trinity, but only insofar as they are made manifest in human form through the mysteries of Passover and Pentecost. See *Christ the Sacrament of the Encounter with God*, 25-36.

[5] As the fundamental basis of all sacramental realities (i.e., representing outward selfless expression and genuine reciprocating reponse), the Trinity itself may be thought of as the perfect sacramental manifestation of itself, i.e., a plurality of loving relationships within the one Divine essence.

ment corresponds respectively to the objective and subjective poles of the Church's sacramental teaching, traditionally expressed by the Latin terms *ex opere operato* (literally, "from the work performed," referring to the accurate performance of the sacramental rite) and *ex opere operantis* (literally, "from the work of the one performing," referring to the actual faith of the recipient).[6] It also reflects the well-known Thomistic distinction between *finis cuius* ("the end for which" a thing is done) and *finis quo* ("the end by which" a thing is done),[7] as well as the inherent tension in sacramental theology existing between doctrinal truth and mystical experience. When stated in terms of sacramental encounter, it is best expressed, on the one hand, as the application of the redemptive effects of the Christ event to historical circumstance and, on the other hand, as the individual's entering more deeply into the mystery of God's redemptive love.[8] In terms of humanity's relationship to the sacramental God, it reflects the underlying twofold movement of the *visio Dei* itself, i.e., the Godhead's own eternal gaze upon created humanity, and the latter's beatific vision into the depths of the divine.[9]

The point being made here is that the notion of sacramentality is concerned not so much with the material manifestation of the divine as it is with the revelatory power of God's salvific love. This reality extends far beyond the bounds of matter and touches upon

---

[6] For the use of *ex opere operato* in magisterial teaching, see Denz.-Schön., 1608. For the origins and historical development of the terms, see Ott, *Fundamentals of Catholic Dogma*, 329-30.

[7] Aquinas makes great use of the *finis quo / finis cuius* distinction. In his discussion of humanity's last end, for example, he uses it to describe the thing itself in which is found the aspect of good (*finis cuius*), and the use or acquaintance of that thing (*finis quo*). See *Summa theologiae*, I-II, q. 1, a.8, resp.

[8] A similar view is held by Aquinas. The sacraments of the Church derive their power from Christ's Passion. In doing so, they take away the defects consequent on past sins and perfect the soul in things pertaining to divine worship. See *Summa theologiae*, III, q. 62, a. 5, resp.

[9] This twofold aspect is found in the phrase *visio Dei* itself, depending on whether *Dei* is taken as an objective or possessive genitive. The *finis quo/finis cuius* distinction can also be employed in this twofold movement. Taken as an objective genitive, *Dei* would refer to the *finis quo*; taken as a possessive, the *finis cuius*.

the realm of pure spirit. That is to say that the twofold movement of outward selfless expression and genuine reciprocating response found in all sacramental realities exists within the very essence of the Godhead itself. The individual sacraments, in other words, are possible only because of the sacramental nature of the Triune God, i.e., the generating Father, the generated Word, and the processing Spirit. To be sure, the Spirit, who according to the Catholic *Filioque* doctrine "proceeds from the Father *and the Son*"[10] as the eternal loving bond which unites them, is the concrete manifestation of the sacramental nature of the Godhead. The greatest single difference between the sacramentality of God and those realities further down the sacramental scale (e.g., Christ's humanity, the Church, the individual sacraments) is that of the former's uncreated nature (as opposed to the contingent, created nature of the latter). This distinction, however, only demonstrates further that the individual sacraments are not mere intermediate steps to God, but real, if somewhat imperfect, manifestations of the divine, destined to reach their fullness in the life to come.[11]

THE SACRAMENTAL KERNEL

At this point, the fundamental principle of sacramental theology ("The Sacramental Kernel") may be summarized as follows: sacraments are proportionately analogous realities manifesting the mystery of God's internal life within a twofold movement of person-to-person encounter: (1) an outward expression of

---

[10] Denz.-Schön., 527 (277), 682 (345). For the origins and historical significance of the *Filioque* doctrine, see J.N.D. Kelly, *Early Christian Creeds*, 3d ed. (New York: Longman, 1972), 358-67.

[11] If Aquinas seemingly disagrees with the above depiction of God's sacramentality (*Summa theologiae*, III, q. 60. a. 4, resp.), it is so mainly because he insists on using the term *"sacramentum"* in the traditional sense of the sacraments of the Church. When understood according to the lines of proportionate analogy and when applied further and further up the divine/human continuum, the concept becomes less and less dependent upon the sensible, material world.

genuine selfless love and (2) a corresponding reciprocating response. The presence of this sacramental dynamic within the very essence of the Godhead makes the element of materiality necessary only when the nature of this encounter is oriented toward the relationship between the human and the divine (e.g., Christ, the Church, the seven sacraments). In this respect, the individual sacraments themselves are visible manifestations of a special gift and reception of divine love which will reach its richest expression only in the fullness of the life to come.

Given the above formulation of "The Sacramental Kernel," a number of observations arise:

(1) To the extent that the Kingdom of God is being realized in this present life, the sacraments already contain an aspect of that fullness towards which they tend. Not to recognize this presence would run the risk of falling into a state of either ethical complacency or naive otherworldliness.[12]

(2) From the perspective of the divine/human encounter, one must also recognize an element of continuity between God, Christ, the Church, and the individual sacraments. Just as Christ is the sacrament of the Godhead, so too is the Church the sacrament of Christ, and the individual sacraments themselves the sacraments of the Church. To break this continuity in any way is to do a disservice to the richness of the Church's sacramental teaching.[13]

(3) From the perspective of the sacramental nature of the Godhead, the Spirit is the concrete sacramental expression of the eternal exchange of divine love between the Father and the Son. In this respect, the Spirit is the primordial sacrament upon which all other sacramental realities, even that of Christ, the God-Man, depend. The authentic manifestation of the Spirit, in other words, is the ultimate end of any sacramental reality.[14]

---

[12] For the notion of "presence" as it pertains to the eschatological nature of the sacraments, see Cooke, *Sacraments and Sacramentality*, 46-50.

[13] For a concise description of this important "sacramental principle," see McBrien, *Catholicism*, 2:731-34.

[14] For the sacraments of the Church, this pneumatological aspect manifests itself most clearly in the bestowal of sanctifying grace by the Holy Spirit. See Ott, *Fundamentals of Catholic Dogma*, 254.

(4) With respect to the relationship between the Spirit (as the sacramental manifestation within the nature of the Godhead) and Christ (as the sacrament of the Godhead in relationship to humanity), it must be recognized that, while the Spirit proceeds from the Father and the Son, it is Christ, the God-Man, who reveals the Spirit to the world. Hence, the significance of the symbol of the dove at Jesus' baptism (Mt 3:16; Mk 1:10; Lk 3:22), and of the ecclesiological doctrine identifying the Spirit with the "soul" of the Church.[15]

(5) The reciprocating response spoken of in the preceding paragraphs involves not only a response to the doctrinal elements of the faith, safeguarded through time in the treasury of the Church's teaching, but also to Christ's revelation of the Spirit. In this respect, the mystical element of sacramental theology complements what all too often appears as an overt and oppressive dogmatism. Both aspects, in fact (i.e., the doctrinal and the experiential), are essential to any orthodox approach to the sacraments and must be kept in balanced relation one to another.[16]

RELIGIOUS AND THE SACRAMENTS

It is precisely this balance which religious seek to preserve in the Church's sacramental tradition. By means of their vowed life in community, they give radical witness to the mysterious action of God's salvific love in the world. In this respect, they manifest the presence of the Spirit in the life of the Church and thus point to the underlying element of cohesiveness uniting all aspects of

---

[15] For the historical sources and an explanation of the doctrine's meaning , see Ott, *Fundamentals of Catholic Dogma*, 294-96.

[16] Keeping such a balance will help the believing community to avoid the pitfalls of a detached rationalism, on the one hand, and an excessive emotionalism, on the other. It corresponds to a similar balance between the rational and the emotional that must be kept within the individual and on every level of Christian community. For more on the mystical quality of the sacraments, see Schillebeeckx, *Christ the Sacrament of the Encounter with God*, 216-21.

the Church's sacramental life.[17] Taken as a whole, their life dedicated to the Lord through the evangelical counsels manifests the twofold movement of sacramental encounter developed above, i.e., outward selfless expression and genuine reciprocating response: (1) in their vow of chastity, their experience of God's creative power inspires them to forego the good of married life, children, and sexual pleasure, and to rely directly on the one eternal source of these goods; (2) in their vow of poverty, their understanding of the significance of Christ's divine κένωσις leads them to empty themselves of the attachment to created things; (3) in their vow of obedience, their experience of the power of God's Word and the sacramental effects of the Incarnation prompts them to trust that the will of their religious superiors will reveal in their lives the very will of God.[18] Taken as such, their concrete commitment to God through their vows enables them to bring to the reception of the sacraments a heightened awareness of the complementary nature of the doctrinal and mystical facets of the Church's sacramental life. In this respect, they serve as a leaven for themselves and others in living a life oriented in its entirety towards the sacramental love of God.[19]

Religious, moreover, demonstrate in a concrete manner the continuity existing between each sacramental reality, i.e., the Godhead, Christ, the Church, and the individual sacraments. They do so by virtue of both the public profession of their vows and the outward orientation of their communal existence. With regard to the former, it is of the essence of the religious life that a

---

[17] It is in this context that recent magisterial documents emphasize the essential ecclesial dimension of religious life. See, for example, John Paul II, "La vita religiosa si comprende essenzialmente nella dimensione ecclesiale," nos. 7-8 [*IGP* 6/2:582-84]; SCRSI, "Norms for Religious Life," *The Pope Speaks* 28 (1983): 318-19 [English original; text does not appear in *AAS*].

[18] For more on the sacramental or "symbolic" significance of the evangelical counsels, see Karl Rahner, "On the Evangelical Counsels," 163-67.

[19] The greatest sign of the orientation religious have toward the sacramental love of God is the centrality they give to their liturgical life and especially the Eucharist as the heart of their community and its source of life. See Paul VI, *Evangelica testificatio*, nos. 47-48 [*AAS* 63 (1971): 521]; English translation: Flannery, *Vatican Council II*, 701-2.

person makes his or her vows freely and openly in the presence of God, Christ, and his Mystical Body, the Church. The profession ceremony highlights these prerequisites (usually in the context of a Eucharistic celebration) not out of mere social appropriateness, but to underscore the sacramental nature of the religious life and, by way of extension, of the Christian life itself. A religious who does not root his or her life in the concrete expression of the mystery of divine love has not understood the full significance of the vows, let alone that of his or her baptismal commitment.[20] With regard to the latter, it is clear that the religious life cannot be separated from a communal sacramental spirituality which, at one and the same time, both removes itself from the rest of the Church membership (hence, their usual practice of living in canonical foundations such as convents, monasteries, etc.), and integrates itself within it (through apostolic activity and/or contemplative prayer). In this regard, it may be said that the religious life reflects the inherent communal aspect of every sacramental reality, from that of the Godhead itself (i.e., the Triune God), to Christ (i.e., in relationship to his Mystical Body), and to the Church (i.e., in its relationship to all of humanity). For religious, therefore, the sacraments are concrete manifestations of that divine communal love which they seek to realize in their own communities, in the Church itself, and in human society as a whole.[21]

The religious life has little significance once it is taken out of the multidimensional context of the Church's sacramental tradi-

---

[20] The public profession of vows in the Church has been identified as an essential element of religious life. See SCRSI, "Norms for Religious Life," 308-9. Such a statement on the part of the magisterium underscores its obligation to provide guidelines for leading the life of the evangelical counsels. See Vatican Council II, *Lumen gentium*, no. 45 [*CDD*, 177-79]; English translation: Flannery, *Vatican Council II*, 405. This effectively places outside the ecclesiastical category of "the religious state" those groups which have recently opted for non-canonical status.

[21] In this respect, the "sacramental principle" of outward selfless expression and genuine reciprocating response forms part of the interior dynamic through which religious seek continually to consecrate themselves to the Lord through their living the evangelical counsels.

tion. To do so would be tantamount not only to denying the circular relationship existing between the sacraments and all vocations within the Church as a whole (in the sense that the sacraments cannot exist outside the context of a call, and vice versa), but also to overlook the particular role played by the sacraments in the spirituality of religious life. In this respect, the well-known depiction of religious life as a fuller expression of one's baptismal consecration, the Vatican's call for religious to frequent the sacrament of reconciliation, and its insistence that they make the Eucharist the center of their devotional lives, all touch the very heart of the Christian vocation, as well as the radical nature of that commitment to the Lord which the religious vows are meant to convey.[22] Religious, in other words, orient themselves toward the Church's sacramental life not only by virtue of their baptismal call to follow Christ (which they share with all Christians), but also by virtue of their vowed life in community (which, for the sake of perseverance, requires the ongoing nourishing grace of the sacraments). From this perspective, an individual's life in the vows may be seen as a function of his or her commitment to the Church's sacramental life and the various analogous continuities involved therein.[23]

---

[22] For the religious life as a fuller expression of one's baptismal consecration, see Vatican Council II, *Perfectae caritatis*, no. 5 [*CDD*, 337-38]; English translation: Flannery, *Vatican Council II*, 614; Paul VI, *Evangelica testificatio*, no. 4 [*AAS* 63 (1971): 499]; Flannery, *Vatican Council II*, 682; John Paul II, *Redemptionis donum*, no. 7 [AAS 76 (1984): 522-24]; English translation: "*Redemptionis Donum*: An Expression of Love for Religious," 486-88. For the importance of frequent confession for religious, see SCRSI, *Dum canonicarum*, nos. 2-3 [*AAS* 63 (1971), 318]; English translation: Flannery, *Vatican Council II*, 676. For the Eucharist as the center of the devotional lives of religious, see Paul VI, *Evangelica testificatio*, no. 48 [*AAS* 63 (1971): 521]; English translation: Flannery, *Vatican Council II*, 701-2; SCRSI, *La plenaria*, no. 9 in *Vatican Council II: More Post Conciliar Documents*, gen. ed. Austin Flannery (Northport, Conn.: Costello Publishing Co., 1982), 249 [Does not appear in *AAS*; translation supplied by SCRSI].

[23] For more on the sacramental dimension of the religious life, see Armando Bandera, "Consigli evangelici e sacramenti." *Vita consacrata* 9 (1973): 97-106, 204-13; Simon Decloux, "La dimension sacramentelle de la vie religieuse," *Vie consacrée* 58 (1986): 197-208; Eric C. Meyer, "Is Religious Life a Sacrament?" *Review for Religious* 33 (1974): 1100-17.

The Sacramental Kernel

CONCLUSION

This chapter roots the fundamental principle of sacramental theology ("The Sacramental Kernel") in that twofold movement of personal encounter (outward selfless expression and genuine reciprocating response) which exists at every level of the Church's theological tradition. In Trinitarian theology, this movement is spoken of, internally, in terms of the Spirit as the processing love shared by the Father and the Son, and, externally, in terms of the twofold aspect of the *visio Dei* (i.e., the Godhead's vision of humanity, and the latter's beatific vision of God). In Christology, it is found in the nature of the relationship between the human and the divine in Christ, while in ecclesiology it exists in the tension between doctrine and mysticism in the Church's theological tradition. In the sacraments themselves, this twofold movement arises in the classical *ex opere operato / ex opere operantis* distinction and, from a more contemporary perspective, in the recognition that the subjective and objective dimensions of sacramental reception parallel closely the experiential dynamics of personal encounter. The sacraments, in other words, are concrete expressions of the mystery of divine love, a reality which, by its very nature, involves a relationship between two or more personal entities. Within this context, the aspect of materiality is necessary in sacramental theology only when it involves the encounter between the human and the divine (and, hence, would be unnecessary when speaking about the sacramental aspects of the inner relations of the Godhead). The sacraments, moreover, are not to be looked upon as mere intermediary steps, but as concrete realities reaching their fullness in the vision of God in the life to come. To the extent that this vision has already been realized, the individual sacraments themselves effect an aspect of this fullness of the Kingdom in the present.[24]

In relation to this fundamental principle, a further purpose of the religious life is to help to maintain the delicate balance between the doctrinal and mystical elements of the Church's

---

[24] For more on the eschatological character of the Church and its sacraments, see Karl Rahner, *The Church and the Sacraments*, trans. W.J. O'Hara (New York: Herder and Herder, 1963), 18-23.

sacramental tradition. It seeks to do so, on the one hand, by means of its incarnational understanding of the vows and, on the other hand, by virtue of the outward orientation of its own communal existence. In this respect, the religious life reveals, at one and the same time, both the analogous nature of the various sacramental realities in question (i.e., the Trinity, Christ, the Church, the individual sacraments themselves) and the intensely personal relationships which, through them, each individual Christian is called to share with God. To the extent that religious nurture their own personal relationships with God on each of these levels, they serve as a leaven for both themselves and others for the deeper realization of the nature of the Christian vocation, which ultimately finds its rest in the fullness of the vision of God. To the extent that they fail, they fall short of the radical witness to Gospel values they claim to profess in their vows. In this respect, the vows themselves take on authentic Christian meaning only within the context of a sacramental interpretation. Religious, in other words, are called to approach the sacraments through the vows and to be nurtured in their vows through their sacramental existence.[25]

In the final analysis, the fundamental principle of sacramental theology upholds the important continuity between Christian doctrine and mystical experience on all levels of the Church's theological tradition. It does so, on the one hand, by virtue of its careful use of proportional reasoning and, on the other hand, by associating the concept of sacramentality with that of personal encounter. Such an emphasis frees the Church's sacramental tradition from too heavy an emphasis on the traditional matter/form distinction and allows it to be developed more within the context of authentic Christian relationship. As visible, concrete expressions of the mystery of God's love, the sacraments — on whatever level one chooses to view them — seek only to bring one ever more deeply into the experience of that love, until one's entire being is oriented toward God and resting in the fullness of the life to come.

---

[25] Recall that the primary teaching of Vatican II on the religious life appears in chapters five and six of "The Dogmatic Constitution on the Church." The opening remarks of this document refer to the mystery of the Church in Christ and its sacramental nature. See Vatican Council II, *Lumen gentium*, no.1 [*CDD*, 93-94]; English translation: Flannery, *Vatican Council II*, 350.

10

THE BREAD KERNEL

Is there a fundamental principle of the theology of the Eucharist? The answer to this question depends on the way in which the Last Supper, as a symbolic foreshadowing of the heavenly banquet, is thought to embody Jesus' enduring presence with the fellowship of the Twelve and incorporate within itself the main features of the salvific drama of the Christ event. It also depends on the particular theological, philosophical, and linguistic categories used to express these various insights into the meaning of Christ's breaking of the bread and drinking from the cup. These categories must resonate with the particular Christian tradition under consideration (in the present case, that of the Roman Catholic Church) and also speak to the human person in a way that is both comprehensible and pertinent to his or her own cultural circumstances. Needless to say, they would be relevant to the whole of theology.

THE EUCHARIST AS A SYMBOLIC ACTION

Jesus' words of blessing on the evening before his death make little sense unless they are understood as a symbolic representation of a New Covenant existing between God and humanity.[1] The bread and wine which he shares with his disciples signify

---

[1] André Feuillet, *The Priesthood of Christ and His Ministers*, trans. Matthew J. O'Connell (Garden City, N.Y.: Doubleday and Co., 1975), 94.

the sacrifice of his body and blood to be given up and poured out for the sake of many.[2] By placing his passion and death in the context of his last Passover meal, Jesus provides his followers with a concrete way of remembrance that exists in continuity with the tradition of their ancestors and that also raises their awareness of a new, definitive action of God in their lives.[3] In this respect, it partakes in those very events which shape his own destiny in the plan of his Father.[4]

Jesus' last meal is linked not only with the events following it, but also with those preceding it. In all three of the Synoptic Gospels, his public ministry both begins and ends with a symbolic action: the former, that of his baptism by John in the Jordan (Mt 3:13-17; Mk 1:9-11; Lk 3:21-22); the latter, that of the first Eucharist (Mt 26:26-29; Mk 14:22-25; Lk 22:19-20). Even in the Gospel of John, which includes neither Jesus' baptism nor the actual words of institution, the account of his public ministry contains many allusions to the Eucharistic banquet, i.e., changing the water into wine at Cana (2:1-12), the miracle of the loaves (6:1-15), his discourse at Capernaum (6:22-66, especially 32-58), the discourse on the vine and the branches (15:1-17), and the meal of bread and fish (21:9-14).[5] The point being made here is that, while Jesus' words of institution (considered authentic even according to the standards of biblical criticism) link the Last Supper with the events of his passion and death, the evangelists (writing under the

---

[2] Karl Rahner, "The Eucharist and Suffering," chap. in *Theological Investigations*, vol. 3, *The Theology of the Spiritual Life*, trans. Karl H. and Boniface Kruger (London: Darton, Longman and Todd, 1974), 161.

[3] For the opinions on whether the Last Supper was actually a Passover meal, see Vawter, *This Man Jesus*, 62-63. Still, it is clear that the early Christian communities understood the Christ event in terms of a New Passover. See, for example, the possible influence of a Christian Passover ritual on the author of John 6 in Raymond E. Brown, *New Testament Essays* (New York: Paulist Press, 1965), 77-92.

[4] For the symbolic relationship between the Last Supper and the Christ event, see Rahner, "The Eucharist and Suffering," 161-64.

[5] For those passages in John's Gospel which, according to the standards of the historical critical method, may be considered acceptable or, at least, possible allusions to the Eucharist, see Brown, *New Testament Essays*, 76.

inspiration of the Holy Spirit) associate it also with the events of his public ministry.[6] The Synoptic authors achieve the latter by using the symbolic actions of the Lord's baptism and Last Supper as a means of defining the limits of his public ministry; the author of the Gospel of John does so by filling the account of Jesus' ministry of teaching and healing with numerous Eucharistic undertones. In this respect, the Eucharist is connected as much to the life as it is to the death of the Lord Jesus. And, in both cases, they point to what obviously stands out as the culminating event of his life and death, i.e., his resurrection on Easter Sunday morning.[7]

In his use of symbolism as a means of communicating the truth of his redemptive mission, Jesus stands in marked continuity with the long tradition of Hebrew prophetic utterance. Hosea's marriage to the faithless Gomer (Ho 1:2-9), Jeremiah's symbols of the loincloth (Jr 13:1-11) and the shattered wine jugs (Jr 12-14), Ezekiel's making of bread from a single pot of wheat, barley, beans, lentils, millet, and spelt (Ezk 4:9) and his mime of the emigrant (Ezk 12:1-20) are all examples of the prophetic use of concrete material signs and actions to convey the message of Yahweh to his people. What is so often forgotten when interpreting these actions is that, as authentic utterances of the Word of God, they actually bring into effect what they symbolize: "God's word does not return in vain" (Is 55:11).[8] In this respect, Jesus' breaking of the bread and drinking from the cup in the company of his disciples brings the event of Calvary into their midst. That

---

[6] In this respect, the Gospels preserve not only Jesus' authentic words of institution, but also theological reflection upon them by early Christian communities in light of his entire life.

[7] The resurrection, in other words, was understood by the Gospel writers as giving light to aspects of Jesus' person and mission which previous to it had not been in any way perceptible. For the other role-requirements assigned to Jesus' resurrection in contemporary theological writing, see James P. Mackey, *Jesus: The Man and the Myth* (New York: Paulist Press, 1979), 89-90.

[8] For the nature of prophetic symbolism, see Raymond E. Brown, Joseph A. Fitzmyer, and Roland E. Murphy, eds. *The Jerome Biblical Commentary*, vol. 1, *The Old Testament* (Englewood Cliffs, N.J.: Prentice-Hall, 1968), s.v. "Introduction to Prophetic Literature," by Bruce Vawter.

is to say that, before his actual death, Jesus makes present the redemptive effects of that first Good Friday in the bread and wine which he eats and drinks with his disciples.[9] These effects culminate in his Easter rising and, as stated earlier, are already anticipated in his ministry of teaching and healing.

IN THE BREAKING OF THE BREAD

Rooted in this long tradition of Hebrew prophetic utterance, Jesus' institution of the Eucharist takes place in the context of a sacred meal, in the midst of his disciples, in an action symbolizing his redemptive suffering and death on the cross. Asked by Jesus to remember him in this sacred action (to be called a sacrament in the developing Church tradition), his disciples and the communities established by them soon came to recognize that the thanksgiving to God which they rendered in their breaking of the bread and drinking from the cup did indeed involve: (1) a foretaste of the heavenly banquet, (2) the continuing presence of the Risen Lord in their midst, and (3) the sacrificial reality of Christ's redemptive death.[10] Disagreement over the precise nature of each of these elements and the way in which they interact with one another has been the cause of much unrest and turmoil in the history of the Church.[11]

---

[9] For the sacrificial aspects of the Last Supper, see Feuillet, *The Priesthood of Christ and His Ministers*, 126-29.

[10] Of the three, the second (i.e., the Eucharistic presence) is the most difficult to establish in early Christian sources. In the words of Pelikan: "The theologians did not have adequate concepts within which to formulate a doctrine of the real presence that evidently was already believed by the church even though it was not yet taught by explicit instruction or confessed by creeds." See *The Emergence of the Catholic Tradition (100-600)*, 168. For one of the clearest assertions in early Christian literature of Christ's real Eucharistic presence, see Ignatius of Antioch, *Letter to the Smyrnaeans*, 7.1 in *Apostolic Fathers I*, The Loeb Classical Library, 274-75 [*PG* 5.713-14].

[11] Such tension normally has its roots in a theological reductionism that tries to limit the meaning of the Eucharist to one of these aspects. Orthodox approaches seek to maintain a dynamic balance between all three and, in doing so, will preserve in their official formulations something more of the sacrament's mystery. See Leech, *Experiencing God: Theology as Spirituality*, 265-88.

The Bread Kernel

(1) The Eucharist as Banquet. Even to the external observer, the relationship that the Eucharist has to the fellowship of a sacred meal is obvious and nearly always presumed. Like the Passover — its Jewish counterpart — the celebration of the Eucharist commemorates the great saving acts of God on behalf of his people. Its purpose is to bond Christians together first through a telling of the great Christian narrative as it has been handed down through the Gospels and interpreted by Paul and other apostolic witnesses of the faith, and then through the ritualistic sharing in the bread and cup which Christ himself likened to the eating of his own body and blood. In this respect, the Eucharist serves as a focus of identity for the Christian people. By remembering the stories and performing the actions that Jesus asked to be done in his memory, they find themselves drawing closer to one another and thus able to build community in what, at times, appears to be the most unlikely of circumstances. As food for wayfaring pilgrims, the Eucharist provides spiritual strength and nourishment for the believing community's earthly pilgrimage in faith.[12] As a foretaste of the heavenly banquet, it preserves the hope that the reign of God manifested in Christ will one day be fully realized in the lives of his followers.[13] It should not be surprising that the Eucharist, when considered as a meal or banquet, receives almost universal acclaim: Christians of all denominations affirm the importance of the great spiritual strength they receive from their gathering in fellowship around the table of the Lord.

(2) The Eucharist as Presence. The Gospel story of "The Road to Emmaus" (Lk 24:13-35) affirms that the Risen Christ was present to his followers in numerous ways: in their walk along the road (24:15), in their discussion of recent events (24: 16-24), in the explanation of the Scriptures (24: 25-27), and, most especially, "in the breaking of the bread" (24: 30-31).[14] The latter involves not only

---

[12] "The Last Supper and our Eucharistic celebration are both an offering to God and *a family meal.*" See Powell, *The Mystery of the Church*, 151 [italics mine].

[13] For the eschatological context of the Church's Eucharistic banquet, see Vatican Council II, *Lumen gentium*, no. 48 [*CDD*, 181-84]; English translation: Flannery, *Vatican Council II*, 407-8. See also Schmaus, *The Church as Sacrament*, 134-38; Jean Galot, "Pasto escatologico," *Vita consacrata* 26 (1990): 783-99.

[14] See chap. 8, "The Resurrection Kernel," 117 n. 19.

the presence of Jesus, but also a knowledge of this presence on the part of his disciples. This recognition comes in the Eucharistic action (i.e., "the *breaking* of the bread") and signifies Christ's dynamic personal presence to the community of believers in their celebration of the great commemorative action of his redemptive love: in their remembering, believers recognize the very person of Christ in the midst of the sacramental action for which they are giving thanks.

Christ is present in similar ways even in today's Eucharistic celebrations: in coming to and going forth; in the explanation of the Scriptures; in the accompanying theological reflection; most especially, in the breaking of the bread.[15] Within Catholic circles, a special reverence is given to the presence of Christ in the person of the priest, who consecrates the Eucharistic species. Since Vatican II emphasis has also been placed on the presence of Christ in the worshipping community. While these various presences of Christ in the Liturgy do not exist in tension with each other in and of themselves (How can Christ exist in conflict with himself?), it is understandable that, for various reasons, persons or communities of differing spiritualities might wish to emphasize one mode of Christ's presence over another (e.g., his presence in the Word over his presence in the community). Be that as it may, one of the identifying characteristics of the Roman Catholic Church is an august theological realism which insists with firm religious conviction that, in the Eucharistic celebration, the bread and wine are actually changed into the body and blood of the Risen Lord.[16] While "transubstantiation" is the term which, since its inception in the twelfth century,[17] has gained the widest acceptance in

---

[15] For the different modes of Christ's presence in the Eucharist, see Vatican Council II, *Sacrosanctum concilium*, no. 7 [*CDD*, 9-10]; Flannery, *Vatican Council II*, 4-5; SCR, *Eucharisticum mysterium* , chap. 1 part E [*AAS* 59 (1967): 547]; English translation: Flannery, *Vatican Council II*, 109.

[16] For the clarities and obscurities in this affirmation, see Karl Rahner, "The Presence of Christ in the Sacrament of the Lord's Supper," chap. in *Theological Investigations*, vol. 4, *More Recent Writings*, trans. Kevin Smyth (London: Darton, Longman and Todd, 1974), 287-311.

[17] The term was first employed by Roland Bandinelli (the future Pope Alexander III) before 1153. From the twelfth century on it appeared increasingly in ecclesiastical documents (see below 156 n. 18). See William J. McDonald, gen. ed. *The New Catholic Encyclopedia* (New York: McGraw-Hill, 1967), s.v. "Transubstantiation," by C. Vollert.

The Bread Kernel

Catholic circles to describe this transformation, it must be remembered that, as with all theological terms, it too is limited by the capacity of the philosophical assumptions which support it, in this case the Aristotelian notions of substance and attribute.[18] While the tradition must remain open to new possibilities for expressing the mystery of the transformation which takes place during the words of consecration, it must also be aware of the philosophical limitations which any new formulation will necessarily bring with it.[19] Special care, moreover, must be taken not to discard a well-tried formulation solely in the name of theological experimentation. To be sure, it would be much more useful to the Church if the theologian were to view new formulations in conjunction with the old, being aware at all times, of course, of the various philosophical limitations of each, and of the particular beliefs which each, in its own time, originally intended to negate. In this way, the Church would not limit the mystery of the Eucharist to the assumptions of any one philosophical school or theological formulation.

---

[18] Aristotle deals with the concepts of substance and attribute in his *Categories*, a work that had been translated into Latin by Boethius in the sixth century, which formed a part of the *Logica vetus* (i.e., Old Logic), and which was known in the West long before the twelfth century. In the late-twelfth and thirteenth centuries, the Old Logic was supplemented by other entries of Aristotle through Arab translators. See Principe, *Introduction to Patristic and Medieval Theology*, 130-31, 251. Generally speaking, the medieval discussion on substance and attribute takes place within a theological context (e.g., the Incarnation of Christ, transubstantiation) and provides no new insights that can be considered an improvement on Aristotle. They amount to nothing more than variations upon Aristotelian themes. See Paul Edwards, ed., *The Encyclopedia of Philosophy* (New York: Macmillan, 1967), s.v. "Substance and Attribute," by D.J. O'Connor.

[19] For the official magisterial use of the term "transubstantiation," see Denz.-Schön., nos. 802 [430], 860 [465], 1642 [877]. According to the latter passage from the Council of Trent's "Decree on the Most Holy Eucharist," the conversion of the bread and wine into the body and blood of Christ is "appropriately and properly" (*conveniter et proprie*) called transubstantiation. Since the development of a more precise formulation using different philosophical categories is not specifically addressed, the possibility would seem to remain an open issue for Catholic theology. As recent as 1965, however, Paul VI insisted that terms such as "transignification" (i.e., a change in meaning) and "transfinalization" (i.e., a change in purpose) did not sufficiently explain the real presence. See *Mysterium fidei*, nos. 10-12 [*AAS* 57 (1965): 755-56]; English translation: *The Pope Speaks* 10 (no. 4, 1965): 311-12.

(3) The Eucharist as Sacrifice. When discussing the way in which the Eucharistic celebration participates in the sacrifice on Calvary, the tendency, in Catholic circles, has been to emphasize the eternal aspect of Christ's redemptive act and its ability to enter the realm of history in whatever manner and whatever moment in time. Hence, the origin of the well-known phrase: "The bloody sacrifice of Calvary is made present in the Mass in an unbloody way."[20] The great strength of such an expression is that it joins the action of the Mass to Christ's sacrifice on the cross without turning the former into a historical reenactment of the latter. Despite the accusations of the sixteenth-century reformers, the Catholic position has always affirmed the unique, unrepeatable nature of the event of Calvary.[21] In fact, it is precisely because Christ's death extends beyond the bounds of time that it may now be invoked at any point along the continuum of history. Rather than a reenactment of Calvary, the celebration of the Eucharist is a sacramental realization of what, by all counts, is the veritable culmination of the whole of salvation history. Indeed, what needs to be brought out more in the discussion of the sacrificial aspects of the Eucharist is the way in which Christ's redemptive offering on Calvary is made present not only in its reality as an event, but also in the two conditions relating to it by way of cause and effect, i.e., the Incarnation and the Resurrection. That is to say that the redemptive truth of Christ's bloody death presupposes both the reality of his becoming a man (the former could not have existed without the latter) and its causal relationship to his being raised on Easter morning by the power of the Father. In this respect, the contours of Christ's redemption of humanity encompasses his entire life — from the manger to the empty tomb — and are made present substantially in the Church's celebration of the Eucharist.[22] In the

---

[20] For the various theories of how this takes place (e.g., destruction, mystery and oblation), see Ott, *Fundamentals of Catholic Dogma*, 410-12.
[21] Schmaus, *The Church as Sacrament*, 108-9.
[22] While Christians should therefore understand their own participation in Christ's redemptive mission as occurring throughout the whole of their lives, it is affirmed most profoundly when they gather for the Eucharistic banquet. In the words of the Second Vatican Council: "As often as the sacrifice of the cross by which 'Christ our Pasch is sacrificed' (1 Cor 5:7) is celebrated on the altar, the work of our redemption is carried out." See *Lumen gentium*, no. 3 [*CDD*, 95]; English translation: Flannery, *Vatican Council II*, 351.

dramatic action of every Mass, Christ's becoming man, his dying on the cross, and his rising from the dead, engage all who partake of the bread that is his body and the wine which is his blood. It is in receiving the body and blood of the Risen Lord in the Eucharistic species that the faithful receive the effects of Christ's redemptive action and are able to carry on his ministry of healing and teaching.[23]

THE BREAD KERNEL

From what has been said, the fundamental principle of the Eucharist ("The Bread Kernel") may be described as a symbolic prophetic action performed by Christ, in the Spirit, through the Church which, effected by the eating and drinking of bread and wine duly consecrated by God's ordained minister, makes present for the community of believers, down through history, and in the form of a sacred meal, the definitive redemptive action of God's love for all of humanity. The scope of this saving event encompasses the whole of Christ's life on earth and manifests itself in the close interrelation of the threefold notion of Eucharist as banquet, presence, and sacrifice. These aspects of the one Eucharistic mystery, which complement each other and should not be understood in isolation, provide the necessary inner logic to show how, in one simple liturgical action, the one redemptive action of Christ can be made present in its cause (i.e., the Incarnation), in its reality (i.e., Christ's death on Calvary), and in its effects (i.e., the Risen Christ). That is to say that, in the breaking of the bread, the Risen Christ becomes our bread and wine, just as these elements are themselves transformed into the body and blood of the Risen Christ. To receive this food is to participate in the sacred meal which Christ shared with his apostles on the night before his death. To partake of his body and blood is to taste beforehand the delicacies of the heavenly banquet over which Jesus himself, even now, presides.

---

[23] That is to say that the work of redemption is accomplished in us in a special way through the Eucharist, the participation in and reception of which enables us to manifest the mystery of Christ and his Church more clearly. See Vatican Council II, *Sacrosanctum concilium*, no. 2 [*CDD*, 3-4]; English translation: Flannery, *Vatican Council II*, 1.

From the above formulation, a number of important corollaries arise:

(1) The mystery of the Eucharist is not bound by the capacity of the philosophical and theological concepts which seek to penetrate its meaning. While a particular doctrinal formulation (including the present one) may be defined as an orthodox expression of the Church's teaching, it could never be said to fully exhaust the meaning of the mystery itself. In this regard, the Church must be ever aware of new ways of understanding the mystery of Christ's action in the breaking of the bread and the drinking of the cup, while, at the same time, paying heed to those well-tried formulas which have served it well in the authentic proclamation of the faith.[24]

(2) While the Risen Christ is present to the Church in any number of ways, he is recognized by its members most profoundly "in the breaking of the bread." The Eucharist is thus the center of the Church's life — the point around which all else revolves. It is when celebrating this sacrament that the Church is at home and most itself. Deprived of this special source of strength and spiritual sustenance, the Church would find it difficult, if not impossible, to survive.[25]

(3) Although it is primarily a communal celebration, the Eucharist can nurture (and, indeed, cannot do without) an intense

---

[24] In this respect, the term "transubstantiation" is an orthodox formulation of the Catholic faith, but does not, in and of itself, exhaust the full meaning of the mystery of Christ's presence in the consecrated Eucharistic species. The possibility therefore remains open for: (1) other formulations to develop over time and be incorporated into the tradition that will express the mystery more fully and (2) other formulations that will capture certain aspects of the mystery more fully and which can then be used in conjunction with the more traditional expressions. See above 141 n. 19. For a postmodern reading of the term "transubstantiation," see David Crownfield, "The Seminal Trace: Presence, Difference, and Transubstantiation." *Journal of the American Academy of Religion* 59 (1991): 361-71.

[25] For the Last Supper in relation to the foundation of the Church, see Powell, *The Mystery of the Church*, 96-98. For the Eucharist as the summit and source from which all the Church's power flows, see Vatican Council II, *Sacrosanctum concilium*, no. 10 [CDD, 11-12]; Flannery, *Vatican Council II*, 6. See also CIC, can. 897 [AAS 75/2 (1983): 163]; English translation: *Code of Canon Law: Latin-English Edition*, (Washington, D.C.: Canon Law Society of America, 1983), 337.

private devotion. The relationship between the individual and communal dimensions of the sacrament should be understood as inclusive and mutually affirming. That is to say that the Eucharist can truly be a communal celebration only if the individuals forming a part of the celebration receive an internal affirmation of the reality and importance of their own personal relationship to the Risen Christ. Private devotions, in turn, are significant in that they give the individual a deeper awareness of the mystery of Christ's redemptive presence and action in the Eucharistic celebration. While tensions are bound to exist, the overall relationship between private and communal devotion should be one which ultimately gives rise to balanced spiritual growth.[26]

(4) As grains of wheat are kneaded into a single loaf and as grapes are pressed and fermented into wine, so too, the Eucharist draws individuals from disparate walks of life and transforms them into a unified body of believers. As the source of Christian unity, the Eucharist affirms the relation of harmony which should exist between believers. To receive the Eucharist in the midst of interior division of soul (i.e., personal sin) or exterior division in the family, community, or society at large (i.e., social sin) denigrates the worth of Christ's sacred action and trivializes the mystery for which it stands. This is true especially in the case of that false irenicism which often exists in the mutual relationships between Catholics and their Protestant brethren.[27]

(5) As a foretaste of the heavenly banquet, the Eucharistic celebration realizes on earth, for the few moments during which the consecrated species has been received by and remains with the

---

[26] It was probably an excessive focus on private Eucharistic devotion in popular piety in the period immediately prior to the Second Vatican Council which led to its demise in many sectors of the post-Conciliar Church. In any case, Eucharistic devotions, both public and private are encouraged by the Church, provided they follow the norms established by legitimate authority. See Vatican Council II, *Sacrosanctum concilium*, no. 13 [*CDD*, 13]; English translation: Flannery, *Vatican Council II*, 7; SCR, *Eucharisticum mysterium*, chap. III, part I [*ASS* 59 (1967): 569]; English translation: Flannery, *Vatican Council II*, 132.

[27] For the Eucharist as the sacrament of Christian unity, see O'Neill, *Meeting Christ in the Sacraments*, 178-80. See also Vatican Council II, *Unitatis redintegratio*, no. 2 [*CDD*, 245]; English translation: Flannery, *Vatican Council II*, 453.

worshipping community, the reign of God on earth. It thus manifests the eschatological orientation of God's people who, through their reception of the Eucharist, anticipate the full establishment of God's reign of peace and justice at the consummation of time. In this respect, the Eucharist gives the believing community a glimpse of the happiness in God which they were intended from all eternity to possess.[28]

(6) As already implied in the statement that Christ's redemptive action in the breaking of the bread is present in its cause (i.e., the Incarnation), its reality (i.e., Calvary), and its effects (i.e., the Risen Lord), the Eucharist is related to the whole of theology. That is to say that Christ is just as much the Lord of theology as he is the Lord of history, and that there exists a particular Eucharistic dimension to every theological discipline — dogmatic, moral, ascetical, mystical, as well as sacramental and liturgical. In this respect, the fundamental principle of the theology of the Eucharist provides a way of looking at the various disciplines of theology that promises to unify what all too often appears to be a field of unrelated enterprises with little bearing on life as it is really lived.[29] Here, as in all else that has been discussed thus far, religious have much to offer — and also much to learn.

THE EUCHARIST AND RELIGIOUS

In their dedication to the Lord through the vows, religious seek to emulate the life led by Christ when he walked the earth. They do so, not as an end in itself, but because such dedication gives a special witness to the presence of Christ in the life of the Church today and in the world at large. Among the deepest yearnings of the sincere and faithful religious is to be chaste as Christ was chaste; poor as Christ was poor; obedient as Christ was

---

[28] Galot, "Pasto escatologico," 797-99.

[29] In this respect, the image in the *Didache* of the broken bread that "was scattered upon the mountains, but was brought together and became one" (chap. 9) has implications not only for the Church as a mystical corporate entity, but also for its ongoing theological reflection. See *Apostolic Fathers I*, Loeb Classical Library, 322-23. On the unity of theology, see Thomas Aquinas, *Summa theologiae*, I, q. 1, a. 3.

The Bread Kernel

obedient.[30] These yearnings take on special significance when religious participate in the sacramental commemoration of Christ's passion and death. There, the evangelical nature of Christ's entire life shines through with matchless clarity, encouraging religious to make the Eucharist the center of their lives and to embody in their own faithful living out of the vows its threefold spiritual significance of banquet, presence, and sacrifice.[31]

Through their vows, religious seek to affirm the transient nature of the present world and point to the ultimate fulfillment of God's reign at the end of time when all of humanity will be invited to partake in the great heavenly banquet. This eschatological dimension of their lives frees them from false pretensions and enables them to enter into fellowship with others on the basic level of their common humanity. In their chastity, which puts them in touch with the loneliness which all people share at the bottom of their hearts, in their poverty, which forces them to confront their human frailties in a more immediate way, in their obedience, which teaches them to put the will of God before their own, religious are constantly inviting others to be aware of the bond of fellowship which all men and women share by virtue of their common humanity.[32]

Through their vows, religious are thus called to be present to others as when Christ walked the earth. Free from the obligations and cares of supporting and raising a family, religious can empty themselves in such a way that they can be present to the person before them as if, at that particular moment, he or she was the only person in existence. Emptying themselves of the goods of marriage in their vow of chastity, of attachment to material goods in

---

[30] In the words of the Second Vatican Council: "...Mother Church rejoices that she has within herself many men and women who pursue more closely the Savior's self-emptying and show it forth more clearly." See *Lumen gentium*, no. 42 [CDD, 173]; English translation: Flannery, *Vatican Council II*, 401.

[31] The Church is most clearly herself while celebrating the Eucharist. See Powell, *The Mystery of the Church*, 151. This is especially true for religious, whose vows deeply reflect and resonate with the threefold Eucharistic significance of banquet, presence, and sacrifice.

[32] The eschatological character of religious life is dealt with specifically in Vatican Council II, *Lumen gentium*, no. 44 [CDD, 176-77]; English translation: Flannery, *Vatican Council II*, 404. See also Powell, *The Mystery of the Church*, 214.

their vow of poverty, of their own private desires in their vow of obedience, religious make room for others to encounter in them the friendship of Christ, who relates to others with no hidden agenda or ulterior motives. That is to say that religious keep alive the presence of Christ in a world that still, more often than not, fails to recognize him.[33]

Religious also seek to emulate Christ's sacrificial love for others. Their vows make little sense outside of the understanding that they are charisms of the Church given to particular individuals and communities for the purpose of serving God's people during their journey through life on their way to God's Kingdom. Religious are thus asked to embrace Christ's dramatic emptying of self as the pattern of their own life of service for God's people. They live in chastity, poverty, and obedience for no other reason than to make the redemptive sacrifice of Christ present in concrete circumstances in the world today. In this respect, they seek to become other Christs to those whom God has given them to love in this life. That is not to say that one may not be "another Christ" in any other state or walk of life (e.g., single, married, priestly), but only that religious seek to do so by embracing the radical lifestyle which Christ himself chose to live. By remaining faithful to their call to live the evangelical counsels, religious present the love of Christ to the world in a truly unique and visible way.[34]

To the extent that they nourish the bonds of fellowship among themselves and others, reveal the presence of the Lord in their midst, and offer themselves in humble service to those in need of God's love, religious extend the influence of the Eucharist in the world and help to make visible in their particular historical

---

[33] The presence of Christ communicated by religious is closely tied to their free decision to imitate the life style that he made his own while on this earth. See Vatican Council II, *Lumen gentium*, no. 44 [*CDD*, 176-77]; Flannery, *Vatican Council II*, 404. By trying to make Christ's poverty, chastity, and obedience their own, religious offer the world a concrete symbol of God's divine redemptive action. This action is concretized for religious and all members of the Church in the celebration of the liturgy.

[34] "... the very practice of evangelical counsels is to be animated and governed by this charity." See Vatican Council II, *Perfectae caritatis*, no. 6 [*CDD*, 338]; English translation: Flannery, *Vatican Council II*, 614.

circumstances the reality, meaning, and ongoing hope of Christ's redemptive mystery. In this respect, they become "eucharist" — bread and wine; body and blood — for others, encouraging all they meet to share in their common thanksgiving around the table of the Lord. There, "in the breaking of the bread," they seek to recognize both the presence and the significance of The Risen One in their lives. Such a recognition brings religious to place the Eucharist more and more at the center of their lives and, in doing so, enables them to acknowledge the presence of their Master even on the periphery of their vision.[35]

CONCLUSION

This chapter has sought a fundamental principle of the Eucharist that is both internally consistent and relevant to the whole of theology. After having rooted this principle in the venerable tradition of Jewish prophetic symbolism, it focused on the complementary notions of "banquet," "presence," and "sacrifice" as the most appropriate way in which both the sound doctrinal teaching and the mystery of the Eucharist may be preserved. Described as a symbolic prophetic action performed by Christ, in the Spirit, through the Church, the principle affirms the efficacious nature of priestly consecration which gives each historical community of believers the definitive redemptive action of God's love in the form of a sacred meal. It is in the breaking of the bread and drinking from the cup that believers, down through the centuries, have recognized this presence of the Risen Christ in their lives. Such a recognition heightens the bonds of fellowship among believers as they dedicate themselves more firmly

---

[35] Jesus' welcome extended to those from the periphery of first century Jewish society (e.g., lepers, tax collectors, prostitutes). By nourishing themselves at the Lord's table and by following him in his radical way of life, religious hope to extend the same kind of welcome to others. On the liberating aspects of the Eucharistic celebration, see Leech, *Experiencing God: Theology as Spirituality*, 294-98. See also Giovanna Della Croce, "La communità eucaristica," *Vita consacrata* 10 (1974): 480-82; Susan Wood, "The Eucharist: Heart of Religious Community," *Review for Religious* 46 (1987): 178-86.

to continuing the ministry of Christ's life of service to his people.

Religious have a special role to play in this regard. In their love of the Lord expressed through their individual and communal dedication to the life of the vows, they find in the Eucharist the source of their spiritual strength and nourishment. In their desire to live as Christ did when he walked the earth, they find in their ritual breaking of the bread and drinking from the cup the unique reminder that, like their Lord and Master, they are called to offer themselves to the Father as a living sacrifice in such a way that their lives will reveal the presence of Christ to those whom they are called to serve. This call to discipleship leads many to the realization that they are called to embody the same kind of spiritual strength and nourishment, deeply personal presence to others, and sacrificial emptying of self that Christ's ritual thanksgiving symbolizes and promises to effect.

In the final analysis, the fundamental principle of the theology of the Eucharist ("The Bread Kernel") offers both believer and non-believer alike a focal point around which they can seek to understand the meaning of the Christian mystery. For the believer, it not only highlights some underlying themes essential to the Catholic faith, but also provides a handy creedal synthesis with definite repercussions for the whole of theology. For the unbeliever, it helps to explain the reason for the highly sacramental character of Catholic worship and presents in coherent fashion some of the most basic reasons for the believer's insistence on the close relation between the events of Holy Thursday, Good Friday, and Easter Sunday morning. If nothing else, the fundamental principle of the theology of the Eucharist is a reflection on the mystery of the Christ event that is, at one and the same time, both continuous with the Catholic tradition and sensitive to the fact that this very tradition must be interpreted anew for every generation seeking to understand the meaning of the action celebrated by Christ "in the breaking of the bread." Not to do so would amount to nothing less than an insensitivity to the ongoing presence of Christ's Spirit in the Church and the significance of what must be numbered among some of Christ's final words to his disciples, "Do this in memory of me."

11

THE MORALITY KERNEL

Is there a fundamental principle of moral theology? The answer to this question depends on the way in which one understands the relationship between moral theology and other theological disciplines, on the one hand (e.g., Trinitarian theology, Christology, ecclesiology, sacramentology, eschatology), and its various internal subdivisions, on the other (e.g., fundamental and special moral). Also important is the way in which one understands the nature of Christian revelation and the relationship it shares with the epistemological foundations of human reason. These relationships form the contours of moral theology as it is known today. To overlook any of them runs the risk of removing the discipline from its larger theological context and isolating it from the roots of the Christian faith.

THE REUNIFICATION OF THEOLOGY

The last five hundred years have witnessed a peculiar breakup of theology into numerous separated disciplines and related fields.[1] Theologians have become "specialists" in very small,

---

[1] For the historical development of this breakdown, see Servais (Th.) Pinckaers, *Les sources de la morale chrétienne: sa méthode, son contenu, son histoire*, Etudes d'éthique chrétienne, no. 14 (Fribourg: Editions universitaires, 1985), 258-62. For a description of the disciplines themselves, see Latourelle, *Theology: The Science of Salvation*, 97-151.

keenly defined areas of knowledge and have often lost sight of the larger role their expertise plays in the service of the whole of theology. Rooted, on the one hand, in the scholastic decadence of the late medieval and Counter Reformation periods, where theological distinctions often became nothing more than extended logical deductions, thus losing their vigor and, ultimately, their credibility as valid starting points of theological inquiry, and, on the other hand, in the Enlightenment's enthronement of univocal reasoning as the accepted norm of all scientific (even theological) investigation, theology today exists in a fragmented state with little hope of returning to its earlier integrated shape.[2]

The task before today's theologians is not an uncritical return, but a calculated retrieval of those elements in the Catholic theological tradition which emphasize the interrelated, cohesive nature of any systematized understanding of the human person in his or her relation to divine revelation.[3] Such an endeavor must focus not only on the level of content, but also on that of method, the former being influenced, indeed, partially determined by the latter. For moral theology, such an endeavor means taking a good hard look at the history of its origins as a separate theological discipline, with special emphasis on the various shifts in theological methodology which have made it possible.[4]

---

[2] These changes in theology roughly parallel the growth in Western culture of the scientific method and are rooted in what one author describes as the "fallacy of imitative form," i.e., the attempt to shape theology along the lines of empirical science. See Louth, *Discerning the Mystery*, 9-11.

[3] One of the primary aims of this effort will be to bridge and eventually to reintegrate the aims of theology (i.e., the explication of the truths of revelation) with those of spirituality (i.e., the sanctification of the human person). For the relationship between theology and spirituality, see Duquoc, "Theology and Spirituality," 46-51; Jones, "Spirituality and Theology," 161-76; Louth, *Discerning the Mystery*, 1-16, 132-47.

[4] Important ground work for this task has been laid by the various recent attempts at a history of moral theology, among which include J. Gallagher, *Time Past, Time Future: An Historical Study of Catholic Moral Theology* (New York: Paulist Press, 1990); Karl-Heinz Kleber, *Einführung in die Geschichte der Moraltheologie* (Passau: Passavia Universitätsverlag, 1984); John Mahoney, *The Making of Moral Theology: A Study of the Roman Catholic Tradition* (Oxford: Clarendon Press,1987); Pinckaers, *Les sources de la morale chrétienne: sa méthode, son contenu, son histoire*; Louis Vereecke, *De Guillaume d'Ockham à Saint Alphonse de Liguori: Études d'histoire de la théologie morale moderne 1300-1787,*

The Morality Kernel

ALLEGORY, SYLLOGISM, AND INDUCTION

One way of describing these changes is in terms of a movement from allegory to syllogism to induction, a progression which roughly parallels the well-known historical succession from monastic theology to its later scholastic counterpart, and finally to the birth of modern scientific method. This evolution is itself a function of the more fundamental epistemological changes involved in the movement from Neoplatonism to Aristotelianism to Nominalism as the predominant philosophical outlook of Western culture.[5]

Best exemplified by its well-known use of the fourfold senses of Scripture — the literal (i.e., relating to history), the allegorical (i.e., relating to Christ and his Church), the tropological (i.e., relating to the moral life), and the anagogical (i.e., relating to the end things) — monastic theology saw no conflict between the literal sense of Scripture and any of its spiritual meanings.[6] Any given word or verse could reveal to its reader any one or more of these dimensions of God's revealed Word, all of which were considered continuous both with the literal sense and with each other. Here, history, Christology, ecclesiology, morality and eschatology were all thought of as intimately tied to one another. Speculative and practical reason, moreover, were hardly distinguished, let alone dichotomized as in later centuries.[7]

While recognizing the existence of the various spiritual

Bibliotheca historica Congregationis SSmi Redemptoris, vol. 12 (Rome: Collegium S. Alfonso de Urbe, 1986); R.E.O. White, *The Changing Continuity of Christian Ethics*, vol. 2: *The Insights of History* (Exeter: The Paternoster Press, 1981).

[5] For a depiction of this evolution within the context of Western society's changing world views, see Wildiers, *The Theologian and his Universe*, 59-78, 130-60, 213-35.

[6] For one of the best contemporary treatments of the fourfold senses of Scripture, see Henri de Lubac, *Exégèse médiévale: les quatre sens de l'écriture*, 2:643-56.

[7] Although evidence of this distinction existed in such widely read philosophical and theological sources as Augustine's *De trinitate*, 12.4 [*CCSL*, 50:358; *PL* 42:989-90] and Boethius' *Philosophiae consolatio*, 4.6 [*CCL* 94:78-85; *PL* 63:813-22], monastic authors made very little practical use of it since they presupposed a natural hierarchical continuity between the two spheres of knowledge.

senses, scholastic theology focused instead on the explanation of the literal sense through the use of syllogistic reasoning.[8] The latter, in fact, eventually became separated from the text of Scripture, which ultimately found itself introduced into scholastic argumentation only as an "authority" ("a proof text," if you will) to support an already previously established "major" and "minor" premise with their logically deduced conclusion.[9] While theology was still looked upon as intricately one, the signs of a breakup were already beginning to appear. Generally speaking, only the literal sense of Scripture could be introduced in a strictly theological line of argumentation; the spiritual senses, by way of contrast, were relegated to the realm of the spiritual edification of the faithful.[10] The distinction between speculative and practical reason, moreover, was made more often, but only in terms of its object, with the former focusing on the contemplation of divine things and the latter on concrete moral actions.[11]

The rise of Nominalism and the systematic application of the newly revered principle of parsimony (Ockham's razor) witnessed a breakdown of the high scholastic synthesis and the consequent proliferation of theological disciplines.[12] Valuing only inductive reasoning as an adequate form of human knowledge, it helped create an atmosphere where a voluntaristic faith in an authoritative divine law became the only compatible theological response to its basic philosophical tenets. The result was a rupture in the relation between nature and supernature, which mani-

---

[8] See Thomas Domanyi, *Der Römerbriefkommentar des Thomas von Aquin: Ein Beitrag zur Untersuchung seiner Auslegungsmethoden*, Basler und Berner Studien zur historischen und systematischen Theologie, no. 39 (Bern: Peter Lang, 1979), 77-80, 267.

[9] For the evolution of scholastic forms, see M.-D. Chenu, *Toward Understanding Saint Thomas*, 3d ed. trans. A.-M. Landry and D. Hughes (Chicago: Regnery Press, 1964), 80-96.

[10] Aquinas, for example, recognizes the existence of the spiritual senses, but states explicitly that a theological argument can be drawn from the literal sense alone. See *Summa theologiae*, I, q. 1, a. 10, ad 1m.

[11] See, for example, Aquinas' discussion of the relationship between higher and lower reason, *Summa theologiae*, I, q. 79, a. 9.

[12] For the influence of Ockham's notorious razor upon the medieval scholastic synthesis, see Gilson, *History of Christian Philosophy in the Middle Ages*, 498-99.

fested itself in both a further estrangement of the theological sciences themselves, and a real dichotomy in the nature, function, and goals of speculative and practical reason.[13] This process was further enforced by the rise of Cartesian dualism and the philosophical agenda of the Enlightenment which, by strengthening the bonds between the inductive method and univocal thought, turned theological inquiry into a purely mathematical endeavor, exemplified most clearly in the widespread replacement of the Christian concept of the Trinitarian God with that of the mechanized God of the Deists.[14] The Kantian break between pure and practical reason represents the final outcome of this centuries-long process.[15]

The point being made in this short summary of the historical movement in theological methodology from allegory to syllogism to induction is that the specialized discipline traditionally known as "moral theology" is a development of relatively recent vintage in the Church's theological tradition (a matter of a few hundred years) and can be properly understood only in the context of its relationship to the rise of Nominalism in Western thought, the Enlightenment's enthronement of univocal reasoning, and the ultimate breakdown in the relationship between speculative and practical reason. A fundamental principle of moral theology should thus take into account not only the philosophical and theological context of its own origins, but also the particular contours of moral reasoning used in the ages preceding the period of its own appearance.[16] Foremost among these elements should

---

[13] For the effects of Ockham's thought on Christian moral discourse, see Mahoney, *The Making of Moral Theology*, 182-84. See also Lucan Freppert, *The Basis of Morality According to William Ockham* (Chicago: Franciscan Herald Press, 1988), 171-81; Pinckaers, *Les sources du morale chrétienne*, 244-62.

[14] For Cartesian dualism (i.e., the separation of cosmology and natural theology) and the influence of Enlightened deistic thought upon Christian self-understanding, see Wildiers, *The Theologian and His Universe*, 148-55.

[15] For the rift in Kantian thought between pure and practical reason, see R.E.O. White, *The Insights of History*, 239-40.

[16] Moral reasoning, in other words, does not take place outside the context of some ongoing tradition of moral discourse. "The person outside all traditions lacks sufficient rational resources for enquiry and *a fortiori* for enquiry into what tradition is to be rationally preferred." See McIntyre, *Whose Justice? Which Rationality?*, 367.

be the recognition of the moral implications of not just a particular part of theology (i.e., moral theology), but of the entire theological enterprise itself. There is, in other words, an ethical dimension to every dogmatic statement — and vice versa.

THEOLOGY AND LIBERATION

The above insight has peculiar relevance for what in recent years has been perceived as a serious tension existing between the proponents of classical Catholic theology, on the one hand, and those of liberation theology, on the other. While the former have often been criticized for being out of touch with the needs and sensibilities of the people they serve and for burdening them with rules and regulations based on outmoded scholastic distinctions, the latter have themselves been accused of placing those needs outside the bounds of the traditional interpretative norms of the Catholic tradition (i.e., the magisterium) and of adopting certain questionable secular methods to achieve their ends (i.e., Marxist social analysis). Putting aside the question of whether or not such a tension is healthy for the Church in its present historical moment (both points of view have much to offer in the debate), one sometimes cannot help but feel that the tension itself is ill-conceived or, at least, poorly articulated by both sides. That is to say that the basis for the tension seems to be rooted not so much in what some might call the inability of classical theology to respond to the needs of the impoverished or what others might call the failure of liberation theology to meet the demands of orthodoxy, but rather in the tendency both sides have to overlook the important ethical implications of the Church's classical doctrinal statements.[17]

---

[17] One cautious yet welcomed attempt at locating the common ground between these two approaches is provided by SCDF, *Instructio de libertate christiana et liberatione* [*AAS* 79 (1987): 554-99]; English translation: "Instruction on Christian Freedom and Liberation," 461-97. This document points out the ethical dimensions of the Church's theological formulations and their implications for both human solidarity and the dignity of the human person.

The Morality Kernel

There are, in fact, not one but at least two different ways of doing liberation theology: (1) the approach of social conscientization, which identifies the experience of the oppressed as virtually the sole valuative norm in the ongoing redemption of humanity and (2) the approach of classical adaptation, which finds room within the traditional doctrinal statements of the Catholic faith for the experience of the oppressed to find validation. The main difference between these two approaches is that the former seeks the voice of God directly and immediately in the response of the poor to very particular, concrete circumstances, while the latter accepts the normative value of the classical formulations (e.g., the Trinity, the Incarnation, the real presence) as a given and uses it to direct the social experience of the oppressed to constructive ends.[18]

Needless to say, each approach has its own particular strengths and weaknesses. The danger with social conscientization is that the experience of the oppressed might never be referred back to the roots of the Christian experience. This could lead to possible distortions of the truth in the search for social justice, as well as possible manipulation by the interpreters of that experience.[19] With classical adaptation, on the other hand, the situation of the oppressed might never be directly averted to, thus allowing the formulations of classical theology to be used by a powerful elite as an ideological tool to further enhance its own structure of power.[20] When compared with each other, conscientization seems more prone to quick, decisive action, while that of classical adap-

---

[18] Yet another classification is provided by Juan Luis Segundo, "Two Theologies of Liberation," in *Liberation Theolgy: A Documentary History*, ed. Alfred T. Hennelly (Maryknoll, N.Y.: Orbis Books, 1990), 353-66.

[19] In this respect, true human liberation can occur only when the process of conscientization takes place within the context of the traditional Christian narrative. See Carlos Mesters, "The Use of the Bible in Christian Communities of the Common People," in *Liberation Theology: A Documentary History*, ed. Alfred T. Hennelly (Maryknoll, N.Y.: Orbis Books, 1990), 14-28.

[20] To avoid this Church leaders must challenge those in positions of power, to reintegrate faith and praxis wherever they have diverged. They will do this by bringing the ethical implications of the classical theological formulations to the fore and by calling for economic and political structures to be in accord with the dignity of the human person.

tation would take a slower, more discerning course. The latter, moreover, would tend to coincide more fully with the tenets of orthodox doctrine, while the former would be more susceptible to the influence of traditionally heterodox teaching. Be that as it may, both need to emphasize further the theologian's need to be aware of the various preconceptions which he or she brings to an issue. To be conscious of such assumptions would enable him or her to break through the rigid classifications of theology, compensate for the weaknesses operative in either approach, and place theology more fully at the service of the people.

THE MORALITY KERNEL

Given all that has been said thus far, a statement of the fundamental principle of moral theology ("The Morality Kernel") would read as follows: Moral theology deals with the ethical implications of all theological and philosophical statements affirmed by the Catholic tradition. It does so by: (1) analyzing the changing methods and contents of that tradition, (2) listening sincerely to the experience of the people of God in their concrete historical circumstances, (3) becoming more deeply aware of the theologian's own assumptions, presuppositions, and prejudices in the matter, and (4) arriving at a concrete judgment as a result of the intense interaction of the previous three. Each element of this process is always allowed to challenge and to receive challenge from another, while at the same time taking special care to preserve the fundamental unity of theology as a whole. To do this, it must itself be keenly aware of its historical origins and development as a theological discipline.

In response to this formulation, the following observations are in order:

(1) The nature of the interaction among the various elements described above will vary in emphasis according to national, regional, and cultural differences, as well as the approaches taken by individual theologians themselves. In this regard, it is important that no single element achieve dominance to the point of

excluding any other. It is also important that the interaction be allowed to take its proper course, but not to the extent of going on indefinitely so as to prevent a judgment on the issue.[21]

(2) When viewed from this perspective, moral theology is not a specialized theological discipline (e.g., as opposed to biblical, historical, or dogmatic theology), but rather the extension of a particular field into the realm of the moral life.[22]

(3) Such an outlook encourages a rearrangement of the traditional understanding of theology as separate disciplines which somehow "fit together" (like pieces of a puzzle) to form an organized and patterned whole. A more appropriate paradigm would be one of concentric circles, with the study of the Scriptures in the center, then moving out respectively to the historical sciences, dogmatic theology (i.e., Trinitarian theology, Christology, ecclesiology, sacramentology), and, finally, moral theology itself.[23]

(4) Even within the traditional discipline of moral theology, the relationship between fundamental and special moral should itself be viewed in a circular manner. That is to say that not only does fundamental have something to contribute to the various

---

[21] In the future, moral theologians will thus be asked to develop the skill of facilitating this process of moral decision making in very specific socio-cultural contexts. They will be able to do so only by integrating their own discipline more and more with the insights of spiritual and pastoral theology. For a useful discussion of pastoral moral guidance and judgment, see Richard M. Gula, *Reason Informed by Faith: Foundations of Catholic Morality* (New York: Paulist Press, 1989), 306-13.

[22] One of the few Catholic moral faculties to have incorporated an interdisciplinary approach into its academic curriculum is the Alphonsian Academy in Rome. The task of this institute is "to work at creating a new moral theology, which would meet the immense needs of priests engaged in the care of souls." See *Academia Alfonsiana: 1957-1982*. (Rome: Pisani, 1982), 59. The full implications of this insight, however, bring out the need in moral faculties not only for specialists in particular fields (e.g., Scripture, Dogma, Church History, Sociology, Philosophy, etc.), but also for generalists who are able to synthesize the insights of the various disciplines into a cohesive synthetic whole.

[23] By seeking out the ethical implications of the Church's theological formulations, moral theologians demonstrate the relevance of Church teaching for its people. According to this model, moral theology is closely related to spirituality (which would seek the spiritual implications of those same formulations) and pastoral theology (which would seek the pastoral).

areas of special moral, but special moral itself has a great deal to say about the way in which fundamental moral should be carried out (e.g., new moral paradigms often arise from attempts to deal with newly emerging personal and social problems).[24]

(5) A means of prioritizing issues, concerns, even conflicts must be developed so as to allow the fullest possible participation by the people of God, while, at the same time, taking into account the concerns presented by the tradition through the interpretative stance taken by the Church magisterium on a given issue. In this respect, moral theologians must take care to preserve that dynamic balance which is indicative of both their pastoral response to the people and their fidelity to those designated as authentic interpreters of God's Word.[25]

(6) Finally, with respect to the two approaches to liberation theology outlined in the previous section (i.e., social conscientization and classical adaptation), the latter reflects a greater concern for the interaction of the various elements outlined above, while the former displays a greater sensitivity to whatever elements which may inadvertently have been omitted. To employ a simple analogy: each approach is a different lan-

---

[24] In this respect, a carefully structured return to case studies as a method of moral inquiry could provide the necessary context within which the relationship between fundamental and special moral theology might be redefined. That is to say that a particular moral case could be studied in the context of the ramifications it would have on every level of ethical reasoning. For the revival of casuistry in contemporary moral discourse, see Albert R. Jonsen and Stephen Toulmin, *The Abuse of Casuistry: A History of Moral Reasoning* (Berkeley: University of California Press, 1988), 304-32.

[25] Guidelines for theologians in their attempt to keep this delicate balance are provided by SCDF, *Instructio de ecclesiali theologi vocatione* [*AAS* 82 (1990): 1550-70]; English translation: "Instruction on the Ecclesial Vocation of the Theologian," *Origins* 20 (1990): 117-26. The vast array of responses to this document includes James Byrne, "Dialogue and Dissent," *The Furrow* 41 (1990): 689-94; Avery Dulles, "The Magisterium, Theology and Dissent," *Origins* 20 (1991): 692-96; Idem, "The Question of Dissent," *The Tablet* 244 (1990): 1033-34; Christian Duquoc, "The Curia Sews It Up," *The Tablet* 244 (1990): 1097-98; Ladislas Orsy, "Magisterium and Theologians: A Vatican Document," *America* 162 (1990): 30-32; Idem, "The Limits of Magisterium," *The Tablet* 244 (1990): 1066-69; Archbishop John Quinn, "Observations on Doctrinal Congregation's Instruction," *Origins* 20 (1990): 201-5. See also my "Dialogue and Dissent II," 303-9.

guage with special idiomatic expressions and rules of grammar and syntax unique to itself. For valuable dialogue to occur, care must be taken to develop a facility with each and to incorporate its insights into the mainstream of moral theology as developed in "The Morality Kernel."[26] Religious, it would seem, have an important role to play in this regard.

RELIGIOUS AND MORAL THEOLOGY

At first glance, one might very well wonder about the appropriateness of discussing the relationship of the religious life to a theological discipline such as moral theology. Why should they be singled out in such a discussion as opposed to those in any other vocational state within the Church? Are they not themselves far removed from many of the burning moral issues in society and the Church today? What kind of a contribution could they possibly bring to these issues?

As probing as such questions appear, they cannot obscure the fact that, traditionally, religious have played an extremely important role in the Church's working out of its moral theological tradition. To substantiate this claim, one need only to point to the role of the Benedictines and Cistercians in the development and preservation of monastic theology, to the Franciscans and Dominicans in the theological syntheses achieved during the scholastic period, or to the role played by the Jesuits and Redemptorists in the casuist approach to moral theology during the modern period.[27]

---

[26] The analogy of language in the dialogue between different philosophical and theological systems is borrowed from Bruce Williams, "Human Rights: A 'Bilingual' Dialogue," TMs [photocopy], pp. 1-3, Simposio Interdisciplinare 'Diritti Umani: Problema Nodale nel Mondo Contemporaneo,' March 9, 1988, Pontifical University of Saint Thomas, Rome.

[27] For the contributions of these orders to Christian moral thought, see F. Vandenbroucke, *Pour l'histoire de la théologie morale: la morale monastique du XIe au XVIe siècle*, Analecta Mediaevalia Namurcensia, vol. 20 (Louvain: Editions Nauwelaerts, 1966), 13-29; Pinckaers, *Les sources de la morale chrétienne*, 244-45, 276-79.

The tack to be taken in this section, however, is slightly different. Rather than focusing on the contributions religious have made to the development of Christian moral thought as a theological discipline (as many as they may be), what will be emphasized here instead are the particular values they, as religious, must simply take for granted as their theological point of departure. Despite the fact that religious differ greatly from order to order and even within themselves from region to region and from age to age, there appear to be some universal values which transcend contingent historical barriers and which should be in some way present at all times, especially in an enterprise as important as moral theology. Each of these values centers upon the meaning of the evangelical counsels.[28]

Firstly, religious bring to moral theology a particular stance towards creation and the beyond (i.e., the world to come). Together, their vows of chastity, poverty, and obedience affirm the fundamental goodness of creation, while at the same time straining toward the ultimate fulfillment of the Kingdom of God. This tension between the already and the not-yet flows from the very essence of the religious vocation and may not be compromised.[29] To the extent that religious convey this tension to others through their actions, attitudes, and words, they remain faithful to that radical commitment to the Lord which the vows seek to express.

Secondly, religious bring to moral theology a genuine understanding of the cost and beauty of love. The asceticism of the vows and the transformation which they can help bring about in a person's life give a very visible witness to that movement from sacrifice to resurrection which forms a part of Christ's own love

---

[28] In this respect, religious are called to bring what they *are* by reason of their vowed life to the specific tasks before them, in the present case, the doing of moral theology. When speaking about religious life, one of the favorite themes of John Paul II is to emphasize the priority of *being* over *doing*. See John Paul II, *Redemptionis donum*, no. 4 [*AAS* 76 (1984): 517-19]; English translation: "Redemptionis Donum: An Expression of Love for Religious," 484-5. See also John Paul II, "La vita religiosa si comprende essenzialmente nella dimensione ecclesiale," no. 6 [*IGP* 6/2:582].

[29] These values are clearly expressed in Vatican Council II, *Lumen gentium*, no. 44 [*CDD*, 176-77]; English translation: Flannery, *Vatican Council II*, 404-5.

The Morality Kernel

for the world. Each of the vows represents something forsaken (sexual pleasure and progeny, the free use of material goods, following one's own will) and something gained (intimacy with God, the provisions of providence, the will of God as one's own).[30] To the extent that religious reveal these aspects of sacrifice and transformation to others, they seek to live out the meaning of their vows to the fullest.

Thirdly, religious bring to moral theology a sense of the social nature of human existence. Their vows are not private possessions, but shared charisms given to the entire community. That is to say that individuals live out their vows in a community which, while respecting the innate dignity of each of its members as persons created in the image of God, calls them to an ever deeper solidarity with all of humanity. To the extent that religious express this sense of shared communal life, they call others to a deeper awareness of the communal nature of their own baptismal promises.[31]

The lives of religious manifest in a concrete manner the moral implications of the Christian life. That is not to say that those in other vocational states (both lay and priestly) cannot manifest similar values and ethical dimensions in their lives; it means only that these aspects are themselves intimately tied to the very meaning of religious life itself. The vows, in other words, give authentic witness to the values of creation and the kingdom, Christ's sacrificial love and resurrected life, the dignity of the human person and the solidarity of God's people. The values

---

[30] With respect to this movement of ascetical transformation, "the profession of the evangelical counsels involves the renunciation of goods that undoubtedly deserve to be highly valued." See Vatican Council II, *Lumen gentium*, no. 46 [CDD, 179]; English translation: Flannery, *Vatican Council II*, 406.

[31] John Paul II refers to "the fundamental communitarian nature of religious life," see *Redemptionis donum*, no. 15 [*AAS* 76 (1984): 543]; English translation: "*Redemptionis Donum*: An Expression of Love for Religious," 499. For other magisterial statements on the importance of the common life for religious, see Vatican Council II, *Perfectae caritatis*, no 15 [CDD, 347-48]; English translation: Flannery, *Vatican Council II*, 620; SCRSI, "Norms for Religious Life," *The Pope Speaks* 28 (1983): 309-11. See also Ernest R. Falardeau, "Religious Life Is a Communion," *Review for Religious* 43 (1984): 65-68; Edward A. Molloy, "The Character of a Religious Community," *Review for Religious* 37 (1978): 748-52.

which religious seek to uphold in their everyday lives are thus meant to be the fundamental points of departure for their entire approach to moral theology. It would be a great tragedy in religious life if such values were simply put on hold or not averted to when doing theology, especially in an area as important as Christian morals. By bringing their life commitments to the forefront of the theological enterprise, and by refusing to compromise them on any level and in any way, religious pay a great service to the Church and its people. They are called to give radical witness to Christ in precisely this way so that others may hear and see the Good News of the Lord.[32]

CONCLUSION

This chapter has sought to place moral theology in the context of its position within the whole of theology. It has done so not only by examining the changing theological methodologies in the Christian tradition (from allegory to syllogism to induction) and the impact that has had on the Christian moral life, but also by pointing out how the current tension between the classical and liberation approaches to theology reflects more a failure to understand the mutual relationship between dogmatic and moral formulations than an irreconcilable clash in their fundamental starting points. In this respect, moral theologians are challenged to delve more deeply into the various assumptions which guide their particular mode of theological inquiry.

In line with this challenge, the fundamental principle of moral theology ("The Morality Kernel") has been shown to be comprised of the interaction of a critical analysis of Church tradition, the experience of the people (with special reference to the poor and the oppressed), and the theologian's awareness of his

---

[32] Their theological integrity may be thought of as yet another way in which religious act as a sign that inspires others to fulfill their Christian duties. See Vatican Council II, *Lumen gentium*, no. 44 [*CDD*, 176]; English translation: Flannery, *Vatican Council II*, 404.

or her own personal investment in the issue at hand. From this interaction, a judgment is formed which states as clearly as possible the appropriate Christian response to the issue in the given circumstances. Each of these elements is necessary for a moral theology that is to be, at one and the same time, both responsive to the needs of the people it serves and faithful to the tradition which gives it life. Only by such an interaction of tradition, experience, and personal investment can new ways of incorporating the continuing experiences of God's people into the tradition of the Church be devised and championed.

Religious have traditionally played an important role in the Church's tradition of moral theology. In the present, they are called on to bring the values affirmed by their vows to the forefront of their examination of the ethical implications of the Catholic theological tradition. The creative tensions between creation and the beyond, between sacrifice and transformation, and between personal dignity and human solidarity, can all do much to move moral theology out of its current deadlock of compromised issues and poorly adapted secular methods. Religious can bring to the discipline that dimension of faith which belongs in any truly theological endeavor, and especially in one as important as the discipline of moral theology.[33] Such is the nature of the radical witness they are called to give.

In the final analysis, the fundamental principle of moral theology is a call for the integration of ecclesiastical tradition, social experience, and the theologian's reflection upon his or her own values. Such an integration is necessary if moral theology is to find its place in the Church once again as a discipline based on authentic teaching, free from inordinate self-interest, and rendered in service for the good of God's people.

---

[33] The following reflection of Albert Dilanni on the prophetic dimension of the religious life is very appropriate when considering the specific role of religious in Catholic moral theology: "Religious must teach by their life that all Christians must be in the world but not of the world; that their greatness will not spring from surrender to the values of the world. If we fail to make a distinction between religious and laity, the significance and identity of the Christian laity is also in danger of being lost." Quoted in Sammon, "The Transformation of Religious Life," 191.

12

THE PRAYER KERNEL

Is there a fundamental principle of prayer? The answer to this question depends on: (1) the relationship of prayer to the whole of theology and (2) whether the various levels of prayer within the Christian tradition are held together by an unbroken, discernible thread of theological unity. These, in turn, depend on the underlying anthropological factors which provide the conditions for the possibility of the hoped for unity. To neglect any one of these factors is to fail to fathom the full significance of prayer for both the personal and social levels of human existence.

THE RELATION OF PRAYER TO THEOLOGY

In its connection to theology, prayer may have: (1) no relation, (2) a supportive, ancillary function, (3) an integral, guiding role, or (4) an absolute identity with it.

Of the above, the first depicts a strict dichotomy between piety and theological inquiry. Here, prayer has absolutely nothing at all to do with a reasoned analysis of the tenets of the Christian faith: theology is utterly rational; *lex orandi* has no relation to *lex credendi*; personal prayer is relegated to the realm of private piety and devotion.[1]

---

[1] This lack of rapport between prayer and theology is yet another reflection of that "dissociation of sensibility" which, manifesting itself at various times in the history of Western culture, culminated in the rationalist project of the Enlightenment. See Louth, *Discerning the Mystery*, 1-16.

The last, in contrast, actually equates theology with prayer. Its proponents often manifest a strong anti-intellectual current by submerging theological reflection in the irrational currents of an unrestrained fideism. In this context, a person seeks to develop his or her relationship with God without any concern for the precise contours of that relationship.[2]

The second stands between these two extremes, but is closer to the first. By assigning to prayer a supportive, ancillary role, it recognizes that, while the scientific discipline of theology must proceed in its analysis of divinely revealed truths according to an organized set of rational principles, a life of prayer strengthens the theologian's adherence to those truths, thus insuring that the theological enterprise remains a journey of faith in search of deeper understanding. In this respect, prayer makes the ongoing enterprise of theology possible, but does not strictly affect its outcome.[3]

The third also stands between these two extremes, but remains closer to the second of them. By giving prayer an integral guiding role in the theological enterprise, it emphasizes the experiential focus of theological reflection. Here, prayer is valued not only for the deeper insights it may uncover about the nature of the divine realities (e.g., the experience of the saints and mystics), but also for the way it brings people together in bonds of human solidarity. In this respect, prayer is a starting point for individual

---

[2] One must not overlook, however, the venerable intellectual tradition of Evagrius of Pontus (d. 399), who understood *theologia* to be nothing more than *theoria*, the contemplation of God: "...if you are a theologian, you pray truly, and if you pray truly, you are a theologian." *Treatise on Prayer*, chap. 60. Cited in Louth, *Discerning the Mystery*, 4. See also *Les leçons d'un contemplatif: le traité de l'oraison de Evagre le Pontique*, trans. I. Hausherr (Paris: Beauchesne, 1960), 85.

[3] This understanding of the relationship between prayer and theology is often reflected in scholastic methodology. Prayer is valued as a means to personal sanctity, but does not play a decisive role in the theologian's attempt to elucidate the content of revelation. In the words of Peter Comestor (d. 1179), "...ita sunt qui orationi magis operam dantes lectioni minus insistunt, et hi sunt claustrales. Sunt alii, qui lectioni invigilant, rarius orantes, et hi sunt scholares" ("There are some who do more praying than reading: they are the cloister dwellers; there are others who spend all their time reading and rarely pray: they are the schoolmen"). See *Sermo* 9 [*PL* 198:1747]. Translation cited in Leclercq, *The Love of Learning and the Desire for God*, 198-99.

and social conscientization, a necessary element for the continuing process of human liberation.[4]

To be specific, of the four possible relationships between prayer and theology, the first describes the dichotomy between prayer and a program in religious studies at a modern secular university; the second, the ancillary connection between prayer and theology as a science in the classical Thomistic sense (*Summa theologiae*, I, q. 1, aa. 1-8);[5] the third, the experiential bond between prayer and mystical theology (e.g., as in the thought of Bonaventure and Meister Eckhart), on the one hand, and between social conscientization and human solidarity as found in many of today's theologies of liberation, on the other;[6] the fourth, the unreflective fideism which many of today's TV evangelists foist upon their quiet, unwitting audiences.[7]

Strictly speaking, theology, as understood in the first and fourth relationships, does not fit the classical definition of "faith seeking understanding" (*fides quaerens intellectum*). The first carries out scientific investigation outside of the context of faith (and thus considers prayer irrelevant); the fourth denies the validity of

---

[4] This understanding closely reflects the approach found in the patristic tradition (especially that of Augustine), and in the continuance of this tradition in the medieval monastic schools and in the mystical theologies of subsequent centuries. It also has striking similarities to the role assigned to prayer by many liberation theologians for the process of conscientization. See Louth, *Discerning the Mystery*, 3-4; Leclercq, *The Love of Learning and the Desire for God*, 217-22; Claude Geffré, "A Prophetic Theology" in *Liberation Theology: A Documentary History*, ed. Alfred T. Hennelly (Maryknoll, N.Y.: Orbis Books, 1990), 185-86.

[5] Although Aquinas' understanding of theology is modeled on Aristotle's notion of science (i.e., the study of a subject whose properties are proved by appeal to principles), it involves more than a mere logical analysis of the propositions of divine revelation. For the important ancillary role of prayer in Thomas' theological methodology, see Ralph McInerny, "St. Thomas: Contemplative in the University," *Communio* 14 (1987): 373-84.

[6] The experiential relationship between prayer and theology judges *per modum inclinationis*; theology as a subalternated science, in contrast, judges *per modum cognitionis*. This does not mean, however, "...that the theologian occupies a different universe from the saint." See McInerny, "St. Thomas: Contemplative in the University," 380.

[7] These examples are mere concretizations and do not exhaust the number of possible applications.

rational investigation into the truths of revelation (and considers both prayer *and* faith sacrosanct). Only in the second and the third relationships would theology qualify as a scientific discipline.[8] Even there, however, one must be quick to recognize the obvious differences in their understanding of the nature of theology itself. When viewed in conjunction with the various forms of prayer, these differences must be viewed not in conflict with one another, but in the context of a sound Christian anthropology.

THE FORMS OF PRAYER: AN ANTHROPOLOGICAL APPROACH

A suitable starting point for the discussion of the various levels of prayer and their connection with theology is the apostle Paul's tripartite division of the human person into spirit, soul, and body (1 Th 5:23).[9] As one of the earliest anthropologies of the New Testament, it provides an important unifying principle for a proper exposition of "The Prayer Kernel."

"Spirit" (πνευμα), for Paul, stands for the innermost depths of the human person as it is open to the divine presence and awake to God's Spirit. It is that part of the person which communes with God beneath the sphere of human consciousness and cries out,

---

[8] Strictly speaking, only the second coincides with the Aristotelian understanding of science as "a knowledge being certain and valid at all times, being the result of logical deduction." See Latourelle, *Theology: Science of Salvation*, 38. Aquinas distinguishes between two types of science: one, whose principles proceed from the natural light of reason; the other (theology), whose principles proceed from a higher science, i.e., the science of God himself. See *Summa theologiae*, I, q. 1, a. 2, resp. The third understanding of the relationship between prayer and theology can be considered a science only from the perspective of its goal, the acquisition of true Christian knowledge or gnosis, i.e. "that kind of higher knowledge which is the complement, the fruition of faith, and which reaches completion in prayer and contemplation." See Leclercq, *The Love of Learning and the Desire for God*, 214.

[9] These Pauline concepts are closely integrated and thus differ vastly from the trichotomized anthropology of Platonic philosophy. See A.M. Festuguère, "La trichotomie de 1 Th. 5:23 et la philosophie grecque," *Recherches de science religieuse* 20 (1930): 385-415.

The Prayer Kernel

"'Abba, Father,'" from the depths of the human heart (Rm 8:15).[10] In the Christian tradition, this is the level of human existence which yearns for the direct experience of God in contemplative prayer. It is that part of the human person which seeks to pierce through the theologian's conceptual constructs of the nature of the Godhead and to encounter the ultimate ground of reality as it is. Since life "in the Spirit" represents the ultimate goal of human existence, one finds here the important role in the life of the Church of mystical theology, i.e., theological reflection on the nature of the human experience of the divine.

"Soul" (ψυχη), for Paul, refers to the conscious, deliberative level of human existence.[11] Here, reason plays an active role in constructing the concepts upon which a positive theology of God is based. This is the level of human existence which speaks to God through the images of mental prayer. Expressions of love, the examination of conscience, resolutions to action, prayers of petition, the meditative reading of Scripture, all find a place on this important constituent aspect of the human person. Here is the appropriate place for the classical understanding of theology as a science which proceeds not from self-evident principles, but from the principles of divinely revealed truths. On this level, prayer supports the pursuit of theological knowledge, but does not participate explicitly in its ongoing rational explication.

"Body" (σωμα), for Paul, refers to corporeal human existence, not in any denigrated sense (as when he contrasts spirit [πνευμα] with flesh [σαρξ]), but as a neutral, albeit essential, element of human existence. It is that part of the person which,

---

[10] Paul's understanding of πνευμα is not always distinguishable from ψυχη (e.g., Ph 1:27; 2 Cor 12:18). If anything, it "suggests the knowing and willing self and, as such, the aspect that is particularly apt to receive the Spirit of God." See Raymond E. Brown, Joseph A. Fitzmyer and Roland E. Murphy, *The New Jerome Biblical Commentary*, vol. 2, *The New Testament and Topical Articles* (Englewood Cliffs, N.J.: Prentice-Hall, Inc., 1990) s.v. "Pauline Theology," by Joseph A. Fitzmyer.

[11] ψυχη expresses "the vitality, consciousness, intelligence, and volition of a human being." See Raymond E. Brown, Joseph A. Fitzmyer and Roland E. Murphy, eds., *The New Jerome Biblical Commentary*, s.v. "Pauline Theology" by Joseph A. Fitzmyer.

although under the sway of "law of the flesh" (σαρξ), has been, is, and will be redeemed by those living according in the Spirit of Christ.[12] Prayer seeks expression even on this, the most visible and concrete of all levels of human existence: through vocal expression (e.g., singing, verbal meditations), symbols (e.g. the sign of the cross, uplifted arms, the holding of hands) and posture (e.g., kneeling, standing, bowing one's head), and the rigors of corporeal sacrifice (e.g., fast and abstinence). A theology of prayer which overlooks, disdains, or overly spiritualizes this very important aspect of human existence, must beware of the charge of Cartesian minimalism, which reduces the body to the level of a mere machine and identifies the human person with its inside inhabiting "ghost."

As developed above, Paul's anthropology and its implications for the relationship among the various forms of prayer should also be considered in conjunction with his understanding of the Church as "The Body of Christ" (Ep 1:23; Col 1:18). Borrowed in part from the Platonic parallel of the human soul as "writ large" in the fabric of human society, the tripartite Pauline division translates into the Spirit, Christ as the head of the Church, and the faithful who form the members of his Body.[13] Here, the social dimension of the Pauline anthropology comes to the fore, doing so in a way which highlights the fundamental communal orientation of each level of human existence. That is to say that, the contemplative, mental, and physical levels of human prayer reach their fullest expression only to the extent that they are done "in Christ" and, hence, in solidarity with all those who, in varying degrees, are incorporated into his Body, the Church. Indeed, the fullest expression of the human person at prayer is that of the community

---

[12] For the various meanings of σῶμα in the Pauline corpus, see Raymond E. Brown, Joseph A. Fitzmyer and Roland E. Murphy, eds., *The New Jerome Biblical Commentary*, s.v. "Pauline Theology" by Joseph A. Fitzmyer.

[13] This philosophical doctrine appears in Plato, *The Republic* no. 441A, The Loeb Classical Library, 404-5. For the Pauline teaching on the Body of Christ, see Raymond E. Brown, Joseph A. Fitzmyer and Roland E. Murphy, eds., *The New Jerome Biblical Commentary*, s.v. "Pauline Theology" by Joseph A. Fitzmyer.

of the Church gathered around the table of the Lord. The contemplative, mental, corporeal, and social aspects of human existence come together at the precise moment when the Church and its members are most fully themselves in the presence of their God.[14]

The point being made in the above analysis is that all of the various levels of prayer in the Church's tradition are *necessary* for human existence. Contemplation is not to be pitted against mental prayer; nor the latter against fast and abstinence, or against liturgical prayer. Because the human person is a complex, multidimensional reality, all of these forms are necessary to orient a particular aspect of the human person toward the transcendent ground of his or her being. That is not to say that a person may not be more disposed to one form than another, but only that all four levels — the spiritual, the mental, the corporeal, and the social — are necessary if he or she wishes to orient the entire self towards God. And because this process takes place within the lived experience of Christian community, each of these forms has a special role to play in the Church's liturgical prayer. This explains the importance of singing, concrete symbols, gesture, silence, imagery, and preaching in the Church's communal celebrations. From this perspective, the key question in the discussion of the types of prayer is not, "Which one level is appropriate for me at this moment in my own spiritual growth?" but "What is the proper balance to strike among all four both within myself and within the community to which I belong?" The question, in other words, has moved from the area of personal choice to that of the proper dynamics of personal and communal prayer.[15]

---

[14] For a comprehensive treatment of Paul's understanding of prayer, see Louis Monloubou, *Saint Paul et la prière*, Lectio divina, no. 110 (Paris: Éditions du Cerf, 1982).

[15] In attempting to strike this balance, it goes without saying that Church directives concerning regular Mass attendance and the reception of the sacraments must be taken into account. See, for example, Vatican Council II, *Sacrosanctum concilium*, no. 106 [*CDD*, 48-49]; English translation: Flannery, *Vatican Council II*, 29-30; *CIC*, cans. 897, 989 [*AAS* 75/2 (1983): 163, 176]; English translation: *Code of Canon Law: Latin-English Edition*, 337, 363.

THE PRAYER KERNEL

From what has been said above, the fundamental principle of prayer ("The Prayer Kernel") may be summarized as the person's dynamic movement toward and the balanced reception of the ultimate ground of reality on the various anthropological levels of his or her individual and communal existence. This movement toward and reception of the divine involves finding the correct equilibrium among the spiritual, mental, physical, and social aspects of human experience. Rather than being imposed from without, this balance must arise from within the individual's discernment of the patterns of grace in his or her own life. That is to say that, while an individual may discern a particular orientation toward a single type of prayer, special care must be taken that every anthropological level is cared for within the individual and as the individual relates to his or her community. In this respect, contemplation, mental prayer, corporeal sacrifice, and liturgical worship all have an appropriate (but not exclusive) role to play in a person's relationship to Christ.

Given the above description, a number of observations arise:

(1) Each of the levels of prayer serves an important function in helping a person to develop and sustain his or her relationship with God. Rather than spending time trying to decide which is more important than the other (e.g., contemplation or mental prayer), efforts should be made to highlight the unique contribution of each to the overall relationship one is trying to develop with God. In this respect, each level of prayer is an indispensable link in the human person's relationship to the divine.[16]

(2) For each level of prayer, a person's relationship with God involves both an orientation towards *and* the reception of the ultimate ground of reality. In this respect, prayer is more than a mere aesthetic experience and makes little sense outside of a context of faith which believes in the reality of a world beyond and

---

[16] A fitting analogy would be to understand a person in prayer as relating to God *symphonically*, i.e., with variously arranged and harmonious movements of the different levels of his or her anthropological makeup.

The Prayer Kernel

in the existence of a personal ground of that reality. To whatever anthropological level one refers, prayer is essentially a dialogical encounter between the human person and the personal ground of his or her existence.[17]

(3) In its relation to the theological process of "faith seeking understanding," prayer, on the level of mental prayer, supports the rational analysis of the truths of divine revelation and, on the level of contemplative prayer, the deeper experiential union between God and the believer. When taken as such, each type of theology complements the other and should be understood as providing the human person with a knowledge of God appropriate to a particular anthropological level of human existence. In this respect, theology in its classical and mystical senses speaks about God in ways commensurate with the most basic foundations of human experience.[18]

(4) Care must be taken to safeguard the place of the physical in the prayerful orientation of the human person towards the divine. If, in the past, this anthropological level has been subject to harmful extremes (e.g., flagellation, starvation) which were due, at least in part, to a negative evaluation of the body in its relationship to progress in the spiritual life, new efforts must be made to offset a reactionary movement to the other extreme, i.e., the complete neglect and denial of the body as having anything at all to do with the development of one's relationship with God. In this context, care must be taken to establish anew the deep significance

---

[17] It is God who provides the privilege and who takes the initiative in this interpersonal dialogue. See the discussion on God's gift of prayer in Simon Tugwell, *Prayer*, vol. 2, *Prayer in Practice* (Dublin: Veritas Publications, 1974), 3-15.

[18] This observation supplies an important anthropological foundation for the unity of theology. The human person, created in God's image, is an intrinsic composite unity of various anthropological factors (i.e., physical, mental, spiritual, social). While certain ways of doing theology may emphasize one of these factors in particular (e.g., scholastic theology, the mental; monastic or mystical theology, the spiritual; liberation theology, the social), they should not do so to the total exclusion of the others. For this very reason, the other approaches provide a necessary reminder that theology, while seeking to discern the mysteries of God's revelation, must preserve at all times the essential unity and fundamental dignity of the human person.

that a balanced program of fasting and abstinence has for life in the Spirit. New ways must also be found in which social justice issues and the very basic activities of human work and play may be integrated into a holistic understanding of Christian spirituality.[19]

(5) The various anthropological levels of the person should be nurtured at every level of human community, from the family, the schools and base communities, to the local parish and surrounding religious communities. Communities, in turn, should recognize that some of their problems may stem from their outright neglect of entire areas of a person's anthropological makeup. While it is to be understood that, in any religiously-oriented community, there is bound to be a wide spectrum of interest and understanding about the nature and goals of the spiritual life (indeed, probably no two persons will be at the exact same point at any one time), efforts must still be made to encourage people to grow from where they are, at whatever developmental stage of maturity they happen to find themselves. It is here where the process of social conscientization can prove most useful for the recognition of the various levels of prayer and their relation to those areas in a person's private and social existence in need of liberation.[20]

(6) For the above reasons, local parish and religious communities should encourage the development of small support groups organized for those who are attracted to one particular prayer form or another. Groups organized for development in contemplative or mental or shared prayer should be strongly encouraged, but only to the extent that they recognize the value of all of the various levels of prayer and the intrinsic connection which all

---

[19] The most comprehensive study to date of the role of the body in the Christian tradition is Ashley's *Theologies of the Body*. See also Margaret R. Miles, *Augustine on the Body*, American Academy of Religion Dissertation Series, no. 31 (Missoula, Mont.: Scholars Press, 1979).

[20] To do so, the process of conscientization, as it is normally understood (e.g., Freire, "Conscientizing as a Way of Liberating," 5-13) must broaden its scope to include not only the social sphere of human existence, but each of the anthropological levels discussed above. Utilized in such a way, it will help to identify with greater accuracy the variety of ways in which the human person experiences oppression in the modern world.

The Prayer Kernel

of them have, in varying degrees, with Christian activity in the world. The goal of these groups should be to make the members of each group feel secure enough at one level of prayer so that they will be willing to take the risk and experiment with another.[21]

(7) The role of the liturgy in a local community would then be to gather these various groups together and in such a way that each of the various anthropological levels of prayer finds a place. In this way, each group will recognize the particular orientation with which it feels most at home. It will also be exposed to the presence of others in the worshipping community with different spiritual orientations and (it is hoped) inspired by the great variety of expressions of relating to God which are at their disposal. From this perspective, the Eucharist has a special unifying function to play in the life of the believing Christian community. There, God comes to the community and encourages both it and each individual member to continue the process of conversion by which every level of his or her existence is completely oriented toward the divine as it manifests itself in the various levels of human existence.[22]

(8) The above principle offers a deeper understanding of the Incarnation and its ongoing significance for the life of the Church. Christ became fully human: body, soul, and spirit. He did so to initiate a process of human divinization, which would reach

---

[21] One of the prerequisites of effective pastoral care is taking as much as possible into account the spiritual inclinations of all concerned. To achieve this, pastors should try to create an atmosphere in which people who feel at home with a particular form of spiritual expression are encouraged to gather regularly for prayer. When encouraged to look upon themselves as complementary rather than competing organizations, such groups (e.g., rosary, charismatic prayer, centering prayer, Bible study) will bring great variety and spiritual strength to the life of the parish community.

[22] As "the summit and source of all Christian worship and life" [*CIC*, can. 897], the celebration of the Eucharist is the time when the Church and its members are most themselves before God and, hopefully, before one another. By seeing the continuity between life and worship, Christians find their private prayers validated in their communal offering with Christ's Body, the Church. When properly understood, there is no dichotomy between private devotion and the Church's liturgical worship. See Vatican Council II, *Sacrosanctum concilium*, no. 13 [*CDD*, 13]; English translation: Flannery, *Vatican Council II*, 7; SCR, *Eucharisticum mysterium*, nos. 7, 58 [*AAS* 59 (1967): 545-46, 569]; English translation: Flannery, *Vatican Council II*, 107, 132-33.

across the centuries, beginning anew in every human heart, whenever and wherever there appears the slightest movement of the human person toward God in prayer. Having been entrusted with the charge of continuing this process of divinization for all of humanity, the Church seeks to remain faithful to the teaching, preaching, and sacramental life it has received from the apostles. It can hope to do so only by trying to avoid the manifold traps of human self-deception and by seeking to remain constantly open to the Spirit on every level of its existence, from the most massive of its institutional structures to the smallest parish, family, and local base community.[23] Through their ongoing participation in the charismatic dimension of the Church's spiritual life, religious have an important role to play in this regard.

PRAYER AND RELIGIOUS

It goes without saying that a life devoted to prayer touches the very core of religious life. Indeed, many types of prayer have been fostered and made popular through their connection with particular traditions of various religious orders (e.g., liturgical prayer with the Benedictines, contemplative prayer with the Trappists and Carmelites, meditation on the humanity and passion of Christ with the Franciscans, the rosary with the Dominicans, spiritual exercises with the Jesuits, mental prayer and the prayer of petition with the Redemptorists).[24] What is perhaps not so clear is the way in which each of the religious vows has a

---

[23] The human element of the Church can get in the way of where the Spirit wishes to move it. The fathers of the Second Vatican Council, for example, acknowledged that "often enough men of both sides were to blame" for the serious dissensions that resulted from the Protestant Reformation. See Vatican Council II, *Unitatis redintegratio*, no. 3 [*CDD*, 248]; English translation: Flannery, *Vatican Council II*, 455. Human error can enter at any level of the Church's life and ministry.

[24] For these contributions, see Gordon S. Wakefield, ed., *The Westminster Dictionary of Christian Spirituality* (Philadelphia: The Westminster Press, 1983), s.v. "Benedictine Spirituality, Benedictines" by Maria Boulding; "Carmelite Spirituality, Carmelites," by Colin P. Thompson; "Cistercian Spirituality, Cistercians," by Benedicta Ward; "Dominican Spirituality, Dominicans" by

The Prayer Kernel

particular orientation towards each of the anthropological levels discussed above.

In their vow of chastity, religious renounce the goods of married life and sexual pleasure. They do so in order to offer an eschatological witness of the existence of a life beyond and to free themselves in the present life for the total dedication which their discipleship in Christ demands. Here, too, the vow makes little sense if it is not given concrete physical expression in the lives of each individual religious and if this expression is not supported by an understanding of the reasons for the vow and a belief in its underlying spiritual benefits. Only in this way will the religious be able to avoid the unwanted dangers of self-deception and unnecessary compromise.[25]

In their vow of poverty, religious live in simplicity, detaching themselves from material gain and a life of luxury. This commitment to austerity entails not only a concrete, physical expression in the life of each individual religious and the community to which he or she belongs, but also a certain mindset or attitude toward the use and procurement of material goods. The vow of poverty is not an end in itself, but a means through which a person's spirit may listen more closely and yearn more strongly for the presence of the Spirit in his or her life. In this respect, there is a contemplative, mental, physical, and social dimension to the vow of poverty. To neglect one of these levels is to call into question one's faithful adherence to the vow.[26]

Simon Tugwell; "Franciscan Spirituality, Franciscans," by Eric Doyle; "Jesus, Society of," by George E. Ganss. For the Redemptorists and the prayer of petition, see Jorge Rafael Colón León, "La oración de petición en la dotrina de San Alfonso Maria de Ligorio" (S.T.D. dissertation, Gregorian University, 1986).

[25] The Second Vatican Council proposes the common life lived in a spirit of true brotherly love as a means by which chastity can be securely preserved and such self-deceptions more easily avoided. See Vatican Council II, *Perfectae caritatis*, no. 12 [*CDD*, 343-44]; English translation: Flannery, *Vatican Council II*, 617.

[26] In this respect, religious poverty cannot be reduced to a single absolutely univocal explanation. See Karl Rahner, "The Theology of Poverty," in *Theological Investigations*, vol. 4, trans. David Bourke (London: Darton, Longman & Todd, 1971), 176. See also Vatican Council II, *Perfectae caritatis*, no. 13 [*CDD*, 345-47]; English translation: Flannery, *Vatican Council II*, 618-19.

In their vow of obedience, religious seek the will of God in that of their superiors. The living out of this vow entails a process of discernment on the part of both the superior and the individual religious, one which can achieve a concrete implementation only to the extent that the contemporary theology of the vow is understood, studied, and seen as important for the spiritual growth of all involved. The vow, in other words, has a particular orientation to each of the anthropological levels discussed in this essay. Rather than being unduly concretized or overly spiritualized, it remains for each individual religious to find a proper balance among these various dimensions and to insure that they remain in sync with the values and goals of the community to which he or she belongs.[27]

As described above, the vows are not the mere private possessions of the individual religious, but charisms given to the religious community and, in a larger context, gifts to the entire Church of Christ. For these reasons, efforts must be made on the community level to insure that each of the vows manifests itself concretely in the lives of its members, becomes the source for ongoing theological reflection, and provides a continuing source of spiritual nourishment for all concerned. In doing so, appropriate medical, psychological, and spiritual care must be available for those who, for whatever reason, experience difficulty in living the life of the vows. Care must also be taken to insure, on the one hand, that the structures of community interaction do not interfere with the growth of the members and, on the other hand, that individuals do not make excessive demands on the community

---

[27] Since the vow of obedience is lived in and through the religious congregation, it follows that the particular sociological type of that community (i.e., intentional, bureaucratic) will shade the interpretation of the vow even with regard to specific magisterial texts. Most religious communities prior to Vatican II fell rather squarely within the "intentional" model. Since that time, many have developed along "associational" lines. See Patricia Wittberg, *Creating a Future for Religious Life: A Sociological Perspective* (New York: Paulist Press, 1991), 6-10. Recent magisterial documents seem to be calling religious to return to the more traditional intentional model. See, for example, SCRSI, "Norms for Religious Life," 308-23.

The Prayer Kernel

which would ultimately compromise its mission.[28] In this respect, communities must beware of an undue privatization of the vows in the lives of their members and, on the other hand, an unhealthy tendency towards across-the-board social uniformity. In all cases, a proper balance must be sought and properly struck.[29]

It is precisely in achieving this balance in prayer on the various anthropological levels of their lives — the physical, mental, spiritual, and social — that religious provide for the Church a visible sign of the types of individual and social integration to which all are ultimately called in Christ. That is not to say that such an integration cannot be achieved in other states of life within the Church (both lay and priestly), but only that the religious life, in its communal life dedicated to the realization of the evangelical counsels, is especially suited to it.[30] In this respect, religious are called to serve as a leaven for both themselves and others in the life of the Church, bringing to consciousness the need for prayer to be nurtured on the various levels of human existence and in such a way that the human person remains balanced within his or her own internal relations, in his or her communal relations, and, most importantly, in his or her relations to God. To neglect any one

---

[28] A proper balance between individual and community needs is of the utmost importance for religious life, possibly the single greatest challenge it faces this day. Religious congregations that have relaxed their strong intentional ties and developed into loose associations of individuals do not have a very good prospectus for survival. They would do well to incorporate some characteristics of intentional groups in an attempt to give the community some more internal cohesiveness. On the other hand, communities with extremely strong intentional ties can be psychologically damaging to the individual. See Wittberg, *Creating a Future for Religious Life*, 22, 80-81.

[29] For more on social conformity and the privatization of the vows, see Leddy, *Reweaving Religious Life: Beyond the Liberal Model* (Mystic, Conn.: Twenty-Third Publications, 1990), 52-74. In this context, one author goes so far as to speak of the deconstruction of religious life. See Elizabeth McDonough, "Beyond the Liberal Model: Quo Vadis?," in *Ius Sequitur Vitam: Law Follows Life, Studies in Canon Law Presented to P.J.M. Huizing*, eds. J.H. Provost and K. Walf (Leuven: University of Leuven Press, 1991), 109-116.

[30] "They have a stable and more solidly based way of Christian life." See Vatican Council II, *Lumen gentium*, no. 43 [CDD, 174-75]; English translation: Flannery, *Vatican Council II*, 403.

of these levels means that, somewhere in their private or communal existence, religious have compromised their dedication to and stalwart perseverance in the vows.[31]

CONCLUSION

As described in this chapter, the fundamental principle of prayer ("The Prayer Kernel") offers an approach to the spiritual life that embraces the human person on every level of his or her existence. It achieves this by noting how each of the major levels of prayer — contemplative, mental, corporeal, liturgical — corresponds to a particular anthropological dimension of human life. Rooted in Paul's tripartite anthropology of spirit ($\pi\nu\varepsilon\upsilon\mu\alpha$), soul ($\psi\upsilon\chi\eta$), and body ($\sigma\overline{\omega}\mu\alpha$) (1 Th 5:23) and supplemented by his ecclesiological doctrine of the body of Christ (Ep 1:23; Col 1:18), it offers not only a way in which the proper function of prayer may be understood in its relation to theology, but also the important insight that prayer is to be nurtured on each of these levels and in a manner that corresponds in a balanced way to the particular spiritual orientation of the individual and the particular community to which he or she belongs. While individuals and, indeed, entire communities are sure to have preferences in the particular type of prayer they feel attracted to and want to promote, these leanings do not dispense them from the responsibility of turning every part of their lives (i.e., on every anthropological dimension) over to the Lord.

Religious play an important role in achieving this balance in the life of the Church. In their individual and communal commitment to the vows, they have at their disposal a way of life which, of its very nature, calls for a life dedicated to God in prayer on each of the above anthropological levels. For them to neglect any of

---

[31] For more on prayer as the foundation of the religious life, see Jean Beyer, "La preghiera nella vita consacrata," *Vita consacrata* 9 (1973): 273-89; Jean Galot, "Il Padre nostro e la vita consacrata," *Vita consacrata* 23 (1987): 1-14, 97-106, 204-14, 261-70.

The Prayer Kernel

these levels would be tantamount to neglecting the full theological and spiritual import of the vows themselves and, hence, the very reason for their existence and particular identity within the Church. If, on the other hand, they advert to these levels and seek to find within their personal lives and communal existence that particular balance of contemplative, mental, corporeal, and liturgical prayer which best corresponds to the particular charism they share within the Church, then they will find themselves truly living out their call to discipleship in Christ and both challenging and encouraging others to do the same within the context of their own circumstances and status in life. In this respect, religious remain for the Church a living embodiment of prayer towards which others, from every walk and state of life, can refer and seek to integrate within their own lives and in their own ways the various levels of prayer necessary for a balanced orientation toward God and life in the Spirit.[32]

In the final analysis, the fundamental principle of prayer ("The Prayer Kernel") seeks to provide a basis not only from which prayer has a particular orientation to every level of human existence, but also from which the theologian can discern the role played by prayer on the various levels of the theological enterprise itself. To be sure, both these endeavors are themselves intimately connected: the goal of prayer is to nurture the human person on every level of his or her existence; that of theology is to help the person understand the basis of his or her relationship to God on each of these levels. If nothing else, the fundamental principle of prayer ("The Prayer Kernel") seeks to integrate theology with life in such a way that it brings to the fore the intimate connection between theology as a scientific discipline and the presuppositions of a life of prayer which surround it.[33] In this

---

[32] A deep life of individual, communal, and liturgical prayer is proposed by recent magisterial teaching as an *essential* characteristic of religious life. See SCRSI, "Norms for Religious Life," 314-15.

[33] While spirituality (and, hence, a focus on prayer) stresses the "principle of coherence," theology serves spirituality "by rescuing it from chronic subjectivism." See Jones, "Spirituality and Theology," 163.

respect, prayer, on all of its levels, may be seen as the theologian's silent partner: supporting, nurturing, and maturing the faith perceptions of the believer and of the entire Christian community which he or she is constantly trying to understand.[34]

---

[34] As the theologian's silent partner, prayer could safely assume a place in either the second or third understanding of the relationship between theology and prayer (see above, 167-70). Such an avowal recognizes different vocations among theologians and highlights even more the great variety of approaches that can be taken to the one discipline of theology.

13

THE ECUMENICAL KERNEL

Is there a fundamental principle of ecumenical theology? The answer to this question depends on whether or not there exists within the call for Christian unity an authentic and wide enough theological basis for diverse doctrinal and moral opinion. Such a finding can be arrived at only through a close examination of the various assumptions of that call, not the least of which concerns the very meaning of the term "oneness" itself. This, in turn, must be integrated with the whole of theology, and in such a way that the integrity of each of the Christian traditions is maintained.

THE THEOLOGICAL BASIS OF ECUMENISM

The theological roots of the call to Christian unity can be traced to a number of well-known New Testament texts. Jesus' priestly prayer for solidarity among those who believe (Jn 17:21), Paul's challenging description of the oneness of those baptized in Christ (Gal 3:27-28), the eloquent call to unity in faith, baptism, and Spirit expressed by the author of Ephesians (4:4-5) are but a few of the many texts which come to mind.[1] When taken together with Irenaeus' understanding of the Church's unity of faith in

---

[1] Other texts include: Jn 14:20; Ac 4:32; Rm 10:12; 1 Cor 12:13; Col 3:11; Heb 6:12.

both heart and soul,[2] Cyprian's notion of the unity of the Church as the source of salvation,[3] and the Nicene-Constantinopolitan definition of the signs of the Church as "*one*, holy, catholic, and apostolic" (italics mine),[4] these texts form a formidable body of teaching to support the classical theological claim of the Church's indivisible nature.

Such evidence, however, must not be taken at face value. Beneath it lies an underlying question concerning why the call for unity holds such a prominent place in the texts of Christian antiquity. Do these texts portray a historical reality or a theologized hope? Do they reveal a concrete picture of the ecclesial circumstances of their times? Or do they point instead to the discouraging and ofttimes embarrassing experience of *disunity* within the ranks of the early Church communities? This latter possibility seems more than likely. One need merely point to the first-century tensions between Jewish and Gentile Christians over the need to adhere to the letter of the Mosaic law,[5] or to the Gnostic threat within the early second-century Church of Antioch which led Ignatius to see the value of a strong monarchical episcopacy,[6] or to the third-century controversy between Carthage and Rome over the re-baptism of the lapsed,[7] or even to the hostile division between Catholic and Arian camps in the pre-Nicene Church of the early fourth century, to support this claim.[8] It must also be

---

[2] *Adversus haereses*, 1.10.2 [*SC* 264:158-61; *PG* 7:551-53].

[3] *De ecclesiae unitate*, 6 [*CCL* 3:253-54; *PL* 4:502-4].

[4] Denz.-Schön., no. 150 [86]. See also Kelly, *Early Christian Creeds*, 296-98.

[5] See, for example, the controversy over circumcision at Jerusalem in Acts 15. For tensions among Jews and Christians and also among Jewish and Gentile Christians in the sub-apostolic period, see Frend, *The Rise of Christianity*, 120-51.

[6] For Ignatius' understanding of the monarchical episcopacy, see Hans von Campenhausen, *Ecclesiastical Authority and Spiritual Power in the Church of the First Three Centuries*, trans. J.A. Baker (Stanford: Stanford University Press, 1969), 97-106. See also Kenan B. Osbourne, *Priesthood: A History of the Ordained Ministry in the Roman Catholic Church* (New York: Paulist Press, 1988), 97-102.

[7] For the particulars of this controversy, see W.H.C. Frend, *Martyrdom and Persecution in the Early Church: A Study of a Conflict from the Maccabees to Donatus* (Oxford: Basil Blackwell, 1965), 415-29.

[8] The historical contours of the Arian controversy are set out in Frend, *The Early Church*, 2d ed. (Philadelphia: Fortress Press, 1982), 146-57. For doctrinal aspects

remembered that so-called heretical ideas often develop within existing ecclesial structures and are labelled as such only when circumstances push the Church's teaching authority to articulate for its members a more precise theological doctrine. In this respect, heterodoxy occasions the historical context within which orthodoxy struggles continually to refine itself.[9] This correlation (which, at times, has resembled more a relation of codependence)[10] is an area in the history of Christian thought in need of much further thought and clarification.

Given the above, it comes as no small surprise that one of the greatest feats of the Second Vatican Council was its dogged attempt to invert the historical dynamics of ecumenical relations from one of negative contrariety (i.e., mutual heterodox/orthodox suspicion) to that of cooperative dialogue. While acknowledging that the one Church of Christ subsists visibly in the Catholic church,[11] the Council fathers recognized varying degrees of incorporation into Christ's Body and the ongoing historical existence of other churches and ecclesiastical communities.[12] They also called for the overcoming of prejudicial attitudes, dialogue between competent experts, more cooperation in working for the

---

of the controversy, see Pelikan, *The Emergence of the Catholic Tradition (100-600)*, 191-210.

[9] For emerging orthodox/heterodox relationships in the early Church, see Walter Bauer, *Orthodoxy and Heresy in Earliest Christianity*, 2d ed., eds. Robert Kraft and Gerhard Krodel (Philadelphia: Fortress Press, 1971), 229-40.

[10] The word "codependence" nowadays refers to a cluster of addictive pathologies. It comes from contemporary family systems analysis, which focuses on how members of dysfunctional family groups can support the ongoing life of disease and addiction of an "identified patient." See Patrick McCormick, *Sin as Addiction* (New York: Paulist Press, 1989), 117-18. For more on the notion of "codependence," see Anne Wilson Schaef, *Co-Dependence: Misunderstood-Mistreated* (Minneapolis: Winston Press, 1986); Melodie Beattie, *Codependent No More* (New York: Harper and Row, 1987). A study of the history of orthodox/heterodox relationships in the context of modern codependence theory may bring some revealing new insights to our understanding of the development of doctrine.

[11] See Vatican Council II, *Lumen gentium*, no. 8 [*CDD*, 104-6]; English translation: Flannery, *Vatican Council II*, 357.

[12] Ibid., nos. 14-16 [*CDD*, 117-22]; English translation: Flannery, *Vatican Council II*, 365-68.

good of humanity, prayer undertaken in common, and the ongoing task of renewal and reform.[13] The intention of these challenging doctrinal innovations was to foster within ecumenical relations: (1) a conciliatory attitude towards the divisions of the past, (2) a realistic attitude towards the possibilities of the present, and (3) a posture of hope for the horizons of the future.[14] The immediate result has been more than two decades of intense dialogue between the Catholic church and virtually every major Christian denomination and non-Christian religion.

THE MEANING OF CHRISTIAN UNITY

From these discussions, a number of questions about the nature of Christian unity have arisen. Is the sought after unity something which exists in the transcendent, other worldly dimension of Christ's Mystical Body? Is it to have visible expressions in the world in which we live? Must these expressions be of a structural or institutional nature? Are these expressions necessary to the nature of the Church? Is an absolute uniformity of doctrine and morals essential to the rule of faith? Is it something that people can and should experience in the concrete expressions of their daily lives? Is greater cooperation in social justice issues enough? Is it sufficient for the Christian churches simply to agree to disagree? If so, then in what does the distinctive Christian witness to the world consist? Since the answers to these and similar questions vary as much as the theological starting points of the numerous denominations involved, it is no small wonder that, on almost every front, ecumenical dialogue is slowly moving towards (and, in some cases, has already arrived at) a discouraging and uneasy state of theological deadlock.[15]

---

[13] See Vatican Council II, *Unitatis redintegratio*, no. 4 [*CDD*, 250-54]; English translation: Flannery, *Vatican Council II*, 456-59.

[14] These and other themes are summarized in Robert McAfee Brown, *The Ecumenical Revolution* (London: Burns and Oates, 1967), 193-202.

[15] The strong reaction from Reformed, Orthodox, and Roman Catholic circles against Heinrich Fries and Karl Rahner, *Unity of the Churches — An Actual*

What is the worth of present attempts to break through this apparent confessional impasse? Is the standstill a sign that the ecumenical process itself has been moving in the wrong direction? This possibility seems worthy of exploration. Rather than being thought of as mutually exclusive, perhaps the relational models of negative contrariety and cooperative dialogue can be juxtaposed — held in tension, if you will — in such a way as to create a heuristic device that would enable the churches to understand the meaning of Christian unity in more dynamic and creative terms.[16] Perhaps the Catholic church needs to examine its tradition of opposition to the classical Protestant theologies (i.e., Lutheranism, Anglicanism, Calvinism) as a means of refining its insights into the richness of its own theological tradition. The various Protestant denominations, in turn, should do the same with Catholic theology and perhaps even with each other. The point being made here is that a theological concept can be fully appreciated and understood only in relationship to those ideas it was originally intended to negate. The history of Catholic dogma, in other words, should be written in the context of its own "anti-history," i.e., in relation to those who, ultimately, could not accept the consequences of its teaching.[17]

Possibility (New York: Paulist Press, 1983), a work which put forth the basic thesis that there was no theological obstacle to the reunion of the mainline churches, is symptomatic of the increasing strains that have entered ecumenical relations in recent years. See, for example, E. Herms, *Einheit der Christen in der Gemeinschaft der Kirchen* (Göttingen: Vanderhoeck und Ruprecht, 1984), 133-59; A. Nichols, "Einigung der Kirchen: An Ecumenical Controversy," *One in Christ* 21 (1985): 139-66. Cardinal Joseph Ratzinger, *Church, Ecumenism and Politics: New Essays in Ecclesiology* (New York: Crossroad, 1986), 137.

[16] The continuity of these notions with the *Decree on Ecumenism* is in the latter's emphasis on avoiding any kind of false irenicism, while at the same time insisting on the importance of cooperative dialogue among the churches. See Vatican Council II, *Unitatis redintegratio*, nos. 11-12 [*CDD*, 259-61]; English translation: Flannery, *Vatican Council II*, 462.

[17] One renowned scholar goes so far as to say that "...the convenient and time-honored labels for the distinction of heretical and orthodox prove to be very dangerous tools, since they threaten to distort the historian's vision and the theologian's judgment." See Helmut Koester, "GNOMAI DIAPHOROI: The Origin and Nature of Diversification in the History of Early Christianity" in *Trajectories through Early Christianity*, eds. James M. Robinson and Helmut Koester (Philadelphia: Fortress Press, 1971), 115.

But how is this to be done? How is a balance between ecumenical relations based on negative contrariety *and* cooperative dialogue to be maintained? Are they not mutually exclusive? Do they not stand in open contradiction to one another? How could they ever be reconciled? Plato's description of justice as a well-tempered harmony of contrary forces proves an invaluable guide in this respect.[18] In subtle contrast to Aristotle's rendering of virtue as hitting a mean (or middle point) between the extremes of excess and deficiency,[19] Plato's understanding allows for a creative interplay of wild and unruly forces.[20] True, mistakes will be made from time to time: one horse may overpower the resistance of the charioteer, resulting in his loss of balance and eventual fall. But with the perfection of the skill comes a mastery of these contrary forces; movement is eventually wrought with ease and grace. The point being made here is that, rather than struggling to reach a theological middle ground acceptable to all concerned, those working for Christian unity should be more involved in trying to help people acquire the skill of dialoguing in the midst of intense confessional conflict.[21] In doing so, future ecumenical efforts will be less threatened by those in the churches who, somewhere along the way, have let themselves be swayed by one or the other extreme.

---

[18] Plato, *The Republic* nos. 443C-444A, The Loeb Classical Library, 412-17.

[19] Even this judgment must be properly nuanced. A close reading of Aristotle shows that the process of arriving at this elusive mean or middle point *does* involve a dynamic of balancing extremes in its own right. See, for example, *The Nicomachean Ethics* 2.9, The Loeb Classical Library, 110-115.

[20] A potent metaphor used by Plato is that of a charioteer driving a pair of veering and unruly horses. See Plato, *Phaedrus* nos. 246-47, The Loeb Classical Library, 470-77.

[21] In this respect, the Second Vatican Council refers to a "fraternal rivalry" ("...*per fraternam hanc aemulationem*...") among the separated churches that will incite all to a deeper understanding and expression of the riches of Christ. See Vatican Council II, *Unitatis redintegratio*, no. 11 [*CDD*, 260]; English translation: Flannery, *Vatican Council II*, 462. Stated in another way: "Here it would therefore be a question of continually learning afresh from the other as other while respecting his or her otherness. As a people who are divided we can also be one." See Ratzinger, *Church, Ecumenism and Politics*, 140.

THE ECUMENICAL KERNEL

From what has been said thus far, the fundamental principle of ecumenical theology ("The Ecumenical Kernel") may be described as an acquired interior disposition of individual Christians and believing church communities who, seeking to understand the historical and theological significance of their own religious traditions, maintain an ongoing, balanced relationship of negative contrariety *and* cooperative dialogue with Christian traditions other than their own. The goal of these relationships is to increase, on both personal and communal levels, a deeper appreciation of the mutual dependence these traditions share in the historical dimensions of space and time. They are to determine as far as possible the extent to which their stated differences prevent them from remaining true to the most basic tenets of their respective faith traditions.

Given the above formulation of "The Ecumenical Kernel," a number of observations arise:

(1) As "an acquired interior disposition," the principle resides within individual members of the believing faith community. This habitual attitude of mind looks upon other faith traditions not as a threat, but as a challenge to question and, hopefully, to grow in the knowledge and love of one's own tradition. Acquired by human cooperation with the intricate working of God's grace, it represents a level of maturity which cannot be presupposed for all members of a particular tradition. In this respect, the principle must be thought of as existing in varying degrees among the members of the faith community. Numerous internal tensions are likely and are to be expected.[22]

(2) The principle contains an important social dimension. The above-mentioned interior disposition of mind is not confined

---

[22] Pertinent to this observation is the Vatican II statement: "There can be no ecumenism worthy of the name without interior conversion. For it is from newness of attitudes of mind, from self-denial and unstinted love, that desires of unity take their rise and develop in a mature way." See Vatican Council II, *Unitatis redintegratio*, no. 7 [*CDD*, 256-57]; English translation: Flannery, *Vatican Council II*, 460.

to the restrictions of private piety, but is oriented, by its very nature, to be shared with others and to grow within groups — often across denominational boundaries — for the purpose of achieving its stated relational goals. In this respect, a person's own interior disposition of mind is strengthened by the growth of this attitude within his or her community. The more this interior disposition of mind grows in its social orientation, the more it will affect the doctrinal outcome of ecumenical relations among the churches.[23]

(3) The principle asserts that the Christian search for self-understanding must be carried out in the context of the relationship a particular faith tradition has to those traditions outside of its official confines and against which the thrust of its doctrine was originally intended to negate. This "knowledge by negation" forces the believer to delve ever more deeply into the roots of his or her own theological tradition and to try to determine the precise historical basis of church doctrinal statements.[24]

(4) From a doctrinal perspective, precedents for the theological balancing of opposing extremes are found in both the classical Trinitarian doctrine established in the fourth- and fifth-century councils (i.e., Three Persons in One God) and in the way the divinity and humanity of Christ were balanced in the definition of Chalcedon (451). In each instance, the orthodox position emerges only in contrast to certain teachings encountered within the ranks of the Church which the authorities ultimately sought to negate (i.e., Arianism, Nestorianism, Monophysitism). From this perspective, the principle challenges the Church to adapt its classical theological approach of balancing opposing extremes to the pressing ecumenical concerns of the present.[25]

---

[23] Stated officially: "If Christians are prepared for dialogue *within* their own Communities, they are equipped to receive the fruits of an interconfessional dialogue" [italics mine]. See SPUC, *Reflections and Suggestions Concerning Ecumenical Dialogue*, no. 5 in Flannery, *Vatican Council II*, 546 [does not appear in *AAS*].

[24] In addition to such "knowledge by negation," one may also apply the concept of "codependence" analogously in order to try to understand the contours of the dysfunctional relationships that have existed among various Christian churches for so long. See above 187 n. 10.

[25] An early thesis of Rahner (i.e., formulated prior to the Fries-Rahner plan)

(5) The balancing of the relationships of negative contrariety and cooperative dialogue also points to the capacity of an individual or group to maintain a steadfast internal equilibrium between two very different ways of dealing with the lack of religious unity in their lives (i.e., polemics and irenics). Rather than seeking to compromise or to water down one approach with the other, the aim here is to develop within believers a sufficient latitude of mind that will enable them not only to challenge and confront, but also to see the intrinsic worth of faith traditions other than their own. By helping believers to recognize the extent to which their own tradition is dependent upon and has, in fact, been enriched by various opposing trends, these relationships should evoke a unity of respect that will go a long way in the pursuit of further ecumenical exchanges.[26]

(6) Since various religious and secular traditions are likely to be involved, the extent and scope of these relationships will vary from place to place and, depending on circumstances, change even within local churches of the same tradition. Stronger and more fruitful relationships of negative contrariety will exist between those traditions sharing a long history of doctrinal controversy. Relationships of cooperative dialogue are constrained only by the limits of constructive theological reflection and exchange. Since each tradition will obviously look within itself for its measure of orthodoxy, progress in ecumenical relations is to be measured not so much in terms of a movement towards doctrinal

---

concerning the ultimate basis of ecumenical theology posits "a unity apprehended in hope" even before an explicit theological formulation in creedal form has been achieved. See Karl Rahner, "On the Theology of the Ecumenical Discussion," chap. in *Theological Investigations*, vol. 11, *Confrontations I*, trans. David Bourke (London: Darton, Longman and Todd, 1974), 33.

[26] In this regard, Ratzinger emphasizes a twofold orientation in ecumenical activity: (1) a continuing search to think up new models of unity and (2) an increasing recognition that it is God who will ultimately bring it about. In his opinion, the "must of division" is a necessary precondition for unity. By focusing on the present unity which Christian churches already do share in the midst of their diversity, he sees developing a kind of respect that "will have as its fruit a peaceful maturation and a joyful thankfulness for so much closeness despite the mysterious 'must.'" See *Church, Ecumenism and Politics*, 140-41.

uniformity, but in the mutual commitment of each tradition to keeping the balanced relationship of negative contrariety and cooperative dialogue alive.[27]

(7) The goal of appreciating the mutual dependence of conflicting religious traditions challenges the members of each community to take the risk of letting go, if ever so briefly, of some of the most precious presuppositions of their faith. They do this, on the one hand, in order to look at their own tradition from without its own self-limiting confines and, on the other hand, to experience the conflicting tradition from within its own framework of hermeneutical preconceptions. The result should be an interpretative turn back to their own tradition with eyes opened anew to both the strengths *and* weaknesses of their most basic doctrinal positions.[28]

(8) From this deeper appreciation of mutual dependence, there arises a concern over the extent to which the differences now articulated between or among opposing traditions prevent them from remaining faithful to even more basic tenets of their faith, tenets which the several traditions may very well share with each other. In this respect, the stated premise is and must always remain a person's faithfulness to his or her own theological tradition.[29] Disagreement between mutually dependent religious traditions is to be expected and cannot be overcome in any or all

---

[27] These healthy relationships should be looked upon as ends in themselves and not merely as the necessary means to achieving some future doctrinal unity. By focusing on maintaining healthy, functional relationships among the various Christian churches, future ecumenical activity may (or may not) arrive at what would be the certainly welcome outcome of closer doctrinal unity.

[28] This is implied in magisterial teaching in the context of ecumenical education where dialogue demands "...a mind open and ready to base life more deeply on one's own faith because of the fuller knowledge derived from dialogue with others, who are to be reckoned as sharing with us the true name of Christian." See SPUC, *Spiritus Domini*, no. 76 [*AAS* 62 (1970): 714-15]; English translation: Flannery, *Vatican Council II*, 524. See also Rahner, "On the Theology of the Ecumenical Discussion," 40.

[29] Thus, dialogue in ecumenical education also demands "sincere and firm fidelity to one's own faith, without which dialogue is reduced to a conversation in which neither side is genuinely engaged." SPUC, *Spiritus Domini*, no. 76 [*AAS* 62 (1970): 714-15]; English translation: Flannery, *Vatican Council II*, 524.

instances. What is more important is that (1) these mutually dependent religious traditions support each other in the beliefs and values which they share and (2) they remain committed to maintaining an open relationship of contrariety, one which will insure that each will continue to refine its own positions and grow in a deeper understanding of their final consequences.[30]

These observations do not exhaust the richness of the fundamental principle of ecumenical theology as set forth in this essay. They seek merely to draw out some of the implications of the principle and to help to provide an overall context by means of which the current efforts of ecumenism may be replenished at the source. In this respect, religious have an important role to play in the renewal of ecumenical theology.

RELIGIOUS AND ECUMENISM

Characterized by a communal lifestyle dedicated to the evangelical counsels, the religious life provides an appropriate environment that can foster the interior disposition of the heart and mind needed to maintain a balanced relationship of negative contrariety and cooperative dialogue.

In their vow of chastity, religious forego the goods of marriage in order to give witness to the existence of a life beyond the confines of the present earthly reality. In an ecumenical context, this translates into a constant reminder to the various proponents of Church unity that the ultimate source of that unity cannot be accounted for by human efforts alone, but is rooted in the Trinitarian harmony of "unity in plurality" within the life of the Godhead itself. In this respect, religious urge their fellow Christians to be aware of the eschatological dimensions of their struggle for Church unity. God's kingdom, in other words, is established on earth only to the extent that the oneness and peace found in the divinity's

---

[30] A similar approach of "unity through diversity" is adopted by Ratzinger. See *Church, Ecumenism and Politics*, 139-40.

inner life manifests itself: (1) within the communal assemblies of the faithful and (2) in the human society where these faithful assemblies gather.[31]

In their vow of poverty, religious seek to empty themselves not merely of an inordinate attachment to material goods, but even of those immaterial attachments of the mind and heart that may get in the way of their service of the Lord. In an ecumenical context, this would mean a willingness to hold own's own theological opinions "in check" so as to cooperate with other faith traditions with a view towards experiencing them for their own intrinsic worth. Such an interior disposition should culminate in a deeper awareness of the various strengths and weaknesses of one's own theological perspective.[32]

In their vow of obedience, religious choose to accept the will of their superiors as a concrete sign of God's design for them in their lives. In an ecumenical context, this would translate into a strong identification of one's own desire for Church unity within the approved ecumenical directives of the Catholic church.[33] In this respect, religious stand as staunch defenders of their Church's theological tradition, who are not only able and willing to confront other religious traditions with challenging questions and

---

[31] In this respect, Ratzinger's emphasis on the eschatological dimensions of ecumenical activity (i.e., "...that we know neither the day nor the hour, nor are we able to determine, when and how unity will come into existence") has great import for religious. See *Church, Ecumenism, and Politics*, 138-42.

[32] In this respect, the distinction between a theological truth and the linguistic formula through which that truth is expressed must be kept in mind. To hold on to the latter when other ways have been found to express the truth more clearly is a sign of stubbornness and inordinate attachment that goes against the spirit of religious poverty.

[33] Such an identification does not rule out the possibility of institutional criticism on the part of religious. No person should be forced to act contrary to the prudently formed judgments of his or her conscience. See Vatican Council II, *Dignitatis humanae*, no. 3 [*CDD*, 515]; English translation: Flannery, *Vatican Council II*, 801. In the case of disagreement on the Church's official stance in particular ecumenical concerns, the directives regarding dissent must be taken seriously. See SCDF, *Instructio de ecclesiali theologi vocatione*, nos. 32-41 [*AAS* 82 (1990): 1562-69]; English translation: SCDF, "Instruction on the Ecclesial Vocation of the Theologian," *Origins* 20 (1990): 123-25.

observations rooted in a sound knowledge of their own faith, but also capable of refining their own theological positions in the light of challenges and observations received from without.[34]

Even more important than the above considerations is the fact that the religious life asks its members to strive constantly towards achieving in many areas of their lives a delicate balance of opposing extremes, i.e., action/contemplation; personal needs/community life ; the ideals of the evangelical counsels/the experience of human weakness and the tendency to sin. Such a life of balanced extremes should make the balance of negative contrariety and cooperative dialogue spoken of in this essay that much easier to incorporate within one's own spirituality and approach to life. That is not to say that a similar balance cannot be developed in other states of life within the Church (both lay and priestly), but only that the religious life is especially suited to it.[35] To be sure, the eschatological orientation of the vows themselves moves the religious to maintain a continually balanced perspective between life in the present and in the beyond. In this respect, realized eschatology refers not to a collapse of the latter into the former, but to the balanced and simultaneous movement of each, bringing the Christian to his or her ultimate end in God.[36]

---

[34] The fundamental ecclesial dimension of the religious life takes on even greater significance in the ecumenical context. See John Paul II, "La vita religiosa si comprende essenzialmente nella dimensione ecclesiale," nos. 7-8 [*IGP* 6/2:582-84]; SCRSI, "Norms for Religious Life," *The Pope Speaks* 28 (1983): 318-19 (English original; text does not appear in *AAS*).

[35] For the role of religious in promoting Church unity, see Pierre-Yves Emery, "Vie religieuse et oecuménisme," *Vie consacrée* 53 (1981): 23-31; Thaddeus Horgan, "Religious Community and Christian Unity," *Review for Religious* 30 (1971): 442-46; Marie-André Houdart, "Communautés religieuses et souci de l'unité chrétienne," *Vie consacrée* 39 (1967): 288-309; Christianne Méroz, "Vie religieuse et unité de l'Église," *Vie consacrée* 53 (1981): 17-22.

[36] It would seem that this circular relationship in realized eschatology between the "already" and "not yet" lies at the heart of the Rahnerian ecumenical thesis of "unity apprehended in hope." See above 192 n. 25.

CONCLUSION

This chapter deals with the present deadlock in ecumenical progress by reexamining some of the basic premises of the discussion and by redirecting many of its current efforts for Christian unity. As put forth in these pages, the fundamental principle of ecumenical theology ("The Ecumenical Kernel") calls for the balancing of the opposing extremes of negative contrariety and cooperative dialogue. While the former refers to the relationship of heterodox/orthodox codependence prevalent in the early Church and in the Catholic church's relation with dissident Christian traditions down through the centuries, the latter represents the more conciliatory, irenic approach employed since the time of the Second Vatican Council. The essay argues that the movement towards Christian unity lies not so much in a calculated agenda for doctrinal uniformity as in the commitment among the churches to maintain the balanced relationship of negative contrariety and cooperative dialogue. The resulting bonds from such a relationship of opposing extremes give rise to a healthy respect for traditions other than one's own and, at the same time, a deeper consciousness of the mutual dependence which so many traditions share but so seldom advert to.

Religious can play an important role in helping to maintain this balance of opposing extremes. Their commitment to the vows provides them with a deep spiritual basis from which they can develop the necessary internal disposition of mind and heart required for the principle to take effect. Since their way of life already asks them to sustain a similar balance of opposing extremes in many areas of their lives, they give witness, on the one hand, to those who believe it cannot be done and set an example, on the other hand, for those seeking to embody the principle in their own lives. In this respect, the faithful dedication of religious to their calling not only serves as a leaven for themselves and others (both within and without the Catholic tradition), but also brings those whose indifference blinds them to the call for Church unity to sit up and take notice. From all that has been said, religious should be in the forefront of the Church's attempt to

The Ecumenical Kernel

maintain with other religious traditions a balanced relationship of negative contrariety and cooperative dialogue.

In the final analysis, the fundamental principle of ecumenical theology ("The Ecumenical Kernel") states that Church unity involves a process of committed encounter between religious traditions whose very existence implies a relationship of concrete mutual dependence. The goal of ecumenical theology must be to highlight this relationship in such a way that it will provide for all concerned a deeper understanding of the issues which unite and separate them. Since such understanding will take place only in the context of the above-mentioned balance of opposing extremes, it would seem that the churches have much to do before the long yearned-for unity "in faith and morals" becomes a reality for future Christian generations.[37]

---

[37] A parting note on the future of ecumenical theology: The notion of "a balance of opposing extremes" is not unlike the phrase in the Christian mystical tradition known as the "coincidence of opposites." Perhaps the next major theological impetus within ecumenical dialogue will be a greater appreciation of the insights that negative theology might have with respect to the mystery of the Church. While negative theology normally focuses on what can be said (or, rather, not said) about the mystery of God, its application to the mystery of the Church is within the realm of theological possibility, but has not yet been adequately explored. For a classic description of the "coincidence of opposites," see Nicholas of Cusa, *De docta ignorantia*, 3.2 in *Nikolaus von Kues Werke*, vol. 1, ed. Paul Wilpert (Berlin: Walter de Gruter and Co., 1967), 73-74.

14

THE MARIAN KERNEL

Is there a continuing theological (i.e., fundamental) principle of Mariology? The answer to this question depends on whether the Church's teaching on Mary can be formulated in such a way that will make it, at one and the same time, both inwardly coherent and intrinsically related to the whole of theology. An adequate response will require a number of important distinctions.

TERMINOLOGY

There is, for example, the question of terminology. In answering the above question it is important that a workable, if not precise, understanding of the terms "continuing," "theological" and "principle" be drawn. At the very outset of any endeavor (and this particular one is no exception), it is important to have at least some idea of just what it is one is looking for. It is important to get hold of one's underlying presuppositions. Otherwise, a person can become a prisoner of his or her own unexamined expectations. It is also possible to spend one's time looking for the wrong thing in the wrong place. To avoid this a person must look carefully at the terms being used. In this context, the word "continuing" is to be understood as "something that endures." A thing, however, can endure in a number of ways. It can, for example, be present from the very beginning and endure in a static, changeless sort of way. It can also endure through evolution and, yes, even through devolution. The concept of change, therefore, need not be excluded from the notion of "continuity." The term "theological" presents a different set of possibilities. There are at least two different ways of doing theology: sapientially or existentially. In the words of Otto Pesch, while the former "is the way of doing theology from outside one's self-actuation in the existence in faith," the latter "is the way of doing theology from within the self-actuation of our existence in faith, as we submit to God in the obedience of faith."[1] The former speaks descriptively, usually in the third person, and looks from God upon humanity; the latter speaks in the mode of confession, usually prototypically within an I-Thou situation, and looks from humanity toward God and then from God back upon humanity. Each approach, having different concerns and modes of expression, often arrives at markedly different conclusions. Finally, there is the term, "principle." This can mean different things to different people. A principle can be something external and applied, or something internal but abstracted. It can also be seen as a motivating force, a veritable "principle of life." These distinctions are made at the beginning to show some of the hidden implications of the question itself. As this essay continues, it will be better not to narrow the meaning of any one term, but to proceed with the consciousness of their multifaceted senses. Indeed, it now proceeds not with one but with many questions within a single formulation: Is there a continuing (static? devolutionary? evolutionary?) theological (sapiential? existential?) principle (external and applied? internal but abstracted? life-giving, motivating force?) of Mariology? The term "Mariology" itself complicates the question even further. In its strictest sense, it refers to the study and sum of anthropological, ecclesiological, Christological, soteriological, and strictly theological statements made in the context of the person and transhistorical symbol of Mary. In its wider sense, it is expanded

---

[1] Otto Hermann Pesch, "Existential and Sapiential Theology: The Theological Confrontation between Luther and Thomas Aquinas," in *Catholic Scholars Dialogue with Luther*, ed. J. Wicks (Chicago: Loyola University Press, 1970), 76. See also chap. 1, "The Theology Kernel," 4 n. 13.

The Marian Kernel

to include the incarnation of these statements in popular piety and devotion.[2] With a mind open to all of the above possibilities, an effort will now be made to outline the essential elements of what may be called "the Marian Kernel." In a later section, an attempt will be made to locate this kernel in the terminologies outlined above.

THE MARIAN KERNEL

Among the titles given to Mary in the New Testament is η δουλη κυριου (female servant of the Lord).[3] This title is given by Luke, placed on Mary's own lips (Lk 1:38, 48) and is expressed in prayer to the Lord. God's response to us through Mary is the birth of his Son in the mystery of the Incarnation. Implied in this gracious act of giving is the reciprocal gift of Mary under her initial title of response: God gives us his Son; along with his Son he has given Mary back to us as η δουλη κυριου. Mary's words of cooperation with the plan of God's providence (the second half of Lk 1:38) as well as her role as Virgin Mother flow from this her first of many titles.[4]

---

[2] See Michael O'Carroll, *Theotokos: A Theological Encyclopedia of the Blessed Virgin Mary* (Wilmington: Michael Glazier, 1982), s.v. "Mariology."

[3] In the Hebrew Scriptures, the title "Servant of the Lord" was used frequently to refer to those chosen by God to carry out his plan for his chosen people or for all of humanity (cf. Gn 24:14; Ex 14:31; 32:13; Nm 12:7; Dt 9:27; Jos 24:29; Ezk 37:25; 2 S 7:8; Am 3:7; Jr 7:25; Is 41:8-9; 42:19; 43:10; 44:1-2; 44:28; 45:1). See McDonald, William J., gen. ed., *The New Catholic Encyclopedia* (New York: McGraw-Hill, 1967), s.v. "Servant of the Lord Oracles," by M.A. Gervais. No other phrase in the New Testament can be placed without hesitation and so naturally in apposition to Mary's name. For Luke, Mary is η δουλη κυριου. See O'Carroll, *Theotokos*, s.v. "Titles of Our Lady."

[4] According to Raymond E. Brown: "...he [Luke] is voicing a Christian intuition that the virginal conception of Jesus must have constituted for Mary the beginning of her confrontation with the mysterious plan of God embodied in the person of her son." See *The Birth of the Messiah: A Commentary on the Infancy Narratives in Matthew and Luke* (Garden City, N.Y.: Doubleday and Co., 1977), 318.

It must be pointed out, however, that, even in Luke, one is already walking along the paths of theological expression. To be sure, within the confines of a strict historical critical examination of the evidence, it is possible to say that the historical Mary is just as obscured as the historical Jesus, if not more. The Catholic tradition, nevertheless, has affirmed what may be termed an *evolutionary* continuity between the historical Mary, the various theological presentations of her in the New Testament (conflicting as they may be), and her transhistorical significance as expressed and defined by later centuries of the Church's tradition.[5] If this is true, then, it follows that Mary's title η δουλη κυριου, can be applied to her at any point along the evolutionary continuum of Mariology. This implies that Mary says now not only to God, but also to the Church vivified by God's Spirit γενοιτο μοι κατα το ρημα σου ("Let it be done to me according to your word"). As in the infancy narrative of Luke, this is achieved by according Mary both a maternal and a virginal function. In other words, just as, traditionally, these roles have been ascribed back to the historical Mary from the evidence in the infancy narratives, it is possible to apply them by real proportionate analogy to the level of her transhistorical significance. Here, Mary's mothering role has taken shape on the level of symbol and myth; her virginal role has functioned through her use as a theological model. In all of this, what unites the Church's view of Mary is that, on whatever level of the continuum she is dealt with, she is perceived as virgin and mother. These very roles, however, are dependent on Mary's fundamental title of being η δουλη κυριου. The following sections will elaborate these claims.

---

[5] The German Catholic theologian Karl Adam expresses this continuity thus: "We know little or nothing of her early life; but from the moment that she appears upon the stage of history, Mary is irradiated with light: 'Hail, full of grace, the Lord is with thee, blessed art thou amongst women (Lk 1:28).' No angel has ever spoken a greater or holier word than that to man or woman. For centuries now the Church has pondered this angelic salutation, prayerfully and lovingly, and has discovered continually in it new glories of Mary. And yet her mystery is still unexhausted." See *The Spirit of Catholicism*, 126.

MARY AS MOTHERING MYTH AND SYMBOL

To understand Mary's mothering role in its transhistorical significance, it is necessary to understand the nature of symbol and myth. While a symbol is a specific act or figure (e.g., a bow or a candle), a myth develops and elaborates many symbols in a story which contains characters and several episodes. The two obviously go together: psychologically, they are humanity's way of expressing and experiencing in a concrete way the yearning of its deepest personal, social and religious hopes. Unlike mere signals and poetic expressions, symbol and myth cannot be constructed and then taken apart. They must be born; their existence ends only by their being allowed to die. Symbol and myth delve beneath the person's conscious self and nurture the unknown, deeper parts. They are at home in the unconscious and work there in a way not dissimilar to that of dreams. Symbol and myth foster a person's hope in a beyond; they give birth to new hopes in humanity's transcendental destiny.[6]

Mary's mothering role in Mariology is best perceived at the levels expressed above. The infancy stories of Luke, her wait at the cross in John, the meditations on her early childhood in *The Protoevangelium of James*, her depiction as The New Eve in Irenaeus and Tertullian, the views of her Assumption and Queenship in heaven,[7] all of the symbols connected with her interrelate to form "The Myth of Mary." This myth expresses theological and psychic

---

[6] Paul Tillich finds six main characteristics of a symbol: (1) It points to something beyond itself; (2) It participates in that to which it points; (3) It opens up levels of reality which are otherwise closed to us; (4) it unlocks dimensions of our soul which correspond to those dimensions and elements of reality; (5) it cannot be produced intentionally; and (6) like living beings, it grows and dies. See *Dynamics of Faith* (New York: Harper and Row, 1957), 41-43. For more on the symbolic structure of theology, see Haight, *Dynamics of Theology*, 142-45.

[7] For a treatment of these and other devotional representations of Mary, see Hilda Graef, *Mary: A History of Doctrine and Devotion*, vol. 1, *From the Beginning to the Eve of the Reformation* (New York: Sheed and Ward, 1963), 1-27, 32-46, 133-38, 142. See also O'Carroll, *Theotokos*, s.v. "Apocrypha, The New Testament"; "Assumption of Our Lady, The"; "Infancy Narratives, The"; "John the Evangelist"; "Queenship, Mary's."

truths about the believer's yearning for salvation and hope that in some sense the fullness of redemption has already taken place. It also touches the interior intuition and yearning of many for a feminine, mothering image of God. The Mary myth, according to Catholic tradition, is continuous with historical fact. This continuity, however, should not be looked upon as something static and changeless. While being continuous, it has at the same time moved beyond fact. In its transhistorical significance the myth itself not only expresses humanity's deepest yearnings, but also, acting not only as object but also as subject, conveys an experience. That experience can be described as the spiritual motherhood of Mary.[8]

MARY AS VIRGIN AND THEOLOGICAL MODEL

Mary in her transhistorical significance, however, is both mother and virgin. While her maternal role in Mariology is played out through symbol and myth, her virginal function is performed through her use as a theological model. A theological model can be defined as a description or analogy used to help visualize a theological truth that cannot be directly observed.[9] Because such models deal with truth on the level of mystery, they can, by their very nature, be nothing more than approximations. There is a logical gap between the model itself and the mystery it seeks to hold. Strictly speaking, therefore, theological models cannot define mystery itself. They themselves, however, can be defined as legitimate, orthodox attempts to hold the truth of revelation.

The Church has used Mary often as a theological model in order to express and preserve the purity of its faith. This correlates

---

[8] For more on Mary's spiritual motherhood, see Frederick M. Jelly, "The Concrete Meaning of Mary's Motherhood," *The Way Supplement* 45 (1982): 30-40. See also Stan Parmisano, "Mary in Contemporary Culture," *Review for Religious* 48 (1989): 328.

[9] Theological models, then, are not "picture (or scale) models," which provide exact pictures of the realities they treat, but "disclosure (or analogue) models," which disclose or re-present the realities they seek to interpret. See Tracy, *Blessed Rage for Order*, 22.

to Mary's virginal role in her transhistorical significance. The models of the virgin birth, the Theotokos, the Immaculate Conception and the Assumption, were "defined" to express either a Christological or a soteriological truth. They have been defined as legitimate, orthodox expressions of the faith and, in varying degrees, can be seen as healthy reactions to the respective Gnostic, Nestorian, rationalist, and Marxist diminutions of the Church's perception of the Gospel.[10] Be that as it may, no single model captures the fullness of the mystery of Mary in her relation to her Son, to the Church, and to humanity in general. Indeed, the very fact that they are models suggests that they are to be held gently and perhaps only in relationship to what they were originally intended to negate. From this perspective, the history of the Church's use of Mary as a theological model can be seen as the history of its struggle for the integrity of its faith.[11]

MARY: VIRGIN AND MOTHER

To be both virgin and mother is a natural contradiction.[12] Just as they are combined in the person of Mary in Luke's infancy narrative and have been ascribed consequently to the historical

---

[10] Thus, the virgin birth offset the docetic tendencies of Gnostic mythology; the Theotokos doctrine countered the Nestorian belief that Mary was the mother of Jesus, but not the mother of God; the Immaculate Conception affirmed the need for God's grace in order (for Mary) to be preserved from sin, thereby contradicting the Enlightenment's naive exaltation of the innate potential human nature; the doctrine of the Assumption emphasized the transcendent character of human destiny in the face of Communist and secular humanist atheism.

[11] For more on the Church's use of Marian doctrine as a way of expressing the purity of its faith, see Frederick M. Jelly, "Mary's Virginity in the Symbols and Councils," *Marian Studies* 21 (1970): 69-93.

[12] For a clear exegetical presentation of the problem of the virginal conception, see Brown, *The Virginal Conception and the Bodily Resurrection of Jesus*, 1-68; Raymond E. Brown, Karl P. Donfried, Joseph A. Fitzmyer, John Reumann, eds., *Mary in the New Testament* (Philadelphia: Fortress Press, 1978), 91-96, 115-25. For a dogmatic perspective on the problem, see Karl Rahner, "Mary's Virginity," chap. in *Theological Investigations*, vol. 19, *Faith and Ministry*, trans. Edward Quinn (London: Darton, Longman and Todd, 1983), 218-31.

Mary by the tradition of the Church, so too they must be combined in her transhistorical significance through the Church's subsequent theological thought and reflection. For the Church today, Mary must be an object of both symbol and intellectual reflection. As in any age, the overriding danger is that she will be relegated to only one of these roles. To do so would seriously harm the important relationship between experience (myth, symbol) and truth (theological models) which the Catholic tradition has endeared to itself for so long. Once again, it is important to remember that Mary's role as the virgin mother followed from her willingness to be η δουλη κυριου. The complexity of the mothering and virginal tensions in Mary, dealing as they do with different concerns and modes of expression, find their focal point in a simple, life-giving principle of service. Mary placed herself in the service of God. God, in turn, has placed Mary at the service of the Church's experience and theology. In doing so, the Church, with Mary, seeks to give birth to Christ in each age subsequent to his departure.

Even in today's Church, Mary is cast in a role that operates on a number of different levels. Regardless of the level, however, Mary, η δουλη κυριου, must be allowed to work within the context of both her mothering and virginal roles. To begin with, individuals must be willing to delve within themselves and discover those personal symbols and images with which a feminine principle is associated. These, in turn, should be reflected upon, theologized upon and related to Mary. An association of fire with a feminine principle, for example, can be related to Mary and the Pentecost event. The image of the early Church in the upper room with tongues of fire over their heads is one that many can relate to strongly. From there a person can develop his or her own personal devotion to Mary in the context of what has become a contemporary model of ecclesiology.

This process should move from individuals to groups as well. Some religious orders, for example, have been fortunate in that they have a single image of Mary that strikes strong emotional chords in their members and has become a focus of their group identity (e.g., the icon of "Our Mother of Perpetual Help" and the

Redemptorists).[13] Given this common image of Mary, it is important (perhaps now more than ever) that such groups reflect on the significance of Mary for the living out of their faith in accordance with their vowed commitment and rule of life.[14] In such groups, there is often a strong mothering image operative in their collective existence; one sometimes suspects, however, that the reflective, virginal side has been left unattended.

Of course, such personal and group relationships to Mary are important only if they contribute to the overall veneration of Mary that is proper to her in the mainstream of the Church as it is depicted in the Council documents, in *Marialis cultus*,[15] and as it should be celebrated in the Liturgy. Anything divisive is not in the genuine spirit of Vatican II's teaching on Mary. It might be added, moreover, that Mary's role as servant, as it is expressed in the mothering and virginal function of her transhistorical significance, also has a peculiarly ecumenical role to play. Given current understandings of both the nature of symbol and myth and the approximating, preservative role of the theological model, it is now possible for Protestants and Catholics alike to come out of their centuries-old trenches and observe mutually, in a spirit of profound respect, each other's approach to Mary.[16] As has been

---

[13] In 1866, the Redemptorists were entrusted with the icon of Our Mother of Perpetual Help. When the picture was enshrined in their church of St. Alphonsus in Rome, Pope Pius IX gave a command to the Redemptorists: "Make Our Mother of Perpetual Help known throughout the world." See William J. McDonald, gen. ed., *The New Catholic Encyclopedia*, (New York: McGraw-Hill, 1967), s.v. "Our Lady of Perpetual Help (Succour)," by C. Henze.

[14] For a useful starting point for such a reflection, see A. Bandera, "La Vergine Maria e la pratica dei consigli evangelici," *Vita consacrata* 9 (1973): 290-302, 380-94.

[15] Paul VI's apostolic exhortation for the right ordering and development of devotion to the Blessed Virgin Mary [*AAS* 66 (1974): 113-68]. For commentary, see E. Carroll, "Mary in the Western Liturgy: *Marialis Cultus*," *Communio* 7 (1980): 140-56.

[16] See, for example, the clear theological presentation of Mary in the context of ecumenical discussion given by Anglican theologian John Macquarrie in *Mary for All Christians* (Grand Rapids: Eerdmans, 1991). See also Donal Flannagan, "Mary in the Ecumenical Discussion," *Irish Theological Quarterly* 40 (1973): 227-49; Mary Eileen Foley, "Some Reflections on Mary, Bridge to Ecumenism," *Review for Religious* 48 (1989): 342-54.

suggested, this would involve close attention to both the images used concerning her as well as strict theological formulations.

MARY AND RELIGIOUS

The fundamental principle of Mariology ("The Marian Kernel") also offers significant insights into the life of the evangelical counsels. In their call to radical discipleship, religious turn to Mary, "the first Christian disciple,"[17] and seek to emulate her humble and genuine acceptance of God's Word in her life. Because her role as η δουλη κυριου is intimately related to her divinely inspired *fiat* (cf. Lk 1:38), it is appropriate that religious should model their own lives after Mary's grace-filled response. In their attempt to do so, they too will look upon themselves as "servants of the Lord" and display in their own lives elements of Mary's virginal and maternal functions. These elements surface most clearly in the vows they profess and live by.

In their vow of chastity, religious give up the goods of sexual pleasure, marriage, and family life in order to give witness to the existence of a beyond and to turn their lives over fully to an intimate relationship with God. In doing so, they remind others of the created (and hence relative) nature of their lives and the goods they enjoy. Such a witness evokes from others a twofold expectation that religious will be able (1) to give them a deeper understanding of what lies beyond and (2) to help them on their journey toward it. Because religious chastity (like the other counsels) is lived in and through an ecclesial context,[18] it follows that the appropriate response of religious to these expectations will involve their opening up and sharing with others the riches of the Catholic spiritual/theological tradition. In responding to the first expectation, religious demonstrate a deep concern for maintain-

---

[17] Brown, *The Birth of the Messiah*, 319.

[18] The ecclesial context of the vows is emphasized in John Paul II, "La vita religiosa si comprende essenzialmente nella dimensione ecclesiale," nos. 7-8 [IGP 6/2:582-84]; SCRSI, "Norms for Religious Life," 308-9, 318-19.

The Marian Kernel

ing the integrity of the faith. This concern corresponds to the virginal role assigned to Mary in maintaining the purity of the faith throughout Church history — and especially in times of turmoil. In responding to the second, they seek to nourish the growth of God's Word in others, just as they experience a similar growth (and eventual birth) within themselves. This relates to the important mothering role that Mary has assumed in Catholic spirituality. Through their vow of chastity, religious can emulate Mary, η δουλη κυριου and Mother of the Church,[19] by making sure that these dual concerns are maintained in a proportionate balance in their own lives and in their relations with others. An excessive movement toward either extreme will not do justice to the demands of Christian discipleship.

In their vow of poverty, religious maintain a simple lifestyle and are careful not to accumulate nonessential material accessories. They also seek to cultivate an inner spirit of humility that will keep them from drawing undue attachments to human goods on any of the various levels of their anthropological makeup (i.e., physical, mental, spiritual, and social).[20] In doing so, they express their deeply rooted belief that God is the only treasure of any lasting worth. From him, all other goods derive their value and significance; without him, they lose their luster and fail to truly satisfy. In the context of the fundamental principle of Mariology, this spirit of simplicity makes religious wary of drawing unnecessary attachments to any spiritual fads or novelties that may arise either outside or on the periphery of Catholic thought. In what amounts to their virginal concern to maintain and espouse the simplicity of the faith, religious are open to and eager to learn from other religious traditions, but always with an eye to how they will deepen and enrich their own understanding of the Catholic faith. Their solid resting in the simple contours of the Church's liturgi-

---

[19] For Mary's ecclesial motherhood, see Vatican Council II, *Lumen gentium*, no. 53 [*CDD*,192]; English translation: Flannery, *Vatican Council II*, 414; see also Jean Galot, "Madre della chiesa. Madre della communità," *Vita consacrata* 22 (1986): 348-54.

[20] These anthropological dimensions of human existence are developed in chap. 12, "The Prayer Kernel," 170-73.

cal/sacramental tradition, moreover, touches upon the important nurturing role that they offer to others. By not giving in to the temptations of spiritual consumerism and by actively making the Church's sacramental spirituality the focal point of their lives, they give eloquent testimony to others of their simple desire to rely solely on the Lord and to be nourished by the ordinary means provided through the Church for their salvation. By underscoring the importance of the sacraments for their own lives and by refusing to compromise this significance, religious help others to recognize the great nourishment that the sacraments offer. Their vow of poverty, in other words, embraces the simplicity of their spirituality which, as suggested above, expresses itself in both a virginal and maternal manner.

In their vow of obedience, religious accept the expressed wishes of their legitimate superiors as the will of God for their lives. This freely chosen act of submission of one's will to another person makes very concrete the otherwise vague and, at times, elusive desire to find God's will in the circumstances of life. Such a vow requires a relationship of mature discernment and openness to dialogue on the part of both the religious and his or her superior. Its spirit is perhaps most clearly expressed in the Annunciation scene of Luke where Mary, despite her fear (1:30) and her "being deeply troubled" (1:29), expresses by the grace of God the unconditional response of her Gospel *fiat*: "Let it be done to me as you say" (1:38). Understood in this important Marian context, religious obedience has an intimate connection with both the virginal *and* the maternal aspects of the fundamental principle of Mariology. With regard to the virginal, religious convey by their vow of obedience the conviction that truth is greater than the self and the self's perception of the truth. From this perspective, the vow is a useful means by which religious can successfully avoid the state of moral self-deception (i.e., the refusal to spell out accurately the limits of one's relationship with the world).[21] A

---

[21] More precisely, Herbert Fingarette describes self-deception as "a patent characteristic that even when normally appropriate he [the person] *persistently* avoids spelling out some feature of his engagement with the world." See *Self-Deception* (New York: Humanities Press, 1969), 38-39.

The Marian Kernel

mature adherence to the vow, in other words, requires religious to form their consciences well before ever openly challenging an explicit obedience of a legitimate superior. To do otherwise is to run the risk of mistaking one's feelings or strong preferences for the binding judgment of conscience.[22] With regard to the maternal, religious display by their vow of obedience a willingness to receive the Word of God as it is mediated through the frail human instrument of their religious superiors. This explicit openness to the reception of God's Word encourages religious to welcome that Word freely in their hearts and to foster its growth for their own spiritual good and for the good of their community. When properly understood, the vow encourages religious to think for themselves while all the time cooperating with God's grace as it is manifested in the concrete circumstances of their lives. As with the other vows, religious must seek to maintain a balance between the virginal and maternal aspects of their vow of obedience. An inadvertent swing to either extreme can remove the vow all too easily from its important ecclesial context and actually deter the spiritual birth of the Word in the minds and hearts of the faithful.

If for no other reason, religious have a close spiritual affiliation with Mary because they, like her, belong undeniably to the Church's life and holiness.[23] By virtue of this close association with the charismatic element of Christ's body, the Church, they seek to emulate that "highly favored daughter" (Lk 1:28) who, filled with the Holy Spirit, accepted so humbly and graciously her vocation as virgin-mother of God's Incarnate Word. In their attempts to follow their Lord by way of the response of Mary, η δουλη κυριου, religious discover the spirit of her virginity and maternity in their faithful and dedicated living of the vows. In doing so, they join

---

[22] That is not to say that emotions have nothing in common with the judgment of conscience. On the contrary, it pertains to the perfection of moral good that they be regulated by reason. See Thomas Aquinas, *Summa theologiae* I, q. 24, a. 3, resp. According to Conrad W. Baars, the emotions have "...an innate need to listen to the voice of reason." See "Christian Anthropology of Thomas Aquinas," *The Priest* 30 (no. 10, 1974): 30.

[23] Vatican Council II, *Lumen gentium*, no. 44 [*CDD*,177]; English translation: Flannery, *Vatican Council II*, 405.

Mary with all their hearts in proclaiming the greatness of the Lord and in finding joy in God their Savior (cf. Lk 1:46-7).[24]

CONCLUSION

To return to the question of precise terminology, it is fair to conclude by saying that the Marian Kernel described in this chapter is an evolutionary, developmental continuity, rooted in a motivating, life-giving principle, which has found and continues to find its expression through a number of ways of doing theology. The kernel itself can be summarized thus: the historical/transhistorical significance of Mary has been given to the Church in both a mothering (symbolic, mythic) and virginal (doctrinal, creedal integrity) capacity; because of this gift, the Church itself is in the process of becoming more fully η δουλη κυριου. From this perspective, the continuing theological principle of Mariology is intrinsic to the Church's view of itself, a part of its very nature (and has special significance for religious). To disregard this principle would be tantamount to disregarding the sacramental nature of the Church itself. It too, in giving birth to spiritual sons and daughters of God through evangelization, has a mothering and virginal role to perform. Mariology, therefore, is closely related to ecclesiology.[25] The continuing theological principle of one must be valid for the other.[26] As η δουλη κυριου, each performs a corresponding maternal and virginal function; each concerns itself with nothing more and nothing less than a giving birth to Christ in the particular circumstances of each succeeding historical age unto the consummation of time itself.

---

[24] The special relationship between Mary and religious has been treated from a slightly different perspective in chap. 4, "The Church Kernel," 61-62.

[25] Thus the final chapter of "The Dogmatic Constitution on the Church" is appropriately devoted to Mary. See Vatican Council II, *Lumen gentium*, nos. 52-69 [*CDD*, 191-206]; English translation: Flannery, *Vatican Council II*, 413-23.

[26] "Marie devient ecclésiale et l'Église devient mariale." See Jean-Marie Hennaux, "Marie, l'église et la femme dans l'évangile de Luc," *Vie consacrée* 47 (1975): 268.

15

THE END KERNEL

Is there a fundamental principle of eschatology? The answer to this question depends on how one relates the Church's teaching on "the last things" to the whole of theology. Careful to steer clear of the extremes of an uncritical literalism, on the one hand, and an unrestrained demythologizing, on the other, the theologian must recognize that such traditional eschatological doctrines as the resurrection, judgment (general and individual), heaven, and hell make little or no sense once they are detached from the larger theological context which originally brought them to light and sustains them. In this regard, eschatology presupposes a certain narrative structure which both unites the various theological disciplines one to another and enables them to anticipate continually the ultimate realization of humanity's redemption. In the Church's theological tradition, this narrative base is usually referred to under the title of "salvation history."

SALVATION HISTORY: THE NARRATIVE BASIS OF ESCHATOLOGY

A literal translation from the German, *Heilsgeschichte*, salvation history recounts the history of God's salvific action on behalf of his people.[1] Rooted in the Hebrew experience of Egyptian

---

[1] For the history of the term *"Heilsgeschichte,"* see Heinrich Fries, ed., *Handbuch Theologischer Grundbegriffe* (Kösel: Verlag München, 1962), s.v. "Heilsgeschichte

captivity, it traces the religious roots of a loosely connected gathering of ancient bedouin tribes from their vague recollections of their patriarchal past, through their experience of liberation from slavery, to their period of Palestinian conquest, prosperity under a united kingdom, internal division, exile in Babylon, return, and ultimate takeover by the military might of Rome's occupational forces. Throughout this time, the belief in God's actions in human affairs was kept alive by the eschatological preaching of the Hebrew prophets, who spoke of the coming of a Messiah and the promise of a New Covenant between God and his people. Jesus of Nazareth saw himself as the fulfillment of these prophecies. His followers consider his passion, death, and resurrection the definitive action of God's redeeming love extended to all peoples. Through the sacraments, the Church continues Christ's redemptive mission on earth during the interim period between his first and second comings.[2]

Even this brief summary of the Christian understanding of salvation history reveals the major premises upon which the narrative basis of eschatology rests: (1) God is involved in human history; (2) the discernible features of that history become visible only to the eyes of faith; (3) God's action in time has a salvific purpose; (4) Christ represents the fullness of that purpose; (5) the Church interprets the meaning of the Christ event; for (6) the Christ event embraces yet far exceeds the bounds of time.[3] Taken together, these premises indicate that all of salvation history is a theological reflection upon the meaning of the Christ event. The eschatological dimensions of this event are present not only at the historical moment of Jesus' death and resurrection or at the consummation of all things in Christ at the end of time, but also at

---

II. Systematisch," by A. Darlapp. For a short English treatment, see McBrien, *Catholicism*, 2:228-29.

[2] For Vatican II's presentation of "salvation history" (*historia salutis*) see Vatican Council II, *Dei verbum* nos. 1-10 [*CDD*, 423-32]; English translation: Flannery, *Vatican Council II*, 750-56.

[3] For an alternative listing, see Karl Rahner, "The Hermeneutics of Eschatological Assertions," in *Theological Investigations*, vol. 4, *More Recent Writings*, trans. Kevin Smyth (London: Darton, Longmann and Todd, 1974), 323-46.

all intervening historical moments. That is to say that eschatology is not so much concerned with "the last things" in the chronological sense of the phrase, but in the sense of it being of ultimate value to human existence. It is for this reason that eschatology is said to be related to the whole of theology. There is, in other words, an eschatological dimension to each and every one of the theological disciplines.[4]

From what has been said, Christian eschatology is not to be thought of as some distant, long-awaited climax of the dramatic religious narrative of God's salvific acts. It has as much, if not more, to do with the past and the present. A slight reformulation of the classical soteriological principle bears this out: "God entered time so that humanity might enter eternity." That is to say that God's decisive entrance into time has ramifications redounding throughout history and affecting the very nature of time itself.[5]

With the coming of Christ, time can no longer be confined to the limitations of scientific quantification. It has been blessed and made holy. Profane time (Χρονος) has been transformed into sacred time (Καιρος), by reason of the presence of that divine perspective which now inhabits its dimensions not as a distant and detached onlooker, but from within its own created limits.[6] God, so to speak, has entered time and now looks out from it through human eyes; all that purports to be of ultimate concern for humanity now has similar significance for the divine. In this respect, the fundamental dimension of all authentic Christian narrative is the belief that God's salvific action is now being

---

[4] For how all of theology is in a sense eschatological (*spes quaerens intellectum*), see Jürgen Moltmann, *Theology of Hope*, trans. James W. Leitch (London: SCM Press, LTD, 1977), 304-38.

[5] The original formula reads: Αυτος γαρ ευηνθρωπησεν ινα ημεις θεοποιηθωμεν ("For He was made man so that we might be made God") [translation mine] Athanasius, *De incarnatione*, 54.3 [SC 199:458-59; PG 25:191-92]. See also Gregory of Nyssa, *De opificio hominis*, 16 [SC 6:151-61; PG 44:178-88].

[6] For a discussion of the sacred and profane dimensions of both time and space, see Mircea Eliade, *Le sacré et le profane*, 2d ed. (Paris: Éditions Gallimard, 1965), 21, 55-63, 90-91.

brought to completion within the historical processes of human activity itself.[7]

It is precisely here where the ethical dimension of eschatology comes to light. To the extent that it is open to the ultimate concerns of life, human action enhances the establishment of the reign of God on earth. To the extent that it is not, it inhibits it. One may even go so far as to say that the eschatological dimension of human action is one of the major identifying characteristics of authentic Christian morality. That is to say that a particular moral standard or ethical system may be considered Christian only to the extent that it is open to the transcendent and oriented to the historical establishment of the beyond. In no other theological discipline is the "already-but-not-yet" character of eschatology manifested to so great an extent. And it is in this respect that eschatology forms the basis of a genuine theology of Christian hope.[8]

ESCHATOLOGY AND HOPE

Along with the other theological virtues of faith and love, the Apostle Paul describes hope as one of but three things that last (1 Cor 13:13). As such, it pertains to values of ultimate human concern and is thus intimately related to Christian eschatology. As a theological virtue, hope is traditionally viewed as an infused gift from God.[9] From this, one may infer that it is a reality shared by both divine and human points of view. Granted the obvious analogical use of the term, a person may rightly conclude that God hopes in humanity just as humanity hopes in the ultimate establishment of God's reign. In Jesus, the unity of the divine and

---

[7] To state it in another way: "Inasmuch as God is the giver of all human life stories, they are the manifestations of his grace and are measured by the demands of his intention." See Navone and Cooper, *Tellers of the Word*, 105.

[8] For the ethical dimensions of Christian eschatology, see Michael Simpson, *Death and Eternal Life*, Theology Today Series, no. 42 (Hales Corners, Wis.: Clergy Book Service, 1971), 90-94.

[9] Thomas Aquinas, *Summa theologiae*, I-II, q. 62, a. 1, resp.; II-II, q. 17, a. 5, resp.

human perspectives enlarges the scope and eschatological dimension of the virtue even further: with his coming, the reign of God has been made manifest and is identified with humanity's struggle to be free from its own inhumanity to itself.

This inhumanity exists on two levels: the individual and the social, each a formidable opponent when encountered in the daily throes of modern life. The current tension experienced in Western society between the individual and his or her relationship to community is reflected not only in the Church's understanding of the connection between personal and social sin, but also in the Church's traditional teaching on particular and universal judgment. That is to say that an overly individualized version of the doctrine of final judgment (e.g., coming exclusively at the moment of a person's death) is just as harmful to the Church's mission as an overly universalized one (e.g., coming only as a generic judgment on the whole human race).[10] In point of fact, the eschatological tension between the two is rooted in a Christian anthropology which recognizes both the singular and communitarian aspects of human personhood. To emphasize one to the exclusion of the other devalues the dignity of the human person and undermines the true meaning of Christian hope. By its very nature, hope cannot affirm one without the other.

Oriented towards those things of ultimate human concern, Christian hope looks forward to: (1) the concrete realization of God's justice for all times and for all peoples; (2) the transformation of the individual into the fullness of his or her created nature; (3) the full incorporation of that resurrected form into union with Christ's Mystical Body; (4) a final determination of the status of God's people (both individually and collectively) in their relation to the persons of the Triune Godhead; and (5) the full creaturely reception of God in the beatific vision (*visio Dei*).[11] Each of these

---

[10] For references pertaining to primary sources and magisterial teaching on the particular and universal judgments, see Ott, *Fundamentals of Catholic Dogma*, 475-76, 492-94.

[11] For a similar description located within the explicit context of Christian eschatology, see Rahner, "The Hermeneutics of Eschatological Assertions," 343-44.

aspects of eschatological hope interrelate. They are united by virtue of their participation in the mystery of Christ, whose entrance into this life marked a turning point in the establishment of God's reign in the world. Rooted in this mystery, Christian hope is possible only in and through the power of Christ, which is made explicit by his promise to be with the believing Christian community forever, "even unto the end of time" (Mt 28:20). In this respect, all that is awaited for in Christian hope is, to some extent, already present, by virtue of the presence in the believing community of that power which will one day bring it fully about.[12] This element of eschatological potency is an essential aspect of any sound formulation of the fundamental principle of eschatology.

THE END KERNEL

From what has been said thus far, the fundamental principle of eschatology ("The End Kernel") may be formulated as follows: Eschatology has to do with all things of ultimate human concern. It points to the concrete establishment of God's justice by means of a final judgment (both universal and particular in scope) which effects the ultimate transformation of human life (i.e., life in the resurrection), the full incorporation into Christ's Mystical Body (i.e., as the Church triumphant), and the fullness of the beatific vision (i.e., the *visio Dei*). Through the virtue of Christian hope, each of these concerns is already potentially present in the believing Christian community.

Given the above formulation, a number of observations arise:

(1) The principle's implicit narrative base must be free from the effects of unnecessary religious dogmatism. The story, in other words, must be allowed to be told without fear of its being forced

---

[12] For pertinent primary texts on Christ as the foundation of Christian hope, see Josef Pieper, *On Hope*, trans., Mary Francis McCarthy (San Francisco: Ignatius Press, 1977), 34-35.

into conforming with any preconceived doctrinal conception of its meaning.[13]

(2) The principle must be viewed in the context of an easily applicable interpretative principle which takes into account both the tradition of the Church's past and the experience of the present. The anagogical sense of pre-modern Biblical exegesis, which relates the sacred text to the last things without isolating them from the other spiritual senses and, hence, from the rest of theology, deserves further investigation for the contribution it made and can still make to the eschatological dimension of each of the theological disciplines.[14]

(3) A way must be found of structuring the various theological disciplines around a single, cohesive eschatological schematic. The Neoplatonic *exitus/reditus* format of Aquinas' *Summa theologiae*, which depicts all of creation as "going out" and "returning" to God, deserves further study with an eye toward applying a similar approach to the structuring of today's theological investigations.[15]

(4) To speak of the concrete establishment of God's "justice" demands clear understanding not only of both the social and personal implications of the term, but also of the way in which God, in Christ, has identified his concerns for justice with those of

---

[13] Jean Daniélou describes this narrative basis thus: "... the substance of the Christian revelation is not in a knowledge of God's existence (which other religions have as well), but in the perception of his activity on the scene of time, his effective interventions in the world of human history. From the Creation to the Resurrection, by way of the choosing of our father Abraham, the Christian revelation is a sacred history, the chronicle of the wonderful works of God, a documentary narrative: alone among the sacred books, the Christian's Bible is not a collection of doctrine but a story." See *The Lord of History* (Chicago: Regnery, 1958), 111.

[14] "Littera gesta docet, quid credas allegoria, / Moralis quid agas, *quo tendas anagogia*" (italics mine). Cited in Robert M. Grant and David Tracy, *A Short History of the Interpretation of the Bible*, 2d ed. (Philadelphia: Fortress Press, 1984), 85. For a discussion of how a return to allegory can help to reintegrate contemporary theology and spirituality, see Louth, *Discerning the Mystery*, 96-131.

[15] For the *Exitus/Reditus* structure of the *Summa theologiae* see Chenu, *Towards Understanding Saint Thomas*, 304-10.

the human struggle for liberation in all its many dimensions. Such an understanding will not allow the cause of personal justice to be achieved at the expense of the social.[16]

5) The notion of "judgment" used in the formulation of the principle should not be understood in terms of an outdated, anthropomorphic notion of "divine wrath," but in the sense of the revelation of the truth upon which all parties (both human and divine) will ultimately concur. In this respect, the judgment of God resembles a mirror held before the critical eye of human conscience, reflecting the truth, but confronting the individual only with that which he or she is able to see.[17]

(6) In order to steer clear of the extremes of uncritical literalism, on the one hand, and unrestrained demythologizing, on the other, "resurrection," as understood in this formulation should be understood as a transhistorical event with historical consequences. In this way, the best of both positions is affirmed, while avoiding those sensitive areas over which they conflict.[18]

(7) Christ's Mystical Body, in contrast, may be understood as a historical reality (i.e., the Church militant) with transhistorical consequences (i.e., the Church triumphant). That is to say that the

---

[16] The classical Thomistic position maintains a fine balance between the individual and communal dimensions of justice: "St. Thomas's answer might have run like this: Justice rules in a community or state whenever three basic relations, the three fundamental structures of communal life, are disposed in their proper order: firstly, the relations of individuals to one another (*ordo partium ad partes*); secondly, the relations of the social whole to individuals (*ordo totius ad partes*); thirdly, the relations of individuals to the social whole (*ordo partium ad totum*). These three basic relationships correspond to the three basic forms of justice: reciprocal, or mutually exchanged justice (*iustitia commutativa*), which orders the relation of individual to individual partner; ministering justice (*iustitia distributiva*), which brings order to the relations between the community as such and the individuals who are its members; legal or general justice (*iustitia legalis, iustitia generalis*), which orders the members' relations to the social whole." See Josef Pieper, *The Four Cardinal Virtues* (Notre Dame: University of Notre Dame Press, 1966), 71-72.

[17] "Intrinsically, the finality and irrevocability of man's status comes from man's own decision and self-judgment, extrinsically it comes from God's judgmental will ratifying and implementing man's decision." See E.J. Fortman, *Everlasting Life After Death* (Staten Island, N.Y.: Alba House, 1976), 125-26.

[18] See chap. 8, "The Resurrection Kernel," 110 n. 2.

Church, which has its origins in a visible earthly reality (i.e., the preaching and teaching of Christ and his followers) is constantly moving toward its eschatological destiny, both through the death and transformation of its members and in its own historical march toward the consummation of time itself.[19]

(8) The *visio Dei* referred to in the principle has both a divine and a human aspect, i.e., God's eternal vision of created humanity and the corresponding human gaze into the mysteries of the divine. While the two must never be equated, it remains clear that the latter is possible only because of the unending, eternal attraction of the former. To overlook this important point runs the risk of compromising the Church's teaching on eschatology with a subtle form of Pelagianism. The beatific vision, in other words, is an utter gift from God and cannot be earned apart from his grace. In this respect, an individual's vision of God is ultimately dependent on God's vision of the individual; the divine vision, in turn, actually sustains the individual and keeps him or her in the act of continued existence.[20]

Taken together, all of the preceding observations are important qualifications of the fundamental principle of eschatology. Not only do they help clarify particular facets of the formulation itself, but they also identify areas in need of further investigation and incorporation into the principle. It should not be surprising that all of these observations are also important for understanding the relation between eschatology and the theology of religious life.

ESCHATOLOGY AND RELIGIOUS LIFE

Through their vowed life, religious give witness to values of ultimate human concern. In their vow of chastity, they forego the goods of marriage, children, and sexual pleasure in order to keep their eyes more firmly fixed on the lasting goodness and pleasure

---

[19] See Vatican Council II, *Lumen gentium*, no. 49 [*CDD*, 184-85]; English translation: Flannery, *Vatican Council II*, 409-10.

[20] See chap. 9, "The Sacramental Kernel," 126 n. 9.

of the beatific vision in the life to come. In their vow of poverty, they point to the common humanity shared by all and which makes all men and women fundamentally equal in the eyes of God. In their vow of obedience, they affirm in the submission of their wills to their religious superiors the existence of a higher will for their lives, one which will lead them to their destiny of union with the ultimate ground of their being. To the extent that religious remain faithful to the vows which they have freely chosen and taken upon themselves, they help make the presence of God's reign visible in the life of the Church and for all to see. In this respect, they orient their entire lives towards the eschatological dimensions of the Christ event and help keep alive the hope of God's coming to a world in dire need of his loving justice.[21]

Religious, moreover, represent a continuation of the living narrative of the eschatological dimension of the Church's life. Each religious vocation represents an individual's response to a divine call which ultimately only he or she can properly articulate. These stories should not be thought of as private possessions of the individual religious, but as the common property of the believing community. For this reason, religious should be encouraged to share the stories of their discovery of God's presence in their lives and the way in which they came to see the value of their witness of transcendency to the world. Their stories will not only contribute to the community's grasp of the ongoing meaning of salvation history in the life of the Church, but also furnish yet a further basis for hope in the ultimate fulfillment of God's eschatological promise.[22]

---

[21] One of the clearest indications of the eschatological dimension of the religious life is the structural location within the Church's official ecclesiological teaching (i.e., *The Dogmatic Constitution on the Church*) of a chapter on religious (chap. 6) between a chapter on the universal call to holiness (chap. 5) and the eschatological (or pilgrim) orientation of the entire People of God (chap. 7). See Vatican Council II, *Lumen gentium* nos. 39-51 [*CDD*, 164-90]; English translation: Flannery, *Vatican Council II*, 396-413. No other state within the Church (neither lay nor priestly) can make this same structural claim.

[22] Recent magisterial teaching identifies this aspect of public witness as an essential characteristic of the religious life: "The very nature of religious vocation involves a public witness to Christ and to the Church... Religious, too,

The End Kernel

From what has been said above, the role of the religious in the life of the Church is to act as a leaven for change, confronting each of its members with the urgency of God's eschatological coming and bringing them to respond by means of an authentic inner conversion. This interior renewal of faith is to make its presence felt in the person's surrounding social environment and should contribute, even if in some seemingly insignificant way, to the establishment of a just and better world. Religious, to be sure, are not the only ones within the Church who can effect such a change in others. Many within the lay and priestly states are already well-equipped to give witness to the transcendental dimension of the Christ event in their lives. The point being made here, however, is that religious are in a unique position to do so. Their style of living a communal life according to the evangelical counsels purports to give a radical witness to this aspect.[23] It may very well be said that the eschatological dimension of the Christ event is preserved, sustained and, to some extent, even realized in their faithful response to their call. In this respect, religious provide an important service to the Church in that they remind its members continually of their transcendent destiny which, from moment to moment, lies always within the grasp of their consciousness.[24]

The religious life cannot be understood apart from its connection with the eschatological dimension of the Christ event and the Church's mission in the world. To separate the two would be

---

in their own times, are called to bear witness to a similar deep, personal experience of Christ and also to share the faith, hope, love and joy which that experience goes on inspiring." See SCRSI, "Norms for Religious Life," *The Pope Speaks* 28 (1983): 307, 316.

[23] For the religious life as a radical following of Christ, see Finbarr B. Connolly, *Religious Life: A Profile of the Future* (Dublin: Reality, 1985), 15-16. See also the Introduction, xxxvi n. 30.

[24] In the words of the Second Vatican Council: "...this state manifests in a special way the transcendence of the kingdom of God and its requirements over all earthly things, bringing home to all men the immeasurable greatness of the power of Christ in his sovereignty and the infinite might of the Holy Spirit which works so marvelously in the Church." See *Lumen gentium*, no. 44 [CDD, 177]; English translation: Flannery, *Vatican Council II*, 404-5.

to effect a process of secularization that would deprive the religious life of its countercultural orientation, as well as reduce its significance for the world today to nothing more than an institution of benign, utilitarian value.[25] When seen, however, from the perspective of its innate transcendental value, the religious life offers both the Church and the world a unique reminder of the transitory nature of the present earthly reality and of the pilgrim orientation of human existence itself. Such a reminder is not only necessary in a world of contingent and constantly changing values, but essential. In this respect, religious, in their faithfulness to their vows and their communal life, keep hope alive in a world which can succumb all too easily to the onslaughts of human despair.[26]

CONCLUSION

This chapter develops the theological discipline of eschatology in the context of its narrative basis in the history of the salvific acts of God. These acts manifest the presence of God and are brought to completion within the historical processes of human activity itself. As a result of these actions, human understanding is capable of transcending the limitations of time. In doing so, it encounters "the last things" as objects of truly ultimate concern. Hope is the means by which humanity awaits the ultimate establishment of God's reign. Sustained by the power of

---

[25] If all of theology has an eschatological dimension, it follows that every vocational state within the Church (lay, priestly, *and* religious) is likewise so oriented. See Karl Rahner, "On the Evangelical Counsels," 145. The religious life, in particular, manifests this dimension "in a special way" by virtue of "its closer imitation of the form of life which Christ himself chose to live while on this earth." In this respect, it "reveals more clearly to all believers the heavenly goods which are already present in this age." See Vatican Council II, *Lumen gentium*, no. 44 [*CDD*, 176]; English translation: Flannery, *Vatican Council II*, 404.

[26] See Fabio Ciardi, "La comunità religiosa segno di speranza," *Vita consacrata* 25 (1989): 222-25.

The End Kernel

Christ in the believing community, it perceives the reality of the eschatological reign to come as already present within the historical parameters of time and place, most especially in the historical mission of the Church to proclaim the Good News of God's loving justice for all.

Religious play an important role in giving witness to these values of ultimate human concern. Their commitment to the evangelical counsels and to life in community make the presence of God's reign visible in the life of the Church and for all to see. They should therefore be encouraged to share their stories of God's presence in their lives not only with other members of their own communities, but also with the Church at large and with all those who are willing to listen. Because their vocations are rooted in the narrative basis of the eschatological dimension of the Church's life, religious confront both themselves and others with the urgency of authentic inner conversion and the necessity of the struggle against the wrongs of injustice. In doing so, they give witness to the presence of the transcendent within the historical circumstances in which they find themselves. In this respect, they remain a source of hope for those who may find it hard to believe or difficult in times of trouble "to call upon the name of the Lord."[27]

In the final analysis, the fundamental principle of eschatology ("The End Kernel") is a theological reflection on the ultimate meaning of the Christ event. It underscores the transcendent nature of divine judgment, resurrection, and the *visio Dei*, while at the same time allowing for certain historical effects to flow from the realized actions of divine salvific intent. In this respect, eschatology forms not only an essential part of the Gospel narratives, but also of the believing Christian community from which they came and in which they continue to be spoken and shared.

---

[27] "All members of the Church should unflaggingly fulfill the duties of their Christian calling. The profession of the evangelical counsels shines before them as a sign which can and should effectively inspire them to do so." See Vatican Council II, *Lumen gentium*, no. 44 [*CDD*, 176]; English translation: Flannery, *Vatican Council II*, 404. For more on the the evangelical counsels as an eschatological sign, see Victor Codina and Noé Zevallos, *Vida religiosa: historia y teología* (Madrid: Ediciones Paulinas, 1987), 145-48.

That is to say that the eschatological dimension of the Church's life is not something to be projected unto some uncertain future date, but to be lived and experienced in hope within the circumstances of daily Christian life. In this and in no other way can Christians continue to be aware of the ultimate concerns of their faith and to back these values up in their present lives with authentic and effective moral action.

16

CONCLUSION

The kernel approach adopted in this book has now been applied to a wide range of theological disciplines. By trying first to recognize the most fundamental principle ("kernel") of each of these areas and then determine their implications for the lives of those committed to the evangelical counsels, important progress has been made in developing a comprehensive theological spirituality of the religious life. One of the distinctive traits of this approach is its attempt to tap the spiritual roots of the Church's theological formulations and to discover their contemporary relevance. By focusing on the significance of these findings for religious, this study has brought to the fore yet another way in which they seek to serve Christ and his Church through the witness of their consecrated lives, i.e., as bearers of the Church's theological tradition.[1]

THEOLOGICAL KERNELS

As a way of validating the above claim, a brief summary of all fifteen kernels will serve both to gather the essential theological findings of this book in one place and provide an appropriate context from which to proceed. They read as follows:

---

[1] For the theological character of the religious life, see Decloux, "La dimension théologique de la vie religieuse," 7-19.

(1) The fundamental principle of theology ("The Theology Kernel") refers to an individual's search for understanding as it is guided by the most basic premises of his or her operative notion of faith (i.e., intellectual, fiducial, performative). Because of the broad cultural context in which such understanding generally takes place, theology embraces both an individual and communal search for truth and moves in a direction beyond that of both the subject's perception of reality and his or her own critical self-reflection. Such understanding coincides with the conclusions of authentic doctrinal insight and reaches its fullest expression in conscientious moral action.

(2) The fundamental principle of Christology ("The Christ Kernel") embraces four closely connected theological movements: The Word of God entered this world, gave of himself completely, became nourishment for the human family, and its source of hope. Each of these corresponds to a different aspect of the mystery of Christ: the first, to his incarnation; the second, to his earthly life and death; the third, to his institution of the Eucharist; the fourth, to his resurrection.

(3) The fundamental principle of Trinitarian theology ("The Trinitarian Kernel") focuses on the Christian God as a community of Love, one in Being yet three in Person. Here, unity and multiplicity find their resolution in a metaphysical juxtaposition of Being and Relation. One may therefore speak of the Triune God as *Ground* (i.e., the Father, ungenerated in his source), *Otherness* (i.e., the Son, as the eternally generated Other) and *Bond* (i.e., the Holy Spirit, eternally processing in its Oneness).

(4) The fundamental principle of ecclesiology ("The Church Kernel") encompasses the community of the faithful, living and dead, who, by reason of their beginning and end in the mind of the Father, interpret (i.e., contemplate, celebrate, formulate, proclaim, and serve) through Christ and in the Spirit, the mystery of their own communal life and the gift of humanity's divinization. Properly speaking, the Church has its origin in the Godhead's external vision of creation and its end in that process of divinization which ultimately leads to the beatific vision.

(5) The fundamental principle of the Church's teaching on original sin ("The Fall Kernel") embraces an analogous under-

standing of the nature of sin (e.g., personal, structural, original) and preserves four essential truths of the Christian tradition: the essential goodness of creation (with the important corollary of humanity's creation in the image and likeness of God); the need for humanity's redemption (i.e., healing and divinization); the salvific inadequacy of human works; and the need for the grace of Christ which comes through baptism.

(6) The fundamental principle of the Church's teaching on grace ("The Grace Kernel") presupposes an analogous understanding of the nature of divine and human encounter. The nature of this encounter is such that there exists an objective *and* a subjective element for each of the members involved. For humanity, the objective element refers to the distinct personal otherness of the divine giver, while the subjective points to the human capacity for the reception of the gift. For God, the objective element refers to the distinct personal otherness of the human receiver, while the subjective refers to the infinite capacity of God to first sustain and then elevate creation for his own greater glory. Such an encounter reaches its fullest expression when it culminates in an ongoing habitation of the divine in the human and the human in the divine.

(7) The fundamental principle of soteriology ("The Redemption Kernel") recognizes four types of salvific relationships: the ransom model touches upon "the cosmic"; the satisfaction, on "the divine-human"; the subjective, on "the inner personal"; and the liberation, on "the societal." Respectively, these models describe the realities of divine-human unrelation, divine-human relation, human self-relation, and human social relation. These relations balance each other out and are to be thought of as complementary elements of the one mystery of redemption.

(8) The fundamental principle of the Resurrection ("The Resurrection Kernel") affirms the proclamation of faith that the *idea* of resurrection has become a *reality* in the Risen Christ. The idea of resurrection contains four distinctive marks: personal life after death, in a transformed state, embracing all the anthropological factors of human existence, in a way continuous with an individual's concrete, earthly life. The reality of resurrection is rooted in the transhistorical nature of the Christ event, whose

historical consequences continue to this day in the ongoing proclamation of the Church.

(9) The fundamental principle of sacramental theology ("The Sacramental Kernel") focuses on proportionately analogous realities that manifest the mystery of God's internal life within a twofold movement of person-to-person encounter: an outward expression of genuine selfless love and a corresponding reciprocating response. The element of materiality is necessary only when the nature of this encounter is concerned with the relationship between the human and the divine (e.g., Christ, the Church, the seven sacraments).

(10) The fundamental principle of the Eucharist ("The Bread Kernel") embraces the symbolic prophetic action performed by Christ, in the Spirit, through the Church which, effected by the eating and drinking of bread and wine duly consecrated by God's ordained minister, makes present for the community of believers, down through history, and in the form of a sacred meal, the definitive redemptive action of God for all humanity. The scope of this saving event encompasses the whole of Christ's life on earth and manifests itself in the close interrelation of the threefold notion of Eucharist as banquet, presence, and sacrifice.

(11) The fundamental principle of moral theology ("The Morality Kernel") deals with the moral implications of all theological and philosophical statements affirmed by the Catholic tradition. It does so by analyzing the changing methods and content of the tradition, listening sincerely to the experience of God's people in their concrete historical circumstances, becoming more deeply aware of the theologian's own assumptions, presuppositions, and prejudices in the matter, and arriving at a concrete judgment as a result of the intense interaction of the previous three.

(12) The fundamental principle of prayer ("The Prayer Kernel") may be summarized as a person's dynamic movement toward and the balanced reception of the ultimate ground of reality on the various anthropological levels of his or her individual and communal existence. This movement toward and reception of the divine involves finding the correct equilibrium

between the spiritual, mental, physical, and social aspects of human experience.

(13) The fundamental principle of ecumenical theology ("The Ecumenical Kernel") may be characterized as the acquired interior disposition of individual Christians and believing church communities who, seeking to understand the historical and theological significance of their own religious traditions, maintain an ongoing, balanced relationship of negative contrariety *and* cooperative dialogue with Christian traditions other than their own.

(14) The fundamental principle of Mariology ("The Marian Kernel") focuses on the historical/transhistorical significance of Mary that has been given to the Church in both a mothering (symbolic, mythic) and a virginal (doctrinal, creedal integrity) capacity. Because of this gift, the Church itself is in the process of becoming more fully η δουλη κυριου.

(15) The fundamental principle of eschatology ("The End Kernel") points to the concrete establishment of God's justice by means of a final judgment (both universal and particular in scope) which effects the ultimate transformation of human life (i.e., life in the resurrection), the full incorporation into Christ's Mystical Body (i.e., as the Church triumphant), and the fullness of the beatific vision (i.e., *visio Dei*). Through the virtue of Christian hope, each of these concerns is already present to some extent in the believing Christian community.

An important corollary to the above summaries is the intrinsic relation of each kernel to the whole of theology. That is not to say that, when taken alone, each of these principles is not internally consistent and unable to withstand the test of coherent theological analysis. It merely implies that each will not be fully understood outside of the cumulative context of the other parts. For example, although internally consistent, the fundamental principle of sacramental theology will make little sense if it is not viewed in relation to the fundamental principle of ecclesiology. The latter, in turn, while also internally consistent, will make little sense if it is not viewed in the context of the fundamental principle of Christology; nor will Christology, if it is not read in light of the fundamental principle of Trinitarian theology, etc. Each of these kernels loses much of its immediate theological significance if it is viewed in isolation (as if in a vacuum) and read with no regard for its relation to the rest of theology.

Each must be examined not only for its own internal consistency, but also for its external coherence with the vast continuum of other fundamental theological principles. Due to the limitations of this study, many of these principles have yet to be formulated.

IMPLICATIONS FOR THE RELIGIOUS LIFE

While each of the above kernels has an influence on all of the vocational states within the Church, this study has focused almost exclusively on their relation to the religious life. What follows is a summary of its more important findings.

(1) "The Theology Kernel" depicts the religious as a person whose "faith in search of understanding" has led him or her to embrace a style of living oriented entirely toward the perfection of that understanding.

(2) "The Christ Kernel" underscores the choice of the religious to follow Christ's call to radical discipleship by imitating closely the particular way of life chosen by Christ during his life on earth.

(3) "The Trinitarian Kernel" demonstrates a correspondence each of the vows has to a particular Trinitarian relation: poverty, to the Father as Ground; obedience, to the Son as Other; chastity, to the Spirit as Bond.

(4) "The Church Kernel" shows how religious benefit the entire believing community by calling it to be ever more conscious of the covenant it shares with its Creator and by challenging its members to examine their own vocations more deeply and to discover the particular way in which they themselves participate in the mystery of the *visio Dei*.

(5) "The Fall Kernel" has each of the vows affirming one or more of the essential elements of the doctrine of original sin (*chastity*, the witness of faith to the existence of a beyond and a countercultural protest against human and sexual relationships

Conclusion

that have gone awry; *poverty*, the goodness of creation, humanity's divine resemblance, and its experience of the need for redemption; and *obedience*, the limitations of human effort).

(6) "The Grace Kernel" describes how the vows point beyond themselves and become for individual religious and particular religious communities the medium through which Christ is personally met, mutually shared, and made continually present within.

(7) "The Redemption Kernel" depicts the religious life as a function and manifestation of its four historically-operative relations: divine-human unrelation, divine-human relation, human self-relation, and human social relation.

(8) "The Resurrection Kernel" encourages religious to strive to center their lives upon the reality of Christ so that they might share in the life of the Resurrection by making the idea of the vows a lived reality in their day-to-day existence.

(9) "The Sacramental Kernel" shows that religious who dedicate their lives to the Lord through the evangelical counsels manifest the twofold movement of sacramental encounter of outward selfless expression and genuine reciprocating response.

(10) "The Bread Kernel" encourages religious to make the Eucharist the center of their lives and to embody in their own faithful living out of the vows its threefold spiritual significance of banquet, presence, and sacrifice.

(11) "The Morality Kernel" informs religious that the values they seek to uphold in their everyday lives are meant to be the fundamental points of departure for their entire approach to moral theology.

(12) "The Prayer Kernel" states that by seeking a proper balance in their lives of prayer on the various anthropological levels of their lives — the physical, mental, spiritual, and social — religious give to the Church a visible sign of the types of individual and social integration to which all are ultimately called.

(13) "The Ecumenical Kernel" finds in the religious life's evangelical lifestyle an appropriate environment that can foster the interior disposition of the heart and mind needed to maintain a balanced relationship between negative contrariety and cooperative dialogue.

(14) "The Marian Kernel" suggests that the deep devotion to Mary characteristic of most religious orders urges all those committed to the evangelical counsels to strike a proper balance between the mothering (symbolic, mythic) and virginal (doctrinal, creedal integrity) facets of the Church's life and worship.

(15) "The End Kernel" encourages religious to orient their entire lives towards the eschatological dimensions of the Christ event and thus help keep alive the hope of God's coming to a world in dire need of his loving justice.

When taken together, these insights point to the way in which the religious life is rooted in the whole of the Church's theological tradition. This means that a deeper understanding of the religious life will come about not by studying each of these implications in lonely isolation, but by appropriating them both individually and in relation to one another. In doing so, the religious life gives direction to other vocational states within the Church by encouraging others to live their own vocations to the fullest.[2] It also serves as a catalyst for new ideas and insights to be incorporated into its own growing self-understanding of the vows. The following is a brief reflection on how the theological spirituality of the religious life developed in this study supports a well-founded yet also innovative approach to the theology of the vows.

THE THEOLOGY OF THE VOWS

To appreciate fully the above application of fundamental theological principles to the religious life, the evangelical counsels must be thought of as being rooted in a person's baptismal consecration and even a fuller expression of it.[3] As such, religious

---

[2] "As such it [the religious life] becomes a sign within the Church, recalling all Christians to follow Christ totally, within their own particular pattern of life." See Connolly, *Religious Life: A Profile for the Future*, 15.

[3] See Vatican Council II, *Perfectae caritatis*, no. 5 [*CDD*, 337]; English translation: Flannery, *Vatican Council II*, 614.

Conclusion

seek and love God above all else, so much so that they possess a countercultural and an eschatological dimension in the very heart of their vocation.[4] This twofold orientation beckons them by virtue of their unequivocal following of Christ to be in the world while not belonging to it. It also has important implications for the role of religious in the Church and the transformation of human society.[5]

Through their vow of chastity, religious offer a radical witness of the sacred character of human sexuality. As a countercultural sign of God's transformative intentions, it underscores the dignity of the human person and the intimate relationships of which he or she is capable. As such, it reminds people that others are not to be treated as objects (and least of all as sexual objects), but rather as individuals created in the image of God and capable of an intimate relationship with their Creator. It is precisely to focus all of their energy on nurturing such a relationship with God, that religious forego the goods of married and family life and embark upon a life that is totally oriented to the beyond even in the most mundane of human activities. This eschatological sign finds in the personal intimacy that the religious shares with God a foretaste of the heavenly banquet and an anticipation of the realization of humanity's deepest hopes.[6]

Through their vow of poverty, religious emphasize the relative worth of earthly wealth and focus their gaze on the

---

[4] Closely related, these dimensions have also been described respectively as the "prophetic" and "mystical" aspects of the religious life: "I can distinguish the mystical aspect of my life...and the prophetic aspect. But I cannot separate them. The prophetic dimension of the religious life makes no sense without the mystical dimension." See Robert Faricy and Scholastica Blackborow, *The Healing of the Religious Life* (Mineola, N.Y.: Resurrection Press, 1986), 3-4. For more on the close link between the mystical vision and prophetic response, see Leech, *Experiencing God*, 349.

[5] As one author puts it: "...our question is no longer how can living poverty, obedience, and celibacy make us perfect. It is, rather, how can we, living poverty, obedience, and celibacy together, transform the world?" Casey, "Toward a Theology of the Vows," 88.

[6] On chastity as an eschatological sign, see Mary Anne Hoope, "Consecrated Celibacy: Gift and Challenge," *Review for Religious* 40 (1981): 910-11; Stephen Rossetti, "The Celibacy Experience," *Review for Religious* 41 (1982): 673-74.

treasures promised them in the world to come. The goal here is not for religious to project human ambition onto a heavenly plane, but to come to appreciate the gifts of the earth for what they are. In their seeking to free themselves from an inordinate attachment to the possession and use of all contingent goods, religious challenge the world, the Church, and their own communities on questions of a disproportionate accumulation and distribution of wealth. They do so out of the conviction that the goods of creation are not ends in themselves, but means to humanity's final destination in God. In this respect, religious poverty pronounces the limitations of earthly wealth and conveys a tangible eschatological sign of the intimate ties between the Creator and his creation. [7]

Through their vow of obedience, religious demonstrate that true Christian freedom means the following of Christ and not the relentless pursuit of an individual's latent psychological needs.[8] Religious obedience challenges the commonly accepted notion that human freedom entails an inherent right to unbridled self-fulfillment. It finds the greatest expression of human freedom in the sincere and humble submission of one's life to the will of a legitimate religious superior. This act of submission does not dispense the individual religious from following the dictates of his or her conscience; it presupposes wise discretion on the part of the religious superior and hopes for an atmosphere of frank and honest discussion. In this respect, religious obedience concerns not the strict adherence to an external discipline of order, but an internal union of wills that finds its model in the self-emptying obediential action of Christ (Ph 2:6-11), who always sought to do the will of his loving Father (Lk 22:42). In their following of Christ, religious offer an eschatological glimpse into that ultimate mo-

---

[7] In the words of Servais (Th.) Pinckaers: "...elle est alors un signe, humain sans doute et par suite imparfait, mais réel tout de même, de la supériorité et de l'amour du Christ." See "La pauvreté religieuse est-elle une vraie pauvreté?" *Vie consacrée* 42 (1970): 64. See also Paul Chapelle, "Méditation sur la pauvreté religieuse," *Vie consacrée* 45 (1973): 143-45.

[8] When coupled with the religious life, the latter can easily lead to "a supermarket spirituality," whereby a person moves from one religious experience to another, "barely digesting one before another is tasted." See Leddy, *Reweaving Religious Life: Beyond the Liberal Model*, 55, 57.

ment out of time when their wills will conform completely to that of their heavenly Father. In the present life, the best indication before them is how they respond to the legitimate requests of their religious superiors.[9]

The mutual inherence of the vows sustains the same double orientation as each of them does when treated individually.[10] On the level of countercultural witness, chastity's witness to the sacredness of human sexuality reinforces poverty's emphasis on the relative worth of earthly wealth, as well as obedience's movement against the flow of worldly self-fulfillment. To be poor, obedient, and chaste run against the very fabric of the normally conceived goals of human endeavor. On the level of eschatological witness, chastity's focus on intimacy with God coincides with poverty's hunger for the one divine good, and obedience's search for the ultimate union of one's will with God's. Intimately connected one to another, the vows offer a consistent picture of heartfelt dedication to the perfect following of Christ which down through the centuries has drawn countless men and women to walk in his footsteps.

This twofold focus of the vows, along with their concurring inherence, extends in different ways to unbelievers, to those variously incorporated into the Church, and to full members in their various vocational states. To unbelievers, it presents the Gospel message in clear, concrete, and uncompromising terms: religious believe in Jesus and his message so much that they are willing to forsake many very legitimate goods of the present life in order to anticipate the fullness of God's love promised them in

---

[9] Thus one author speaks of the ascetical, mystical, apostolic, and unitive dimensions of religious obedience. See Brian O'Leary, "Christian and Religious Obedience," *Review for Religious* 44 (1985): 518-20.

[10] The source of this mutual inherence is the love of God: "They who make profession of the evangelical counsels should seek and love above all else God who has first loved us. In all circumstances they should take care to foster a life hidden in Christ in God, which is the source and stimulus of love of the neighbor, for the salvation of the world and the building-up of the Church. Even the very practice of the evangelical counsels is animated and governed by this charity." See Vatican Council II, *Perfectae caritatis*, no. 6 [CDD, 338]; English translation: Flannery, *Vatican Council II*, 614 .

the kingdom. To those variously incorporated into the Church (i.e, those who believe in God, Moslems, Jews, the Protestant and Orthodox brethren), it makes a statement not only of Christ but also about the Catholic Church as the subsistent source of his body on earth: religious live the consecrated life in a very specific ecclesial context, i.e., within the various rites of the Catholic Church. This context is not accidental to their commitment but an essential prerequisite for their vocations as religious.[11] In this respect, they give witness not only to Christ, but also to the Catholic Church as the universal sacrament of salvation. To official members of the Church, religious serve as leaven through which they are called to a greater fidelity to their various vocational states (i.e., the laity and priesthood). The double orientation of their lives serves to remind each Catholic believer that he or she is called to make specific choices about how to live in the world and how to prepare for life in the next. In this respect, religious do not offer their fellow Catholic believers a superior spirituality or a higher road to sanctity,[12] but call them to follow Christ in a more determined way along the path upon which they have already started.[13] As leaven for the faithful, they help the faithful to participate in the greatest of all countercultural and eschatological actions entrusted to the Church — the gathering of the faithful for the breaking of the bread.[14]

---

[11] According to John Paul II: "The ecclesial dimension is absolutely essential for a proper understanding of religious life. Religious are who they are because the Church mediates their consecration and guarantees their charism to be religious." See "La vita religiosa si comprende essenzialmente nella dimensione ecclesiale," no. 7 [*IGP*, 6/2:582].

[12] Schneiders, *New Wineskins*, 39.

[13] Connolly, *Religious Life: A Profile for the Future*, 15; Powell, *The Mystery of the Church*, 215.

[14] The Eucharist both aptly *signifies* and admirably *realizes* the unity of the People of God. See Vatican Council II, *Lumen gentium*, no. 11 [*CDD*, 112]; English translation, Flannery, *Vatican Council II*, 362. In this respect, the eschatological and countercultural aspects of the Eucharist are intricately connected. The former points to a unity not fully realized; the latter shows how Christians, united by the bonds of Christian community, stand against the forces in society that would seek to undermine the dignity of the human person.

CONCLUSION

When applied to the religious life, the kernel approach to theological spirituality characterizes religious as bearers of the Church's theological tradition. The same can of course be said for all vocational states within the Church. Indeed, to the extent that the whole of theology has concrete implications for all Christian states of life, any Christian bears the Church's theological tradition "in the flesh" whenever these teachings are accepted and incorporated into his or her daily existence. Be that as it may, the title "Bearers of the Church's Theological Tradition" seems particularly appropriate to the religious state.

In making this claim, there is no intention whatsoever to set religious up as contenders for privileges and rights normally assigned to the magisterium. Since they are traditionally associated with the charismatic element of the Church,[15] their role as bearers of the Church's theological tradition is meant to support and vivify the teaching of the magisterium[16] and, at the same time, keep the latent cultic and separatist tendencies of Christianity within the bounds of institutional orthodoxy.[17] While tensions are bound to exist, it cannot be denied that, throughout the history of

---

[15] According to Angela Berríos: "When the religious life is faithful to its true spirit, it is capable of making all that is contrary to its charismatic power disappear: fear, routine, lukewarmness, insecurity, and uncertainty. The future must require of religious life a greater consciousness of, and connaturality with, its charismatic audacity." See "Religious Life Ahora y Manana, Today and Tomorrow," in *The Future of Religious Life: The Carondelet Conference*, ed. Dolores Steinberg (Collegeville, Minn.: The Liturgical Press, 1990), 25.

[16] In this respect, "the state of life... which is constituted by the profession of the evangelical counsels, while not entering into the hierarchical structure of the Church, belongs undeniably to her life and holiness." See Vatican Council II, *Lumen gentium*, no. 44 [*CDD*, 117]; English translation: Flannery, *Vatican Council II*, 405. See also Casey, "Toward a Theology of the Vows," 121-26.

[17] Note the relevancy of John Paul II's exhortation to religious that they "think with the Church and always act in union with her, in conformity with the teachings and directives of the magisterium of Peter and of the pastors in communion with him, fostering at the personal and community level a renewed ecclesial awareness." See *Redemptionis donum*, no. 14 [*AAS* 76 (1984): 539]; English translation: "*Redemptionis Donum*: An Expression of Love for Religious," 497.

the Church, religious institutes dedicated to a life consecrated to the vows have kept rigorist (and potentially heterodox) religious movements within the sphere of ecclesiastical control by challenging the faithful to lead lives of conversion within the context of the Church's structures and sacramental life.[18] In this respect, religious complement the institutional role of the magisterium by both their staunch dedication to Christ and his Church and their radical call to imitate the life of Jesus through their following of the evangelical counsels.

The title "Bearers of the Church's Theological Tradition" is appropriate to religious not because they are particularly skilled in the theological disciplines (although they have certainly contributed more than their share of outstanding theologians in the history of the Church) or because their state in life has the trappings of magisterial authority associated with it (which it certainly does not), but because the counterculturual and eschatological orientation of the vows has a tendency to make them more keenly aware of the necessity of integrating the Church's theological tradition with their own spiritual lives. That is to say that their radical commitment through their life of the vows to Jesus, the Word made flesh, moves them to incorporate ever more deeply in their lives the Church's ongoing reflection of the meaning of the Christ event. In this respect, to say that religious are bearers of the Church's theological tradition underscores both the ecclesial context in which religious live out their vowed commitment and the incarnational basis for their appropriating this ongoing reflection and incorporating it into their lived spirituality. In their integrating the Church's ongoing reflection on the meaning of the Christ event with their spiritual lives, religious purport to be doing nothing more than remaining true to the stress the vows place on

---

[18] For example, the latent heterodox leanings of the medieval movement of evangelical poverty were curbed only by the legitimate institutional expression of the movement in the great mendicant orders of the thirteenth century, i.e., the Franciscans and Dominicans. See John W. O'Malley, "Priesthood, Ministry, and Religious Life: Some Historical and Historiographical Considerations," *Theological Studies* 49 (1988): 231; Little, *Religious Poverty and the Profit Economy in Medieval Europe*, 165.

Conclusion

the imitation of Christ (*imitatio Christi*).[19] In this respect, chastity, poverty, and obedience, stand not for the mere outward imitation of the evangelical lifestyle of Jesus, but for an existential stance toward life that can only be appropriated by an ongoing dialogue with the living tradition of the Church.

The stated purpose of this study was to draw the general parameters of a theological spirituality of the religious life. For all practical purposes, the kernel approach has offered a distinctive way of implementing this goal. If nothing else, the fundamental principles of theology proposed in these chapters have opened up new venues for understanding some of the most characteristic features of the religious life. Close to the heart of Christ, religious have here been depicted as a transforming leaven and a fermenting grace for the Church and all its members. Whatever their particular focus in life — be it contemplation, action, a mixture of each — they are a visible sign of the dedication and commitment that all are called upon to incorporate into their own search for holiness. Such a sign does not mean that religious never fall short of the many and great expectations placed upon them. On the contrary, it is the resiliency with which they respond to their shortcomings and the way in which they seek to balance the ideal with the real, their divine calling with their human limitations, their struggle against sin with their hope in the resurrection, that encourages others not to give up whenever they fall short of their ideals and to respond with each new day and with renewed vigor to the demands of their Christian calling. This is the final and perhaps the best of reasons why religious may be thought of as bearers of the Church's theological tradition. It is certainly the most difficult of convictions to translate from the lofty level of ideals to that of concrete reality.

---

[19] Christ is described as the "exemplar" (*exemplum*) of a life lived in chastity, poverty, and obedience. See Vatican Council II, *Perfectae caritatis*, no. 25 [*CDD*, 352]; English translation: Flannery, *Vatican Council II*, 623.

SELECTED BIBLIOGRAPHY

I. PRIMARY SOURCES

A. Historical Documents

Anselm of Canterbury. *Cur Deus homo*. In *Anselmi opera omnia*, 2:37-133. Edited by F.S. Schmitt. Stuttgart: Friedrich Frommann Verlag, 1984.

_____. *Proslogion*. In *Anselmi opera omnia*, 1:89-123. Edited by F.S. Schmitt. Stuttgart: Friedrich Frommann Verlag, 1984.

Aristotle. *The Nicomachean Ethics*. Loeb Classical Library, 1982.

Athanasius of Alexandria. *De incarnatione*. SC 199. Edited and translated by Charles Kannengiesser. Paris: Éditions du Cerf, 1973. [PG 25:95-198].

_____. *De synodis*. PG 26:681-794.

Augustine of Hippo. *De civitate Dei (libri 13-22)*. CSEL 40/2. Edited by Emanuel Hoffmann. Prague: F. Tempsky, 1900. [PL 41:377-804].

_____. *De nuptiis et concupiscentia*. In *De perfectione iustitiae hominis, De gestis Pelagii, De gratia Christi et de peccato originali, De nuptiis et concupiscentia*. CSEL 42:207-319. Edited by Carl F. Urba and Joseph Zycha. Prague: F. Tempsky, 1902. [PL 44:413-74].

———. *De trinitate.* CCL 50-50A. Edited by W.J. Mountain. Turnhout: Brepols, 1968. [*PL* 42:819-1098].

———. *Epistola* 120. In *Epistolae. CSEL* 34:704-22. Edited by Al. Goldbacher. Prague: F. Tempsky, 1895. [*PL* 33:452-462].

———. *Sermo* 89. *PL* 38:553-58.

———. *Sermo* 212. *PL* 38:1058-60.

———. *Tractatus in Iohannis evangelium.* CCL 36. Edited by D.R. Willems. Turnhout: Brepols, 1954. [*PL* 35:1379-1976].

Biblia sacra vulgata. Edited by Robert Weber. 2 vols. Stuttgart: Württembergische Bibel-anstalt, 1969.

Boethius. *Philosophiae consolatio.* CCL 94. Edited by L. Bieler. Turnhout: Brepols, 1957. [*PL* 63:547-862].

Cyprian of Carthage. *De ecclesiae unitate.* CCL 3.243-68. Edited by R. Weber. Turnhout: Brepols, 1972. [*PL* 4:493-520].

The Didache. In *Apostolic Fathers I.* The Loeb Classical Library, 1977.

The Greek New Testament. 3d ed. Edited by Kurt Aland, Matthew Black, Carlo M. Martini, Bruce M. Metzger, and Allen Wikgren. New York: American Bible Society, 1976.

Gregory Nazianzus. *Oratio* 29. In *Orationes. SC* 250:176-225. Edited by Paul Gallay. Paris: Éditions du Cerf, 1978. [*PG* 36:73-104].

Gregory of Nyssa. *De opificio hominis. PG* 44:123-256.

Ignatius of Antioch. *Letter to the Smyrnaeans.* In *Apostolic Fathers I.* The Loeb Classical Library, 1977.

Irenaeus. *Adversus haereses (liber 1). SC* 264/2. Edited by Adelin Rousseau and Louis Doutreleau. Paris: Éditions du Cerf, 1979. [*PG* 7:433-706].

———. *Adversus haereses (liber 4). SC* 100/2. Edited by Adelin Rousseau. Paris: Éditions du Cerf, 1965. [*PG* 7:971-1118].

Selected Bibliography

Leibniz, G.W. *Essai de théodicée sur la bonté de Dieu, la liberté de l'homme et l'origine du mal.* Chap. in *Opera philosophica,* ed., J.J. Erdmann. Berlin: G. Eichleri, 1840.

Newman, John Henry. *The Idea of a University.* Westminster, Md.: Christian Classics, Inc., 1973.

_____. *On the Development of Christian Doctrine.* Foreword by Ian Ker. Notre Dame Series in Great Books. Notre Dame: University of Notre Dame Press, 1989.

Nicholas of Cusa. *De docta ignorantia.* In *Nikolaus von Kues Werke.* 1:2-100 Edited by Paul Wilpert. Berlin: Walter de Gruter and Co., 1967.

Peter Abelard. *Commentaria in epistolam Pauli ad Romanos.* In *Opera theologica.* CCCM 11:41-340. Edited by E.M. Buytaert. Turnhout: Brepols, 1969.

Peter Comestor. *Sermo 9.* PL 198:1744-48.

Plato. *Phaedrus.* The Loeb Classical Library, 1982.

_____. *The Republic.* The Loeb Classical Library, 1982.

Pseudo-Dionysius. *De divinibus nominibus.* PG 3:585-996.

Thomas Aquinas. *Summa theologiae.* Leonine ed. Turin: Marietti, 1952.

B. Magisterial Documents

1. Papal

John Paul II. *Redemptionis donum.* AAS 76 (1984): 513-46.

_____. "La vita religiosa si comprende essenzialmente nella dimensione ecclesiale." In *IGP* 6/2:578-90 [English original].

Paul VI. *Evangelica testificatio.* AAS 63 (1971): 497-526.

_____. *Marialis cultus.* AAS 66 (1974): 113-68.

_____. *Mysterium fidei.* AAS 57 (1965): 753-74.

2. Conciliar

Council of Trent. *Decretum de justificatione*. Denz.-Schön. nos. 1520-83 [792a-843].

Second Vatican Council. *Dei verbum*. CDD, 423-55.

_____. *Dignitatis humanae*. CDD, 509-40.

_____. *Gaudium et spes*. CDD, 681-835.

_____. *Lumen gentium*. CDD, 93-217.

_____. *Perfectae caritatis*. CDD, 333-53.

_____. *Sacrosanctum concilium*. CDD, 3-70.

_____. *Unitatis redintegratio*. CDD, 243-74.

3. Ecclesiastical Law

Codex iuris canonici. AAS 75/2 (1983): 1-301.

4. Vatican Congregations and Secretariats

SCDF. *Instructio de ecclesiali theologi vocatione*. AAS 82 (1990): 1550-70.

_____. *De libertate christiana et liberatione*. AAS 79 (1987): 554-99.

_____. *De quibus rationibus "Theologiae Liberationis."* AAS 76 (1984): 876-909.

SCR. *Eucharisticum mysterium* . AAS 59 (1967): 539-73.

SCRSI. *Dum canonicarum*. AAS 63 (1971): 318-19.

_____. *La plenaria*. In *Vatican Council II: More Post Conciliar Documents*, gen. ed. Austin Flannery, 244-59. Northport, NY: Costello Publishing Co., 1982 [Text does not appear in *AAS*. Translation issued by SCRSI].

_____. "Norms for Religious Life." *The Pope Speaks* 28 (1983): 304-29 [English original. Text does not appear in *AAS*].

SPUC. "Reflections and Suggestions Concerning Ecumenical Dialogue." In *Vatican Council II: The Conciliar and Post*

Selected Bibliography

Conciliar Documents, gen. ed. Austin Flannery, 535-53. Northport, NY: Costello Publishing Co., 1975 [Text does not appear in *AAS*. Translation issued by SPUC].

_____. *Spiritus Domini*. *AAS* 62 (1970): 705-24.

5. Reference

H. Denzinger. *Enchiridion symbolorum*. 32d ed. Revised by H. Schönmetzer. Freiburg im Breisgau: Herder, 1963 [also listed under *Abbreviations*, xiii as "Denz.-Schön."].

C. Kernel Articles

Billy, Dennis J. "The Bread Kernel," *Review for Religious* 50 (1991): 749-58.

_____. "The Christ Kernel," *Review for Religious* 47 (1988): 594-603.

_____. "The Church Kernel," *Review for Religious* 48 (1989): 897-906.

_____. "The Ecumenical Kernel," *Review for Religious* 51 (1992): 24-33.

_____. "The End Kernel," *Review for Religious* 49 (1990): 917-25.

_____. "The Fall Kernel," *Review for Religious* 49 (1990): 760-67.

_____. "The Marian Kernel," *Review for Religious* 43 (1984): 415-20.

_____. "The Morality Kernel," *Review for Religious* 50 (1991): 438-46.

_____. "The Prayer Kernel," *Review for Religious* 50 (1991): 607-16.

_____. "The Redemption Kernel," *Review for Religious* 49 (1990): 256-64.

_____. "The Resurrection Kernel," *Review for Religious* 51 (1992): 206-16.

_____. "The Sacramental Kernel," *Review for Religious* 50 (1991): 282-89.

_____. "The Theology Kernel," *Review for Religious* 49 (1990): 581-90.

_____. "The Trinitarian Kernel," *Review for Religious* 48 (1989): 602-11.

II. SECONDARY SOURCES

A. Translations

Code of Canon Law: Latin-English Edition. Washington, D.C.: Canon Law Society of America, 1983.

Dionysius the Areopagite. *On the Divine Names and the Mystical Theology*. 2d ed. Translated by C. E. Rolt. New York: Macmillan, 1940; reprint ed. 1951.

Evagrius Pontus. *Les leçons d'un contemplatif: le traité de l'oraison de Evagre le Pontique*. Translated by I. Hausherr. Paris: Beauchesne, 1960.

John Paul II, "*Redemptionis Donum*: An Expression of Love for Religious." *Review for Religious* 43 (1984): 481-502.

The New American Bible, Washington, D.C.: The Confraternity of Christian Doctrine, 1970.

Paul VI. *Mysterium fidei*. *The Pope Speaks* 10 (no. 4, 1965): 309-28.

SCDF. "Instruction on Certain Aspects of the 'Theology of Liberation.'" In *Liberation Theology: A Documentary History*, ed. Alfred T. Hennelly, 393-414. Maryknoll, NY: Orbis Books, 1990.

_____. "Instruction on Christian Freedom and Liberation." In *Liberation Theology: A Documentary History*, ed. Alfred T. Hennelly, 461-97. Maryknoll, NY: Orbis Books, 1990.

_____. "Instruction on the Ecclesial Vocation of the Theologian." *Origins* 20 (1990): 117-26.
Vatican Council II: The Conciliar and Post Conciliar Documents. Edited by Austin Flannery. Northport, NY: Costello Publishing Co., 1975.
Vatican Council II: More Post Conciliar Documents. Edited by Austin Flannery. Northport, NY: Costello Publishing Co., 1982.

B. Books

Academia Alfonsiana 1957-1982. Rome: Pisani, 1982.
Adam, Karl. *The Spirit of Catholicism*. London: Sheed and Ward, 1924; 8th reprint ed., 1969.
Arbuckle, Gerald A. *Out of Chaos: Refounding Religious Congregations*. New York: Paulist Press, 1988.
Ashley, Benedict M. *Theologies of the Body: Humanist and Christian*. Braintree, Mass.: The Pope John Center, 1985.
Aulén, Gustaf. *Christus Victor: An Historical Study of the Three Types of the Idea of the Atonement*. Translated by A.G. Herbert. Foreword by Jaroslav Pelikan. New York: Macmillan, 1931; reprint ed., 1969.
Barrett, William. *Irrational Man: A Study in Existential Philosophy*. Garden City, NY: Doubleday and Co., 1958.
Barth, Karl. *Church Dogmatics*. 2d ed. Vol. 1/1, *The Doctrine of the Word of God*. Translated by G.W. Bromiley. Edinburgh: T. and T. Clark, 1975.
_____. *The Epistle to the Romans*. 6th ed. Translated by C. Hoskins. London: Oxford University Press, 1933.
Bauer, Walter. *Orthodoxy and Heresy in Earliest Christianity*. 2d ed. Edited by Robert Kraft and Gerhard Krodel. Philadelphia: Fortress Press, 1971.
Beattie, Melodie. *Codependent No More*. New York: Harper and Row, 1987.

Black, Max. *Models and Metaphor*. Ithaca: Cornell University Press, 1962.

Brown, Raymond E. *The Birth of the Messiah: A Commentary on the Infancy Narratives in Matthew and Luke*. Garden City, NY: Doubleday and Co., 1977.

_____. *The Churches the Apostles Left Behind*. New York: Paulist Press, 1984.

_____. *The Critical Meaning of the Bible*. New York: Paulist Press, 1981.

_____. *New Testament Essays*. New York: Paulist Press, 1965.

_____. *The Virginal Conception and the Bodily Resurrection of Jesus*. New York: Paulist Press, 1973.

Brown, Raymond E., Karl P. Donfried, Joseph A. Fitzmyer, John Reumann, eds. *Mary in the New Testament*. Philadelphia: Fortress Press, 1978.

Brown, Robert McAfee. *The Ecumenical Revolution*. London: Burns and Oates, 1967.

Brueggemann, Walter. *Prophetic Imagination*. Philadelphia: Fortress Press, 1978.

Bugge, John. *Virginitas: An Essay in the History of a Medieval Ideal*. International Archives of the History of Ideas, no. 17. The Hague: Martinus Nijhoff, 1975.

Cada, Lawrence, et al. *Shaping the Coming Age of Religious Life*. New York: The Seabury Press, 1979.

Campbell, Joseph. *The Masks of God: Creative Mythology*. New York: The Viking Press, 1968; 2d reprint ed., New York: Penguin Books, 1978.

Campenhausen, Hans von. *Ecclesiastical Authority and Spiritual Power in the Church of the First Three Centuries*. Translated by J.A. Baker. Stanford: Stanford University Press, 1969.

Chenu, M.-D. *The Scope of the Summa*. Translated by R.E. Brennan and A.-M. Landry. Washington, D.C.: The Thomist Press, 1958.

Selected Bibliography

_____. *Toward Understanding Saint Thomas*. 3d ed. Translated by A.-M. Landry and D. Hughes. Chicago: Regnery Press, 1964.

Clift, Wallace B. *Jung and Christianity: The Challenge of Reconciliation*. New York: Crossroad, 1982.

Codina, Victor and Noé Zevallos. *Vida religiosa: historia y teología*. Madrid: Ediciones Paulinas, 1987.

Connolly, Finbarr B. *Religious Life: A Profile for the Future*. Dublin: Reality, 1985.

Cooke, Bernard. *Sacraments and Sacramentality*. Mystic, Conn.: Twenty-Third Publications, 1983.

Cullmann, Oscar. *The Christology of the New Testament*. Translated by Shirley C. Guthrie and Charles A.M. Hall. Philadelphia: The Westminster Press, 1963.

Daniélou, Jean. *The Lord of History*. Chicago: Regnery, 1958.

Dockes. Pierre. *Medieval Slavery and Liberation*. Translated by Arthur Goldhammer. Chicago: University of Chicago Press, 1979.

Domanyi, Thomas. *Der Römerbriefkommentar des Thomas von Aquin: Ein Beitrag zur Untersuchung seiner Auslegungsmethoden*. Basler und Berner Studien zur historischen und systematischen Theologie, no. 39. Bern: Peter Lang, 1979.

Dulles, Avery. *Models of the Church*. Garden City, NY: Image Books, 1974.

_____. *Models of Revelation*. Garden City, NY: Doubleday and Co., 1983.

Dupré, Louis. *A Dubious Heritage: Studies in the Philosophy of Religion After Kant*. New York: Paulist Press, 1977.

Durwell, F.X. *In the Redeeming Christ*. Translated by Rosemary Sheed. New York: Sheed and Ward, 1963.

Eliade, Mircea. *Le sacré et le profane*. 2d ed. Paris: Éditions Gallimard, 1965.

Faricy, Robert and Scholastica Blackborow. *The Healing of Religious Life*. Mineola, NY: Resurrection Press, 1986.

Ferré, Frederick. *Language, Logic and God*. New York: Harper and Row, 1961.

Feuillet, André. *The Priesthood of Christ and His Ministers*. Translated by Matthew J. O'Connell. Garden City, NY: Doubleday and Co., 1975.

Fiddes, Paul S. *Past Event and Present Salvation: The Christian Idea of Atonement*. London: Darton, Longman and Todd, 1989.

Fingarette, Herbert. *Self-Deception*. New York: Humanities Press, 1968.

Fortman, E.J. *Everlasting Life After Death*. Staten Island, NY: Alba House, 1976.

Fowler, James W. *Stages of Faith: The Psychology of Human Development and the Quest for Meaning*. San Francisco: Harper and Row, 1981.

Frend, W.H.C. *The Early Church*. 2d ed. Philadelphia: Fortress Press, 1982.

_____. *Martyrdom and Persecution in the Early Church: A Study of a Conflict from the Maccabees to Donatus*. Oxford: Basil Blackwell, 1965.

_____. *The Rise of Christianity*. Philadelphia: Fortress Press, 1984.

Freppert, Lucan. *The Basis of Morality According to William Ockham*. Chicago: Franciscan Herald Press, 1988.

Fries, Heinrich and Karl Rahner. *Unity of the Churches - An Actual Possibility*. New York: Paulist Press, 1983.

Funkenstein, Amos. *Theology and the Scientific Imagination: From the Middle Ages to the Seventeenth Century*. Princeton: Princeton University Press, 1986.

Gallagher, John. *Time Past, Time Future: An Historical Study of Catholic Moral Theology*. New York: Paulist Press, 1990.

Gilson, Etienne. *History of Christian Philosophy in the Middle Ages*. London: Sheed and Ward, 1955.

Selected Bibliography

_____. *The Philosophy of St. Thomas Aquinas*. Translated by Edward Bullough. New York: Dorset Press, 1948.

Graef, Hilda. *Mary: A History of Doctrine and Devotion*. Vol. 1, *From the Beginnings to the Eve of the Reformation*. New York: Sheed and Ward, 1963.

Grant, Robert and David Tracy. *A Short History of the Interpretation of the Bible*. 2d ed. Philadelphia: Fortress Press, 1984.

Grillmeier, Aloys. *Christ in the Christian Tradition: From the Apostolic Age to Chalcedon (451)*. Translated by J.S. Bowden. New York: Sheed and Ward, 1965.

Grimm, Harold J. *The Reformation Era: 1500-1650*. 2d ed. New York: Macmillan, 1973.

Gula, Richard M. *Reason Informed by Faith: Foundations of Catholic Morality*. New York: Paulist Press, 1989.

Gunton, Colin E. *The Actuality of Atonement: A Study of Metaphor, Rationality and the Christian Tradition*. London: T. and T. Clark, 1989.

Haight, Roger. *Dynamics of Theology*. New York: Paulist Press, 1990.

Harvey, Van A. *The Historian and the Believer: The Morality of Historical Knowledge and Christian Belief*. Philadelphia: The Westminster Press, 1986.

Haughton, Rosemary. *The Theology of Experience*. Paramus, N.J.: Newman Press, 1972.

Hellwig, Monika. *The Meaning of the Sacraments*. Dayton: Pflaum Press, 1972.

Hermes, E. *Einheit der Christen in der Gemeinschaft der Kirchen*. Göttingen: Vanderhoeck und Ruprecht, 1984.

Hill, Edmund. *Being Human: A Biblical Perspective*. London: Geoffrey Chapman, 1984.

Hopkins, Jasper. *A Companion to the Study of St. Anselm*. Minneapolis: University of Minnesota Press, 1972.

Horkheimer, M. *Die Sehnsucht nach dem ganz Anderen*. Hamburg: Furche-Verlag, 1970.

Hostie, Raymond. *The Life and Death of Religious Orders: A Psycho-sociological Approach*. Washington, D.C.: Center for Applied Research in the Apostolate, 1983.

Hoy, David Couzens. *The Critical Circle: Literature, History, and Philosophical Hermeneutics*. Berkeley: University of California Press, 1978.

Jalabert, J. *Le dieu de Leibniz*. Paris: Éditions du Cerf, 1960.

Jedin, Hubert and John Dolan, eds. *History of the Church*. Vol. 5, *Reformation and Counter Reformation*, by Erwin Iserloh, Joseph Glazik and Hubert Jedin. Translated by Anselm Biggs and Peter W. Becker. New York: The Seabury Press, 1980.

_____. *History of the Church*. Vol. 9, *The Church in the Industrial Age*, by Roger Aubert, Günter Bandmann, Jakob Baumgartner, Mario Bendidcioli, Jacques Gadille, Oskar Köhler, Rudolf Lill, Bernhard Stasiewski and Erika Weinzierl. Translated by Margit Resch. New York: The Seabury Press, 1981.

Johnston, William. *The Inner Eye of Love*. London: Collins, 1977.

Jonsen, Albert R. and Stephen Toulmin. *The Abuse of Casuistry: A History of Moral Reasoning*. Berkeley: University of California Press, 1988.

Jung, Carl Gustaf. *The Collected Works of Carl Jung*. Bollingen Series, no. 20. 2d ed. Edited by Sir Herbert Read. Translated by R.F.C. Hull. Vol. 18, *The Symbolic Life*. Princeton: Princeton University Press, 1970.

Kasper, Walter. *The God of Jesus Christ*. Translated by Matthew J. O'Connell. New York: Crossroad, 1984.

_____. *Jesus the Christ*. Translated by V. Green. London: Burns and Oates, 1976.

Kelly, J.N.D. *Early Christian Creeds*. 3d ed. New York: Longman, 1972.

_____. *Early Christian Doctrines*. San Francisco: Harper and Row, 1978.

Kleber, Karl-Heinz. *Einführung in die Geschichte der Moral theologie*. Passau: Passavia Universitätsverlag, 1984.

Selected Bibliography

Koester, Helmut. *Introduction to the New Testament.* Vol. 2, *History and Literature of Early Christianity.* Philadelphia: Fortress Press, 1982.

Kuhn, T.S. *The Structure of Scientific Revolutions.* 2d ed. Chicago: University of Chicago Press, 1970.

Lane, Dermot. *The Reality of Jesus: An Essay in Christology.* New York: Paulist Press, 1975.

Latourelle, René. *Theology: Science of Salvation.* Translated by Sister Mary Dominic. Staten Island, NY: Alba House, 1969.

Leclercq, Jean. *The Love of Learning and the Desire for God.* Translated by Catharine Misrahi. New York: Fordham University Press, 1982.

Leddy, Mary Jo. *Reweaving Religious Life: Beyond the Liberal Model.* Mystic, Conn.: Twenty-Third Publications, 1990.

Leech, Kenneth. *Experiencing God: Theology as Spirituality.* San Francisco: Harper and Row, 1989.

Lewis, C.S. *Mere Christianity.* New York: Macmillan, 1952.

Little, Lester K. *Religious Poverty and the Profit Economy in Medieval Europe.* Ithaca: Cornell University Press, 1978.

Lonergan, Bernard. *Insight: A Study of Human Understanding.* San Francisco: Harper and Row, 1958.

Louth, Andrew. *Discerning the Mystery: An Essay on the Nature of Theology.* Oxford: Clarendon Press, 1983.

Lubac, Henri de. *Exégèse médiévale: les quatre sens de l'écriture.* 2 vols. Aubier: Editions Montaigne, 1959.

_____. *The Mystery of the Supernatural.* Translated by Rosemary Sheed. New York: Herder and Herder, 1967.

MacIntyre, Alasdair. *After Virtue: A Study in Moral Theory.* 2d ed. London: Duckworth, 1985.

Mackey, James P. *Jesus: The Man and the Myth.* New York: Paulist Press, 1979.

_____. *Whose Justice? Which Rationality?* Notre Dame: University of Notre Dame Press, 1988.

Macquarrie, John. *Mary for All Christians.* Grand Rapids: Eerdmans, 1991.

_____. *Principles of Christian Theology.* London: SCM Press, 1966.

Mahoney, John. *The Making of Moral Theology: A Study of the Roman Catholic Tradition.* Oxford: Clarendon Press, 1987.

Mascall, Eric. *Existence and Analogy.* London: Longmans, Green, 1949.

McBrien, Richard P. *Catholicism.* 2 vols. Oak Grove, Minn.: Winston Press, 1980.

McCormick, Patrick. *Sin as Addiction.* New York: Paulist Press, 1989.

McFague, Sally. *Models of God: Theology for an Ecological, Nuclear Age.* Philadelphia: Fortress Press, 1987.

Miles, Margaret R. *Augustine on the Body.* American Academy of Religion Dissertation Series, no. 31. Missoula, Mont.: Scholars Press, 1979.

Moltmann, Jürgen. *Theology of Hope.* Translated by James W. Leitch. London: SCM Press, 1977.

Monloubou, Louis. *Saint Paul et la prière.* Lectio divina, no. 10. Paris: Éditions du Cerf, 1982.

Murray, Alexander. *Reason and Society in the Middle Ages.* Oxford: Clarendon Press, 1978.

Navone, John and Thomas Cooper. *Tellers of the Word.* New York: LeJacq Publishing, 1981.

O'Collins, Gerald. *The Case Against Dogma.* New York: Paulist Press, 1975.

O'Meara, Thomas F. *Holiness and Radicalism in Religious Life.* New York: Herder and Herder, 1970.

O'Murchu, Diarmuid. *The Prophetic Horizon of Religious Life.* London: Excalibur Press, 1989.

O'Neill, Colman E., *Meeting Christ in the Sacraments.* Revised by

Selected Bibliography

  Romanus Cessario. Staten Island, NY: Alba House, 1991.
Osbourne, Kenan B. *Priesthood: A History of the Ordained Ministry in the Roman Catholic Church.* New York: Paulist Press, 1988.
Ott, Ludwig. *Fundamentals of Catholic Dogma.* 4th ed. Translated by James Canon Bastible. Rockford, Ill.: Tan, 1960.
Owens, Joseph. *An Elementary Christian Ethics.* 2d ed. Houston: Center for Thomistic Studies, 1985.
Pelikan, Jaroslav. *The Christian Tradition: A History of the Development of Doctrine.* Vol. 1, *The Emergence of the Christian Tradition (100-600).* Chicago: University of Chicago Press, 1971.
_____. *Jesus Through the Centuries: His Place in the History of Culture.* New Haven: Yale University Press, 1985.
Pesch, Otto Hermann. *Die Theologie der Rechtfertigung bei Martin Luther und Thomas von Aquin.* Mainz: Matthaias Grunewald, 1967.
Peters, Edward. *Inquisition.* Berkeley: University of California Press, 1988.
Pieper, Josef. *The Four Cardinal Virtues.* Notre Dame: University of Notre Dame Press, 1966.
_____. *On Hope.* Translated by Mary Francis McCarthy. San Francisco: Ignatius Press, 1977.
Pinckaers, Servais (Th.). *Les sources de la morale chrétienne: sa méthode, son contenu, son histoire.* Etudes d'éthique chrétienne, no.1. Fribourg: Éditions universitaires, 1985.
Powell, John. *The Mystery of the Church.* Milwaukee: The Bruce Publishing Co., 1967.
Principe, Walter H. *Introduction to Patristic and Medieval Theology.* 2d ed. Toronto: Pontifical Institute of Mediaeval Studies, 1982.
Rahner, Karl. *The Church and the Sacraments.* Translated by W.J. O'Hara. New York: Herder and Herder, 1963.

Ramsey, I.T. *Christian Discourse.* London: Oxford University Press, 1964.
———. *Models and Mystery.* London: Oxford University Press, 1964.
———. *Religious Language: An Empirical Placing of Theological Phrases.* New York: Macmillan, 1967.
Ratzinger, Joseph. *Church, Ecumenism and Politics: New Essays in Ecclesiology.* New York: Crossroad, 1986.
Ricoeur, Paul. *De l'interprétation: essai sur Freud.* Paris: Éditions du Seuil, 1965.
Rivière, J. *Le dogme de la rédemption.* 2d ed. Paris: Librairie Victor Lecoffre, 1905.
Rosenwein, Barbara. *Rhinoceros Bound: Cluny in the Tenth Century.* Philadelphia: University of Pennsylvania Press, 1982.
Royo Marin, Antonio. *Teología de la perfección cristiana.* 5th ed. Biblioteca de autores cristianos, no. 114. Madrid: La editorial catolica, 1968.
Schillebeeckx, Edward. *Christ the Sacrament of the Encounter with God,* Foreword by Cornelius Ernst. New York: Sheed and Ward, 1963.
———. *Jesus: An Experiment in Christology.* Translated by Hubert Hoskins. New York: Crossroad, 1985.
Schmaus, Michael. *Dogma.* Vol. 5, *Church as Sacrament.* London: Sheed and Ward, 1975.
Schneiders, Sandra M. *New Wineskins: Re-imagining Religious Life Today.* New York: Paulist Press, 1986.
Schoonenberg, Piet. *Man and Sin: A Theological View.* Translated by Joseph Donceel. Notre Dame: University of Notre Dame Press, 1965.
Senior, Donald. *A Gospel Portrait of Jesus.* Dayton: Pflaum Press, 1981.
Simpson, Michael. *Death and Eternal Life.* Theology Today Series, no. 42. Hales Corners, Wis.: Clergy Book Service, 1971.

Selected Bibliography

Southern, R.W. *The Making of the Middle Ages.* New Haven: Yale University Press, 1953.

⎯⎯⎯. *Saint Anselm and His Biographer: A Study of Monastic Life and Thought, 1059-1130.* Cambridge: The University Press, 1963.

Stock, Brian. *The Implications of Literacy: Written Language and Models of Interpretation in the Eleventh and Twelfth Centuries.* Princeton: Princeton University Press, 1983.

Tillich. Paul. *Dynamics of Faith.* New York: Harper and Row, 1957.

Tixeront, J. *History of Dogmas.* Vol. 2, *From St. Athanasius to St. Augustine (318-430).* Translated by H.L.B. Westminster, Md.: Christian Classics, 1984.

Toon, Peter. *The Development of Doctrine in the Church.* Grand Rapids: William B. Eerdmans, 1979.

Tracy, David. *The Analogical Imagination: Christian Theology and the Culture of Pluralism.* London: SCM Press, 1981.

⎯⎯⎯. *Blessed Rage for Order: The New Pluralism in Theology.* Minneapolis: The Seabury Press, 1975.

Tugwell, Simon. *Prayer.* Vol. 2, *Prayer in Practice.* Dublin: Veritas Publications, 1974.

Vandenbroucke, F. *Pour l'histoire de la théologie morale: la morale monastique du XIe au XVIe siècle.* Analecta Mediaevalia Namurcensia, vol. 20. Louvain: Éditions Nauwelaerts, 1966.

Vanneste, Alfred. *The Dogma of Original Sin.* Translated by Edward P. Callens. Louvain: Éditions Nauwelaerts, 1971.

Vawter, Bruce. *This Man Jesus: An Essay Toward a New Testament Christology.* Garden City, NY: Doubleday and Co., 1973.

Vereecke, Louis. *De Guillaume d'Ockham à Saint Alphonse de Liguori: Etudes d'histoire de la théologie morale moderne 1300-1787.* Bibliotheca historica Congregationis SSmi

Redemptoris, vol 12. Rome: Collegium S. Alfonso de Urbe, 1986.
Vidal, Marciano. *Moral de actitudes*. Vol. 1, *Moral fundamental*. 5th ed. Madrid: P.S. Editorial, 1981.
Wadell, Paul J. *Friendship and the Moral Life*. Notre Dame: University of Notre Dame Press, 1989.
White, R.E.O. *The Changing Continuity of Christian Ethics*. Vol. 2, *The Insights of History*. Exeter: The Paternoster Press, 1981.
Wildiers, N. Max. *The Theologian and His Universe: Theology and Cosmology from the Middle Ages to the Present*. New York: The Seabury Press, 1982.
Wilson Schaef, Anne. *Co-Dependence: Misunderstood-Mistreated*. Minneapolis: Winston Press, 1986.
Wittberg, Patricia. *Creating a Future for Religious Life: A Sociological Perspective*. New York: Paulist Press, 1991.
Young, Frances M. *Sacrifice and Death of Jesus Christ*. Foreword by Maurice Wiles. Philadelphia: The Westminster Press, 1975.

C. Book Components

1. Chapters

Rahner, Karl. "The Concept of Mystery in Catholic Theology." Chap. in *Theological Investigations*. Vol. 4, *More Recent Writings*. Translated by Kevin Smyth. London: Darton, Longman and Todd, 1974.

_____. "Concerning the Relationship Between Nature and Grace." Chap. in *Theological Investigations*. Vol. 1, *God, Christ, Mary and Grace*. Translated by Cornelius Ernst. London: Darton, Longman and Todd, 1974.

_____. "The Eucharist and Suffering." Chap. in *Theological Investigations*. Vol. 3, *The Theology of the Spiritual Life*. Translated by Karl -H. and Boniface Kruger. London: Darton, Longman and Todd, 1974.

Selected Bibliography

_____. "The Hermeneutics of Eschatological Assertions." Chap. in *Theological Investigations*. Vol. 4, *More Recent Writings*. Translated by Kevin Smyth. London: Darton, Longman and Todd, 1974.

_____. "Jesus' Resurrection." Chap. in *Theological Investigations*. Vol. 17, *Jesus, Man, and the Church*. Translated by Margaret Kohl. London: Darton, Longman and Todd, 1981.

_____. "Mary's Virginity." Chap. in *Theological Investigations*. Vol. 19, *Faith and Ministry*. Translated by Edward Quinn. London: Darton, Longman and Todd, 1983.

_____. "On the Evangelical Counsels." Chap. in *Theological Investigations*. Vol. 8, *Further Theology of the Spiritual Life 2*. Translated by David Bourke. London: Darton, Longman and Todd, 1971.

_____. "On the Theology of the Ecumenical Discussion." Chap. in *Theological Investigations*. Vol. 11, *Confrontations I*. Translated by David Bourke. London: Darton, Longman and Todd, 1974.

_____. "The Presence of Christ in the Sacrament of the Lord's Supper." Chap. in *Theological Investigations*. Vol. 4, *More Recent Writings*. Translated by Kevin Smyth. London: Darton, Longman, and Todd, 1974.

_____. "The Theology of Poverty." Chap. in *Theological Investigations*. Vol. 4, *More Recent Writings*. Translated by Kevin Smyth. London: Darton, Longman and Todd, 1974.

_____. "The Theology of Symbol." Chap in *Theological Investigations*. Vol. 4, *More Recent Writings*. Translated by Kevin Smyth. London: Darton, Longman and Todd, 1974.

_____. "Remarks on the Dogmatic Treatise 'De Trinitate.'" Chap. in *Theological Investigations*. Vol. 4, *More Recent Writings*. Translated by Kevin Smyth. London: Darton, Longman and Todd, 1974.

---------. "Some Implications of the Scholastic Concept of Uncreated Grace." Chap. in *Theological Investigations*. Vol. 1, *God, Christ, Mary and Grace*. Translated by Cornelius Ernst. London: Darton, Longman and Todd, 1974.

2. Essays

Berríos, Angela. "Religious Life Ahora y Manana, Today and Tomorrow." In *The Future of Religious Life: The Carondelet Conference*, ed. Dolores Steinberg, 21-32. Collegeville, Minn.: The Liturgical Press, 1990.

Casey, Juliana, "Toward a Theology of the Vows." In *Turning Points in Religious Life*, ed. Carol Quigley, 78-126. Wilmington: Michael Glazier, 1987.

Dulles, Avery. "The Meaning of Faith in Relationship to Justice." In *The Faith that Does Justice: Examining the Christian Sources for Social Change*, ed. John C. Haughey, 10-46. New York: Paulist Press, 1977.

Friere, Paulo. "Conscientizing as a Way of Liberating." In *Liberation Theology: A Documentary History*, ed. Alfred T. Hennelly, 5-13. Maryknoll, NY: Orbis Books, 1990.

Geffré, Claude. "A Prophetic Theology." In *Liberation Theology: A Documentary History*, ed. Alfred T. Hennelly, 179-86. Maryknoll, NY: Orbis Books, 1990.

George, Emily. "Canonical Status." In *Turning Points in Religious Life*, ed. Carol Quigley, 174-88. Wilmington: Michael Glazier, 1987.

Gutiérrez, Gustavo. "Toward a Theology of Liberation." In *Liberation Theology: A Documentary History*, ed. Alfred T. Hennelly, 62-76. Maryknoll, NY: Orbis Books, 1990.

Hennelly, Alfred T. "The Red-Hot Issue: Liberation Theology." In *Liberation Theology: A Documentary History*, ed. Alfred T. Hennelly, 507-13. Maryknoll, NY: Orbis Books, 1990.

Selected Bibliography

Koester, Helmut. "GNOMAI DIAPHOROI: The Origin and Nature of Diversification in the History of Early Christianity." In *Trajectories through Early Christianity*, eds. James M. Robinson and Helmut Koester, 114-57. Philadelphia: Fortress Press, 1971.

McDonough, Elizabeth. "Beyond the Liberal Model: Quo Vadis?" *In Ius Sequitur Vitam: Law Follows Life, Studies in Canon Law Presented to P.J.M. Huizing*, eds. J.H. Provost and K. Walf, 89-119. Leuven: University of Leuven Press, 1991.

Mesters, Carlos. "The Use of the Bible in Christian Communities of the Common People." In *Liberation Theology: A Documentary History*, ed. Alfred T. Hennelly, 14-28. Maryknoll, NY: Orbis Books, 1990.

O'Shea, Kevin. "The Reality of Sin: A Theological and Pastoral Critique." In *The Mystery of Sin and Forgiveness*, ed. Michael J. Taylor, 91-112. Staten Island, NY: Alba House, 1971.

Pesch, Otto Hermann. "Existential and Sapiential Theology: The Theological Confrontation between Luther and Thomas Aquinas." In *Catholic Scholars Dialogue with Luther*, ed. J. Wicks, 61-81. Chicago: Loyola University Press, 1970.

Romero, Oscar. "The Political Dimension of the Faith from the Perspective of the Option for the Poor." In *Liberation Theology: A Documentary History*, ed. Alfred T. Hennelly, 292-303. Maryknoll, NY: Orbis Books, 1990.

Rorty, Richard. "Introduction: Metaphilosophical Difficulties of Linguistic Philosophy." In *The Linguistic Turn: Recent Essays in Philosophical Method*, ed. Richard Rorty, 1-39. Chicago: University of Chicago Press, 1967.

Schneiders, Sandra M. "Reflections on the History of the Religious Life and Contemporary Development." In *Turning Points in Religious Life*, ed. Carol Quigley, 13-77. Wilmington: Michael Glazier, 1987.

Schoonenberg, Piet. "Original Sin and Man's Situation." In *The Mystery of Sin and Forgiveness*, ed. Michael J. Taylor, 243-52. Staten Island, NY: Alba House, 1971.

Schüller, Bruno. "Autonomous Ethics Revisited." In *Personalist Morals*, ed. Joseph A. Selling, 61-70. Leuven: University of Leuven Press, 1988.

Segundo, Juan Luis. "Two Theologies of Liberation." In *Liberation Theology: A Documentary History*, ed. Alfred T. Hennelly, 353-66. Maryknoll, NY: Orbis Books, 1990.

Treston, Kevin. "Living in a Unitary Age." In *Creation Spirituality and the Dreamtime*, ed. Catherine Hammond, 51-71. Newtown, N.S.W.: Millennium Books, 1991.

Vidal, Marciano. "Structural Sin: A New Category in Moral Theology?" In *History and Conscience: Studies in Honour of Sean O'Riordan, C.SS.R.*, eds. Raphael Gallagher and Brendan McConvery, 181-98. Dublin: Gill and Macmillan, 1989.

D. Journal Articles

Aichele, George Jr. "Literary Fantasy and Postmodern Theology." *The Journal of the American Academy of Religion* 59 (1991): 323-37.

Baars, Conrad W. "Christian Anthropology of Thomas Aquinas." *The Priest* 30 (no. 10, 1975): 29-33.

Balthasar, Hans Urs von. "Radicalisme évangélique." *Vie consacrée* 47 (1975): 238-40.

Bandera, Armando. "Consigli evangelici e sacramenti." *Vita consacrata* 9 (1973): 97-106, 204-13.

_____. "La Vergine Maria e la practica dei consigli evangelici." *Vita consacrata* 9 (1973): 290-302, 380-94.

Bechtle, Regina. "Convergences in Theology and Spirituality." *The Way* 23 (1985): 305-14.

Bernardin, Joseph. "Dimensions of the Church in the Third Millennium." *Origins* 21 (1992): 592-97.

Beyer, Jean. "La preghiera nella vita religiosa." *Vita consacrata* 9 (1973): 273-89.

Billy, Dennis J. "Dialogue and Dissent II." *The Furrow* 42 (1991): 303-9.

———. "The Penitentials and The Making of Moral Theology.'" *Louvain Studies* 14 (1989): 142-51.

———. "Traducianism as a Theological Model in the Problem of Ensoulment." *The Irish Theological Quarterly* 55 (1989): 18-38.

Breton, Jean-Claude. "Retrouver les assises anthropologiques de la vie spirituelle." *Studies in Religion/Sciences religieuses* 17 (1988): 97-105.

Byrne, James. "Dialogue and Dissent." *The Furrow* 41 (1990): 689-94.

Carroll, E. "Mary in the Western Liturgy: *Marialis Cultus*." *Communio* 7 (1980): 140-56.

Chapelle, Albert. "La vie religieuse dans le mystère de l'Église." *Vie consacrée* 51 (1979): 104-18.

Chapelle, Paul. "Méditation sur la pauvreté religieuse." *Vie consacrée* 45 (1973): 143-55.

Ciardi, Fabio. "La communità religiosa segno di speranza." *Vita consacrata* 25 (1989): 216-26.

Congar, Y. "La vie religieuse vue dans l'Église selon Vatican II." *Vie consacrée* 43 (1971): 65-88.

Cousins, Ewert. "Models and the Future of Theology." *Continuum* 7 (1969): 78-91.

Crownfield, David. "The Seminal Trace: Presence, Difference, and Transubstantiation." *Journal of the American Academy of Religion* 59 (1991): 361-71.

Daly, Gabriel. "Theological Models in the Doctrine of Original Sin." *The Heythrop Journal* 13 (1972): 121-42.

Daniélou, Jean. "Il carattere specifico della vita religiosa," *Vita consacrata* 10 (1974): 521-31.

Danneels, Godfried, "Le don de la rédemption." *Vie consacrée* 56 (1984): 267-83.

Decloux, Simon. "La dimension sacramentelle de la vie religieuse." *Vie consacrée* 58 (1986): 197-208.
———. "La dimension théologale de al vie religieuse." *Vie consacrée* 57 (1985): 7-19.
Deeken, Alfons. "A Trinitarian Spirituality for Today." *Review for Religious* 31 (1972): 237-46.
Della Croce, Giovanna. "La communità eucaristica." *Vita consacrata* 10 (1974): 414-27, 474-82.
Dulles, Avery. "The Magisterium, Theology and Dissent." *Origins* 20 (1991): 692-96.
———. "The Question of Dissent." *The Tablet* 244 (1990): 1033-34.
Duquoc, Christian. "The Curia Sews It Up." *The Tablet* 244 (1990): 1097-98.
———. "Theology and Spirituality." *Concilium* 9 (no. 2, 1966): 46-51.
Emery, Pierre-Yves. "Vie religieuse et oecuménisme." *Vie consacrée* 53 (1981): 23-31.
Falardeau, Ernest R. "Religious Life Is a Communion." *Review for Religious* 43 (1984): 65-68.
Fatula, Mary Ann. "*Contemplata Aliis Tradere*: Spirituality and Thomas Aquinas, The Preacher." *Spirituality Today* 43 (1991): 19-35.
Festuguère, A.M. "La trichotomie de 1 Th 5:23 et la philosophie grecque." *Recherches de science religieuse* 20 (1930): 385-415.
Foley, Mary Eileen. "Some Reflections on Mary, Bridge to Ecumenism." *Review for Religious* 48 (1989): 342-54.
Galot, Jean. "L'azione di grazie nella vita consacrata." *Vita consacrata* 24 (1988): 705-18, 785-97.
———. "Madre della chiesa. Madre della communità," *Vita consacrata* 22 (1986): 348-60.
———. "Il Padre nostro e la vita consacrata," *Vita consacrata* 23 (1987): 1-14, 97-106, 204-14, 261-70.

Selected Bibliography

---. "Pasto escatologico." *Vita consacrata* 26 (1990): 783-99.

---. "Profetismo della vita religiosa." *Vita consacrata* 13 (1977): 487-96, 529-42.

---. "Redenzione e vita religiosa." *Vita consacrata* 13 (1977): 129-44, 193-204, 257-68, 321-28, 419-36.

Giardini, F. "Una vita interemente consacrata alla ss. Trinità." *Vita consacrata* 22 (1986): 630-38, 721-32, 817-32.

Griéger, Paul. "La conversione personale." *Vita consacrata* 22 (1986): 361-66.

Henn, William. "The Hierarchy of Truths Twenty Years Later." *Theological Studies* 48 (1987): 439-71.

Hennaux, Jean-Marie. "Marie, l'église et la femme dans l'évangile de Luc." *Vie consacrée* 47 (1975): 257-68.

Hoope, Mary Anne. "Consecrated Celibacy: Gift and Challenge." *Review for Religious* 40 (1981): 902-11.

Horgan, Thaddeus. "Religious Community Life and Christian Unity." *Review for Religious* 30 (1971): 442-46.

Hosmer, Rachel. "Current Literature in Christian Spirituality." *Anglican Theological Review* 66 (1984): 423-41.

Houdart, Marie-André. "Communautés religieuses et souci de l'unité chrétienne." *Vie consacrée* 39 (1967): 288-309.

Jelly, Frederick M. "The Concrete Meaning of Mary's Motherhood." *The Way Supplement* 45 (1982): 30-40.

---. "Mary's Virginity in the Symbols and Councils." *Marian Studies* 21 (1970): 69-93.

Jones, Alan. "Spirituality and Theology." *Review for Religious* 39 (1980): 161-76.

Kinerk, Edward. "Toward a Method for the Study of Spirituality." *Review for Religious* 40 (1981): 3-19.

Leclercq, Jean. "Spiritualitas." *Studi medievali* 3 (1963): 279-96.

Malloy, Edward A. "The Character of a Religious Community." *Review for Religious* 37 (1978): 748-52.

Markey, John J. "Towards A Trinitarian Model of Religious Life." *Review for Religious* 49 (1990): 22-35.

Mascall, Eric. "The Doctrine of Analogy." *Cross Currents* 1 (1951): 38-57.
Megyer, Eugene. "Theological Trends: Spiritual Theology Today." *The Way* 21 (1981): 55-67.
Méroz, Christianne. "Vie religieuse et unité de l'Église." *Vie consacrée* 53 (1981): 17-22.
Meyer, Eric C. "Is Religious Life a Sacrament?" *Review for Religious* 33 (1974): 1100-17.
Murphy-O'Connor, Jerome. "Christological Anthropology in Ph., II.6-11." *Revue biblique* 83 (1976): 25-50.
Nichols, A. "Einigung der Kirchen: An Ecumenical Controversy." *One in Christ* 21 (1985): 139-66.
O'Leary, Brian. "Christian and Religious Obedience." *Review for Religious* 44 (1985): 513-20.
O'Malley, John. "Priesthood, Ministry, and Religious Life: Some Historical and Historiographical Considerations." *Theological Studies* 49 (1988): 223-57.
Orsy, Ladislas. "The Limits of Magisterium." *The Tablet* 244 (1990): 1066-69.
_____. "Magisterium and Theologians: A Vatican Document." *America* 162 (1990): 30-32.
Parmisano, Stan. "Mary in Contemporary Culture." *Review for Religious* 48 (1989): 323-36.
Pinckaers, Servais (Th.). "La pauvreté religieuse est-elle une vraie pauvreté?" *Vie consacrée* 42 (1970): 55-64.
Principe, Walter. "Toward Defining Spirituality." *Studies in Religion/Sciences religieuses* 12 (1983): 127-41.
Queralt, Antonio. "La espiritualidad como disciplina teológica." *Gregorianum* 60 (1979): 321-76.
Quinn, John. "Observations on Doctrinal Congregation's Instruction." *Origins* 20 (1990): 201-5.
Rollin, B. "Le radicalisme des conseils évangéliques." *Nouvelle revue théologique* 108 (1986): 532-54.
Rossetti, Stephen. "The Celibacy Experience." *Review for Religious* 41 (1982): 660-77.

Selected Bibliography

Sammon, Sean. "The Transformation of Religious Life." *Origins* 21 (1991): 185-96.

Scharlemann, Robert M. "Theological Models and Their Construction." *Journal of Religion* 53 (1973): 65-82.

Schneiders, Sandra M. "Spirituality in the Academy." *Theological Studies* 50 (1989): 676-97.

Sheets, John R. "The Call to the Renewal of Religious Life." *Review for Religious* 43 (1984): 175-90.

Tripole, Martin R. "Suffering with the Humble Christ in Religious Life." *Review for Religious* 40 (1981): 192-202.

Walgrave, Jan. "Prayer and Mysticism." *Communio* 12 (1985): 276-92.

Wood, Susan. "The Eucharist: Heart of Religious Community." *Review for Religious* 46 (1987): 178-86.

Wright, N.T. "*Harpagmos* and the Meaning of Philippians 2:5-11." *Journal of Theological Studies* 37 (1986): 321-52.

E. Encyclopedia and Dictionary Articles

Brown, Raymond E., Joseph A. Fitzmyer, and Roland E. Murphy, eds. *The Jerome Biblical Commentary*. Vol. 1, *The Old Testament*. Englewood Cliffs, N.J.: Prentice-Hall, Inc., 1968. S.v. "Introduction to Prophetic Literature," by Bruce Vawter.

_____. *The Jerome Biblical Commentary*. Vol. 2, *The New Testament and Topical Articles*. Englewood Cliffs, N.J.: Prentice-Hall, Inc., 1968. S.v. "The Gospel According to Luke," by Carroll Stuhlmueller.

_____. *The Jerome Biblical Commentary*. Vol. 2, *The New Testament and Topical Articles*. Englewood Cliffs, N.J.: Prentice-Hall, Inc., 1968. S.v. "The Letter to the Philippians," by Joseph A. Fitzmyer.

_____. *The New Jerome Biblical Commentary*. Vol. 2, *The New Testament and Topical Articles*. Englewood Cliffs, N.J.:

Prentice-Hall, Inc., 1990. S.v. "The Letter to the Philippians," by Brendan Byrne.

_____. *The New Jerome Biblical Commentary*. Vol. 2, *The New Testament and Topical Articles*. Englewood Cliffs, N.J.: Prentice-Hall, Inc., 1990. S.v. "Pauline Theology," by Joseph A. Fitzmyer.

Edwards, Paul, gen. ed., *The Encyclopedia of Philosophy*. New York: Macmillan, 1967. S.v. "Substance and Attribute," by D.J. O'Connor.

Fries, Heinrich, ed. *Handbuch Theologischer Grundbegriffe*. Kösel: Verlag München, 1962. S.v. "Heilsgeschichte II. Systematisch," by A. Darlapp.

McDonald, William J., gen. ed. *The New Catholic Encyclopedia*. New York: McGraw-Hill, 1967. S.v. "Our Lady of Perpetual Help," by C. Henze.

_____. *The New Catholic Encyclopedia*. New York: McGraw-Hill, 1967. S.v. "Servant of the Lord Oracles," by M.A. Gervais.

_____. *The New Catholic Encyclopedia*. New York: McGraw-Hill, 1967. S.v. "States of Life," by S.V. Ramge.

_____. *The New Catholic Encyclopedia*. New York: McGraw-Hill, 1967. S.v. "Transubstantiation," by C. Vollert.

O'Carroll, Michael. *Theotokos: A Theological Encyclopedia of the Blessed Virgin Mary*. Wilmington: Michael Glazier, 1982. S.v. "Apocrypha, The New Testament."

_____. *Theotokos: A Theological Encyclopedia of the Blessed Virgin Mary*. Wilmington: Michael Glazier, 1982. S.v. "Assumption of Our Lady, The."

_____. *Theotokos: A Theological Encyclopedia of the Blessed Virgin Mary*. Wilmington: Michael Glazier, 1982. S.v. "Infancy Narratives, The."

_____. *Theotokos: A Theological Encyclopedia of the Blessed Virgin Mary*. Wilmington: Michael Glazier, 1982. S.v. "John the Evangelist."

_____. *Theotokos: A Theological Encyclopedia of the Blessed*

Selected Bibliography

Virgin Mary. Wilmington: Michael Glazier, 1982. S.v. "Mariology."

_____. *Theotokos: A Theological Encyclopedia of the Blessed Virgin Mary*. Wilmington: Michael Glazier, 1982. S.v. "Titles of Our Lady."

Vacant, A. , E. Mangenot and E. Amann, eds., *Dictionnaire de théologie catholique*. Paris: Librairie Letourzey et Ané, 1924. S.v. "Grace," by J. Van der Meersch.

Wakefield, Gordon S., ed. *The Westminster Dictionary of Christian Spirituality*. Philadelphia: The Westminster Press, 1983. S.v. "Benedictine Spirituality, Benedictines," by Maria Boulding.

_____. *The Westminster Dictionary of Christian Spirituality*. Philadelphia: The Westminster Press, 1983. S.v. "Carmelite Spirituality, Carmelites," by Colin P. Thompson.

_____. *The Westminster Dictionary of Christian Spirituality*. Philadelphia: The Westminster Press, 1983. S.v. "Cistercian Spirituality, Cistercians," by Benedicta Ward.

_____. *The Westminster Dictionary of Christian Spirituality*. Philadelphia: The Westminster Press, 1983. S.v. "Dominican Spirituality, Dominicans," by Simon Tugwell.

_____. *The Westminster Dictionary of Christian Spirituality*. Philadelphia: The Westminster Press, 1983. S.v. "Franciscan Spirituality, Franciscans," by Eric Doyle.

_____. *The Westminster Dictionary of Christian Spirituality*. Philadelphia: The Westminster Press, 1983. S.v. "Imitation of Christ," by E.J. Tinsley.

_____. *The Westminster Dictionary of Christian Spirituality*. Philadelphia: The Westminster Press, 1983. S.v. "Jesus, Society of," by George E. Ganss.

Wiener, Philip P., gen. ed. *Dictionary of the History of Ideas*. New York: Charles Scribner's Sons, 1973. S.v. "Death and Immortality," by Jacques Choron.

F. Proceedings

The Catholic Theological Society of America: Proceedings of the Forty-Second Annual Convention (Philadelphia, June 10-13, 1987), ed. George Kilcourse. Louisville: The Catholic Theological Society of America, 1987.

Cunningham, Agnes. "Modernity/Postmodernity: The State of the Question For Contemporary Catholic Theology." In *The Catholic Theological Society of America: Proceedings of the Forty Sixth Annual Convention (Atlanta, June 12-15, 1991)*, ed. Paul Crowley, 156-57. Santa Clara: The Catholic Theological Society of America, 1991.

Principe, Walter H. "Presidential Address: Catholic Theology and the Retrieval of its Intellectual Tradition: Problems and Possibilities." In *The Catholic Theological Society of America: Proceedings of the Forty Sixth Annual Convention (Atlanta, June 12-15, 1991)*, ed. Paul Crowley, 175-94. Santa Clara: The Catholic Theological Society of America, 1991.

G. Dissertations

Colón León, Jorge Rafael. "La oración de petición en la dotrina de San Alfonso Maria de Ligorio." STD dissertation, Gregorian University, 1986.

H. Unpublished Manuscripts

Williams, Bruce. "Human Rights: A 'Bilingual' Dialogue." TMs [photocopy]. Simposio Interdisciplinare 'Diritti Umani: Problema Nodale nel Mondo Contemporaneo,' March 9, 1988. The Pontifical University of Saint Thomas, Rome.